ADVANCED LEVEL

Vocabulary Drills

ADULT LEARNING CENTER
2 EAST SECOND STREET
DULUTH, MN 55802
218-733-2075

EDWARD B. FRY, Ph.D.
Professor Emeritus
Rutgers University

JAMESTOWN PUBLISHERS

a division of NTC/Contemporary Publishing Company
Lincolnwood, Illinois USA

Vocabulary Drills
Advanced Level

Cover and text design: Deborah Hulsey Christie
Cover photograph: Warren Jagger
Illustrations: Richard Bishop

ISBN: 0-89061-447-4

Published by Jamestown Publishers,
a division of NTC/Contemporary Publishing Company,
4255 West Touhy Avenue,
Lincolnwood (Chicago), Illinois 60646-1975 U.S.A.
© 1986, 1989 by Edward B. Fry
All rights reserved. No part of this book may be reproduced,
stored in a retrieval system, or transmitted in any form or by any means,
electronic, mechanical, photocopying, recording, or otherwise,
without prior permission of the publisher.
Manufactured in the United States of America.

8 9 0 BA   13 12 11 10 9

CONTENTS

To the Teacher 5
To the Student 9

UNIT 1
1: Meeting Words in Context 14
2: The Roots of Our Language 17
3: Meeting Words in Context 19
4: The Roots of Our Language 22
5: Extending Your Word Power 24

UNIT 2
1: Meeting Words in Context 32
2: The Roots of Our Language 35
3: Meeting Words in Context 37
4: The Roots of Our Language 40
5: Extending Your Word Power 42

UNIT 3
1: Meeting Words in Context 50
2: The Roots of Our Language 53
3: Meeting Words in Context 55
4: The Roots of Our Language 58
5: Extending Your Word Power 60

UNIT 4
1: Meeting Words in Context 68
2: The Roots of Our Language 71
3: Meeting Words in Context 73
4: The Roots of Our Language 76
5: Extending Your Word Power 78

UNIT 5
1: Meeting Words in Context 86
2: The Roots of Our Language 89
3: Meeting Words in Context 91
4: The Roots of Our Language 94
5: Extending Your Word Power 96

UNIT 6

1: Meeting Words in Context	104
2: The Roots of Our Language	107
3: Meeting Words in Context	109
4: The Roots of Our Language	112
5: Extending Your Word Power	114

UNIT 7

1: Meeting Words in Context	122
2: The Roots of Our Language	125
3: Meeting Words in Context	127
4: The Roots of Our Language	130
5: Extending Your Word Power	132

UNIT 8

1: Meeting Words in Context	140
2: The Roots of Our Language	143
3: Meeting Words in Context	145
4: The Roots of Our Language	148
5: Extending Your Word Power	150

UNIT 9

1: Meeting Words in Context	158
2: The Roots of Our Language	161
3: Meeting Words in Context	163
4: The Roots of Our Language	166
5: Extending Your Word Power	168

UNIT 10

1: Meeting Words in Context	176
2: The Roots of Our Language	179
3: Meeting Words in Context	181
4: The Roots of Our Language	184
5: Extending Your Word Power	186

Student Words	193
Answer Key	199
Glossary	217

To the Teacher

Introduction

Is learning vocabulary important? You'd better believe it is! By every measure of common sense, and from research statistics, we know that vocabulary knowledge has a tremendous bearing on reading ability and on most standardized test scores, including those for IQ tests and the SAT.

As long ago as 1916, Lewis Terman, the author of the *Stanford-Binet Tests of Intelligence,* reported a correlation of .91 between the vocabulary section of the test and the total test score. That means that a test-taker's score on the vocabulary section was found to be an accurate predictor of his or her score on the test as a whole. Invariably, those with high vocabulary scores tested high on the entire test. Later studies, done on the *Wechsler Intelligence Scale for Children,* showed correlations that were comparable, though slightly lower. Most major standardized tests—reading achievement tests, college entrance exams (SAT and ACT), graduate school entrance exams (GRE, LSAT, GMAT), and various armed forces selection and placement tests—include a major section on vocabulary.

Vocabulary also plays an extremely important part in reading comprehension. Research by Robert Thorndike has shown that in English-speaking countries such as the United States, England, Scotland and New Zealand there is a correlation of .70 between vocabulary test scores and reading comprehension scores. Vocabulary difficulty is also the most important variable in most of the widely used readability formulas, which are used to calculate the level of difficulty of reading materials.

So, on the basis of solid research results, as well as from a commonsense perspective, it is clear that vocabulary is important. It is a major factor in reading comprehension, and a substantial portion of numerous standardized tests is devoted to the testing of vocabulary knowledge.

Let's spend a minute on the question How large is an average student's vocabulary? This simple question is nearly unanswerable.

First of all, you could ask which vocabulary—reading, writing, listening or speaking. Our *receptive vocabularies,* those that comprise the words we recognize and understand when we hear or read them, tend to be larger than our *expressive vocabularies,* those that comprise the words we use in speaking and writing. The receptive vocabularies of children and young people usually far exceed their expressive vocabularies. In well-educated or well-read adults, the gap is much narrower. This leads us to our first important piece of information related to vocabulary improvement: vocabulary increases through education and through the reading of a wide range of materials.

Let's limit our original big question to How large is a student's *meaning vocabulary?* This encompasses those words whose meanings the student knows, as opposed to *sight vocabulary*—those words that the student recognizes and can pronounce but does not understand.

The results of various research studies vary widely in their estimates of the size of the average student's meaning vocabulary. For example, the lowest estimate for grade seven is 4,600 words, and the high estimate is 51,000. At grade fourteen, which is college sophomore, the range is 7,900 words to 200,000 words. Quite a difference. Part of the discrepancy stems from confusion over what is meant by a "word." Do variant forms constitute different words—are *run, runs* and *running* to be considered different words? Is *ran* different from the other three because its vowel changes? The different decisions that are reached in answer to such questions cause the estimates to differ by several hundred percent. Confusion about how to treat multiple meanings is also a factor that affects estimates. If you understand *run,* as in *Sally can run,* do you automatically understand three other words if you understand the meanings of *run* in the sentences *Sally has a run in her stocking, There is a run on the banks,* and *The fence on the dog run is broken?* The lowest research estimates exclude both variants and multiple meanings, as well as technical and foreign words.

All estimates, however, high or low, reflect constant growth in vocabulary size as students progress through the educational system. As an example, below is some data from the *Basic Word Vocabulary Test* by Harold J. Dupuy, Ph.D.

Grade	Number of Words Known
7	4,600
8	5,300
9	5,900
10	6,400
11	6,700
12	6,900

Note that the table shows greater vocabulary growth in the junior high years than in senior high. This certainly indicates that junior high is a time in which many new words and ideas are being introduced to students, but the apparent difference in growth rate is probably also due to the fact that the test does not reflect the many technical and subject-specific words that senior high school students learn.

An Overview of the Book

The reading selections, lessons and exercises in *Vocabulary Drills* concentrate mainly on two of the best-known and most reliable approaches to vocabulary improvement: the use of context clues and the analysis of the roots of unfamiliar words. Students will learn a fairly large number of words in this book, but, more importantly, they will learn some important skills that will help them to decipher the meanings of new words that they encounter in their own reading.

Context. Sections 1 and 3 of each unit are titled Meeting Words in Context. Each of these sections contains a reading selection that provides the context for ten vocabulary words, followed by four exercises. The reading selections have been drawn from sources representing the broad variety of reading materials that students regularly encounter: newspapers, textbooks, general fiction and nonfiction, and reference books. The exercises following the reading selections have two purposes: (1) to develop a student's ability to perceive the meanings of unfamiliar words based on context clues, and (2) to associate the new words encountered in the reading selection with related words and ideas. The latter is accomplished primarily through synonym and antonym exercises and analogies. Such exercises link the new word with words that the student may already know, thereby helping the student retain the word and better understand it.

Student Words. The students are encouraged to find in each reading passage in the Meeting Words in Context sections one or two words that are unfamiliar to them or whose meanings they are uncertain of. They are asked to try to guess from the context of the passage what the words mean, and to write the words and their guess at a definition in a space provided beneath the passage. They are then asked to look up the words in a dictionary and find the correct definitions, and to write the words and definitions in the pages marked Student Words in the back of the book. Through this exercise, the students will be learning to apply to words of their own choosing, some of the skills they are learning in this book.

Roots. Sections 2 and 4 of each unit, which are titled The Roots of Our Language, feature lessons that teach common Greek and Latin roots and some of the English words that contain them. Three exercises related to each lesson drill the roots and the words, and provide students with practice in deciphering unfamiliar words that contain the roots taught in the lesson.

Extension and Review. The fifth and last section of each unit, called Extending Your Word Power, contains five exercises that expand students' understanding of the words that have been taught in the unit. One exercise deals with multiple meanings of selected words, another deals with variant forms of selected words, and a third introduces synonyms for some of the words, and calls for the students to recognize fine distinctions between the synonyms and the vocabulary words. A fourth exercise serves as a review of ten words from the roots lessons, and the fifth and final exercise is a review, usually in game format, that draws on selected vocabulary from both the unit at hand and the previous unit.

Glossary. At the back of the book is a glossary that contains all of the words and roots that are introduced in *Vocabulary Drills*. The definitions given for the words are limited to those meanings that are dealt with in the book. If you would like to expand your students' understanding of any of the words, have them work with a good dictionary and with other word reference books such as a thesaurus and books on usage.

Answer Key. A complete answer key is provided at the back of the book, following the Student Words pages.

How to Use *Vocabulary Drills* in Class

A complete step-by-step guide to the use of *Vocabulary Drills* with your students is contained in the To the Student section, which begins on page 9. You should go through that section with your students, so that they will have a clear understanding of the purpose of the book and of its contents.

Vocabulary Drills has been designed to encourage students to participate completely in the lessons and exercises without fear of making errors. As has been stated previously, the main thrust of the book is on the teaching of skills that will help students learn to build their own vocabularies, and on presenting English as a lively and interesting language, not on the teaching of definitions. Consequently, the book contains no scoring sheets or progress charts. Students should, however, be encouraged to check their answers, to examine their errors and correct them, and to try to figure out why the correct responses are correct. Discussion is also tremendously helpful in learning vocabulary. The more students hear and use new words, the better they will understand the words, learn their fine points of meaning and usage, and remember them. Students should do the exercises on their own, but it is recommended that, whenever possible, they discuss their responses and correct the exercises as a group. This is especially helpful in the Roots Review exercises in the fifth section of each unit, for those exercises have no specific answers. The students must complete sentences so as to demonstrate their understanding of the meanings of the boldfaced words in the sentence stems. Again, discussion will help the students clarify and refine their understanding of the words.

Vocabulary Extension Activities

This book provides a good starting place for helping your students increase both their receptive and expressive vocabularies. But you can certainly extend the kinds of activities that are presented here, and help your students to increase their vocabularies in many other ways. Following are some suggestions.

(1) *Vocabulary Drills* contains a wide variety of exercise types: multiple-choice, cloze, matching, analogies, substitutions, sentence completion, and a variety of word puzzles and games. You may wish to create similar drills for words of your own choosing. Another effective activity is to challenge your students to create exercise items of their own, using words from their Student Words pages, and to try them out on each other.

(2) Make part of every subject lesson a vocabulary lesson. Whether you are teaching science, grammar or physical education, it is important to teach the specialized vocabulary of the subject. Write any new words on the chalkboard, help students make connections between the new words and subject vocabulary they may already know. Use the new terms in your oral lessons.

(3) Connect new words you teach in as many ways as possible with words and concepts your students are already familiar with. Explore the various meanings of any words that have multiple meanings. Teach any distinctions in meaning, pronunciation or spelling between homophones and homographs. Generate synonyms and antonyms for the words, if appropriate. Explore the fine distinctions between synonyms, comparing and contrasting them. Present the synonyms in sentences that exhibit their proper use, and encourage your students to generate sentences that use the words appropriately.

(4) Teach your students to categorize new words with other words they know or are learning that deal with the same concept. For example, if you are teaching the word *thyroid,* the students could categorize it with the names of other organs of the body, such as *liver, heart, thymus,* and *kidney.* Have the students label their lists, so the words will be linked in their minds with a concept. Another example: If you are teaching the word COBAL, related words might be FORTRAN,

BASIC, and LISP, and the category heading might be Computer Programming Languages.

(5) Teach word continuums related to various concepts with which you are dealing in your subject area. For instance, if you are studying urban communities, and perhaps dealing with the word *metropolis,* you might introduce words related to communities of various sizes and arrange them on the chalkboard in a continuum from smallest community to largest:

hamlet → village → town → city → metropolis → megalopolis

You could then explain the meanings of any words with which the students are unfamiliar, and explore the differences between the various concepts. A metropolis, for instance, is a large city, but it is smaller than a city that is classified as a megalopolis. Also, a megalopolis may encompass several cities, or the highly populated area surrounding an extremely large city. Again, give examples to help your students understand the distinctions between the related concepts.

As a related exercise, you could extend the continuum to a "concept map," drawing lines out from the continuum in a circle and writing words and terms related to the concept. A concept map based on the continuum above, for instance, might include the terms *county, urban core, transport corridor* and *suburb.*

(6) Explore class/example and coordinate relationships. For example, if you were teaching the word *dictator* and the concept of dictatorship, you could classify a dictator as a ruler, and then bring up other types of rulers. You could then generate a discussion of the various types of rulers, comparing and contrasting them according to their individual properties and characteristics. Interesting class discussions can arise when students are asked to list the ways in which two related concepts are alike and how they are different. Conversely, using *dictator* as a class heading, you could discuss examples of dictators, such as Hitler and Peron, and discuss the similarities and the differences between them.

(7) The most important thing you can do to help your students widen their vocabularies is encourage them to read as much and as widely as possible. Encourage them to explore their interests through reading. Recommend good books and magazine articles to them. Bring in interesting newspaper articles that are relevant to the subjects you are discussing in class, and encourage your students to do the same. Remember that it is almost universally true that good readers have good vocabularies, and that it is difficult to develop a good vocabulary without reading.

Finally, there is one last thing that I would like to stress to you and to your students. Vocabulary development is a lifelong learning necessity. It is very important to success both in school and in life, and it can be a fascinating pursuit as well.

E.F.

I would like to thank the following people for their many valuable contributions to *Vocabulary Drills:*

Dr. Donna Fountoukidis, Montclair State College
Ms. Nancy Schwindinger, Rutgers University
Ms. Katharine M. Archambault
Ms. Lee Teverow

To the Student

Introduction

Why build your vocabulary?

If you go into a bookstore and browse through the shelves containing books on language usage and writing, you'll notice that there are many that are intended to help people improve their vocabularies. More are published each year. What makes such books popular? Many people have discovered that being able to write and speak well is a key to success in school, in their careers, and in life in general. An important factor in writing and speaking well is a good vocabulary.

The Importance of Reading

The easiest and most natural way to improve your vocabulary is to read as much as you can, on a variety of subjects and from many kinds of materials. You will meet many new words that way, and you will become familiar with how the words are used. The more often you meet a word, the better you understand its meaning. The better you understand a word, the more comfortable you will be using it. And the more you use a word, the more likely it is to become a standard part of your working vocabulary. That is how a person's vocabulary grows. If you don't use the new words you learn, you will tend to forget them.

Using Context

The aim of *Vocabulary Drills* is to help you learn how to approach new words and to become more comfortable with the language—free to explore new words and their meanings. In the book you will work with useful vocabulary that is presented in reading selections on a variety of subjects and from many different types of sources. As you read the selections and do the exercises that accompany them, you will be developing your skills in dealing with new words—skills that you can carry over to your own reading. One of the most important skills is learning to use context to gain some idea of the meaning of an unfamiliar word. Context is the setting of the word—the ideas contained in the words and sentences that surround it. A word in a sentence carries an idea that fits in with the idea of the sentence as a whole, and of the paragraph in which the sentence is located.

When you are reading on your own and you come across an unfamiliar word, you don't usually want to stop reading to check the word in a dictionary. You should just try to get a fair sense of the word from its context, and keep on reading. You can often come quite close to the meaning of a word by making a guess at it, based on the context. That is a skill you will develop in this book.

Through your work with the exercises, you will also be making the vocabulary words a part of your working vocabulary.

Learning About Roots

Another way by which people build their vocabularies is by learning about the roots of the language—the parts of English words that are based on other, older languages. Many English words are based on word parts borrowed from the ancient Latin and Greek languages. This book contains lessons and exercises that will help you learn the meanings of some Greek and Latin roots and of some words that contain those roots. You can then use your knowledge of roots to help you decipher the meanings of unfamiliar words that you come upon in your reading.

When you have completed this book, you will have learned many new words. More importantly, however, you will have learned how to go on learning new words wherever and whenever you encounter them.

How to Use This Book

Vocabulary Drills is divided into ten units. Each unit is divided into five sections. The first and third sections present reading passages followed by exercises related to vocabulary words that are presented in the passages. Sections two and four contain lessons and exercises related to Greek and Latin roots. Section five extends your understanding of some of the words in the unit, and reviews some of them, as well.

The ideal way to approach the lessons and exercises is to work through them on your own, and then to go over your answers in a group. There are many advantages to this method. Using words aloud and hearing them spoken helps to make them a part of your vocabulary. Talking about the words and discussing the answers to the exercises will help you better understand the words and how they should be used. Such discussions will help you to become more aware and precise in your own speech and writing. This is an admirable goal, for, after all, words are our primary means of communication with each other.

Now let's examine a unit closely.

Working Through a Unit

Section 1 and 3: Meeting Words in Context

Reading selections of three to four hundred words form the basis for each of these sections. They contain the vocabulary words you will work with. The selections represent most types of reading material that people encounter on a regular basis: newspapers, magazines, general fiction and nonfiction, textbooks and reference materials.

The vocabulary words in each selection appear in boldfaced type. There are ten in each passage. As you read a selection, try to figure out the meanings of the boldfaced words from the way they are used. Pay close attention to the ideas contained in the words and sentences surrounding each word, and try to understand how the vocabulary word fits in with those ideas.

Immediately following the selection are spaces in which to write two words from the passage, other than the boldfaced words, that are unfamiliar to you or whose meanings you are uncertain of. (Choose two words even if you think you know what they mean; you may be surprised to learn that a word has a slightly different meaning than you thought it had, or that it has many other meanings.) Make a guess at the meaning of each word, based on context clues, and write that meaning beside the word. Then compare your definition with the definition given in a good dictionary. Be sure to choose the dictionary definition that is appropriate to the word as it is used in the reading selection. Check to see how close your definition came to the one given in the dictionary. Finally, enter your two words and their correct definitions on the Student Words pages that begin on page 193.

Four exercises follow each reading selection. Through the exercises you will explore the meanings of the ten vocabulary words, *as they are used in the selection*. This is an important point, for, as you know, many words have more than one meaning. In these exercises you will be examining only the meanings used in the reading selection. There are a wide variety of exercise types, including multiple-choice, matching, sentence completion, analogies, word substitutions and fill-in-the-blanks. Read the directions for each exercise carefully, to be sure you understand what you are to do.

Each of the four exercises deals with five of the ten words from the reading selection. Exercises 1 and 2 work with the same five, and exercises 3 and 4 use the other five. Exercises 1 and 3, which are called Using Context, ask you to deduce the meanings of the words from the way in which they are used in the passage—from their context. In exercises 2 and 4, Making Connections, you are asked either to associate the words with synonyms and antonyms, to pair the words with their definitions, to use the words in sentences, or to complete analogies (an analogy is a type of comparison made up of word pairs that are related in some way). Work through the exercises on your own. Then, if possible, correct your answers in a group with other classmates. Share your answers, talk about the words, and correct any errors you may have made. An answer key is provided beginning on page 199.

Sections 2 and 4: The Roots of Our Language

A lesson that teaches several Latin and Greek roots and some words that contain those roots form the basis for each of these sections. Following the lesson are three exercises in which you will work with the roots and words that were taught. Exercise 1 is a matching exercise in which you are asked to match five roots and words with their definitions. Exercise 2 is a true-false exercise, containing five statements based on roots and words from the lesson. Exercise 3 may contain questions, fill-in-the-blanks, or a series of multiple-choice questions.

Section 5: Extending Your Word Power

Five exercises that build on your understanding of the words you have worked with in the first four parts of the unit make up this section. Let's look at each type of exercise individually.

Multiple Meanings. Many words in the English language have multiple—two or more—meanings. This exercise is based on words from the Meeting Words in Context sections. Each of the words has at least two meanings. You may be asked to find the other meanings of the words in the glossary at the back of the book, or you may be given the alternate meanings at the beginning of the exercise. To complete the exercise you will have to choose which of the meanings of the words explain the way the words are used in particular sentences.

Roots Review. This exercise asks you to complete ten sentences. Each incomplete sentence contains a word you learned about in a Roots Lesson. You must complete the sentence to demonstrate that you understand what the word means.

Choosing Just the Right Word. Careful writers and speakers try to choose just the right words to express their ideas clearly and completely. Many words have synonyms—other words that have almost the same meaning. But synonyms rarely mean *exactly* the same thing. Each usually carries its own specific meaning. This exercise has you examine and work with words that are very close in meaning but that serve different purposes when it comes to expressing ideas.

Recognizing Word Forms. This exercise develops your awareness of other forms of the words you have studied in the Meeting Words in Context sections of the unit. For instance, if you worked with the word *discriminate* earlier in the unit, this exercise might introduce *discrimination* or *discriminating*.

Putting Your Vocabulary To Use. This exercise provides a review of selected words from the present unit and from the previous unit, as well. This last activity is usually in the form of a game—a word search, a crossword, a bubblegram or the completion of humorous rhyming word pairs.

Checking Your Work

As mentioned earlier, *Vocabulary Drills* contains no grading system or scoring charts. Although you will be adding many new words to your vocabulary as you work in this book, your primary goal is *to develop your ability to acquire and use words,* rather than to gather an impressive list of words that you are only slightly acquainted with.

Answer Key. Check your work by using the Answer Key that begins on page 199. Again, we recommend that you go over the exercises in a group. There is, however, no grading involved in *Vocabulary Drills*. The Answer Key is there to allow you to check your answers, not to test you. It takes time to come to a clear, refined understanding of the meaning of a word, so it is expected that you will not always get the right answers to the exercise questions. Just do your best, check your answers, and then go back and try to figure out why the right answer was right. If you are confused by an answer, discuss it with the other members of your group or with your teacher.

Glossary. The Glossary on pages 217-240 contains definitions of all the vocabulary words that have been introduced in the book. Some exercises require the use of the glossary, others suggest that you use it if you cannot recall what a word means. We suggest that you do not use the glossary when you are working on the Using Context exercises in the Meeting Words in Context sections, for in those exercises you are being asked to try to figure out the meanings of the words only from the way they are used. Be sure when you consult the glossary that if more than one definition is given for a word you choose the one that provides the meaning you are looking for.

Research has shown over and over again that there is a direct link between vocabulary size and success, not just in school, but in all of life. This book gives you a good beginning toward achieving that success.

UNIT 1

1: Meeting Words in Context

    Reading Selection   The Ancient Olympics

    Words Introduced   disdained meager melancholy moratorium pilgrimage prowess revered rituals rubble subsequent

2: The Roots of Our Language

    Roots Introduced   mono- chroma ocul- -gram tele- -graph -gamos -tonous -arch matri- patri-

3: Meeting Words in Context

    Reading Selection   The Contests

    Words Introduced   augment bestowed comprised contenders factor pinnacle prestige simultaneously traverse vied

4: The Roots of Our Language

    Roots Introduced   uni- cycle prime prima genus gener

5: Extending Your Word Power

Multiple Meanings
Roots Review
Using Words Precisely
Recognizing Word Forms
Putting Your Vocabulary to Use

1: Meeting Words in Context

The Ancient Olympics

Today in western Greece, Olympia is quiet and **melancholy**. The **rubble** of monuments lies scattered among the trees. There are few reminders of the glory that once was.

The origin of the Ancient Games has been lost in the mists of time. Sports events and religious **rituals** are known to have occurred at Olympia long before the first recorded date of the Olympic Games, 776 B.C.

The early facilities at Olympia were **meager**. The program of events was also limited. Then, in the sixth century B.C., there began a great cultural surge that lasted two hundred years. Olympia became a center of Greek culture and the focal point of the Mediterranean world.

The ancient Greeks worshiped the earth and the sun. They valued clarity of mind and youthful vigor. They believed that man's physical **prowess** and athletic skills should be honored along with the talents of his mind. Thus, their festivals combined sports, creative arts and religious ceremonies.

Nothing was more important to the Greeks than the Games. Every four years a truce was declared among enemies. The **moratorium** remained in effect for a month. Tens of thousands made the **pilgrimage** to Olympia. They witnessed running, jumping, throwing, wrestling and equestrian matches. Contests of poetry, drama and music were also held.

Each Greek city-state sent its best men. The athletes sought only victory. Second place was equal to failure. A victory at Olympia was the highest honor possible in Greece. When the victors returned home, their cities gave them huge payments. Crowds cheered them. Poets wrote odes to their triumphs, and sculptors immortalized them in bronze and stone.

The glory of the Games peaked at the height of classical Greek culture. The **subsequent** period of decline was long and slow. As the center of world power moved to Rome, the ideals of Olympia became less important.

The deathblow to the Games came with the introduction of Christianity. Glorification of the body was **disdained**. The celebration of the Greek gods was viewed as a pagan ritual. Finally, the emperor Theodosius decreed the Games forbidden in A.D. 394.

Soon the destruction of Olympia began. The statues and temples were dismantled by looters and toppled by earthquakes. Finally, floods slowly buried the area under a layer of silt. Once the most **revered** site in the ancient world, Olympia was forgotten for a thousand years.

Choose from the story two words that are unfamiliar to you or whose meanings you are not completely sure of. (Do not choose words that appear in boldfaced type.) Write the words on the lines provided below. Then, beside each word, write what you think it means, based on how it was used in the story.

1. _____ : _____

2. _____ : _____

When you have finished the exercises in this lesson, go to your dictionary and find the definitions for the words you entered above. If a word has more than one meaning, look for the one that defines the word as it is used in the story. Then write the words and their dictionary definitions in the Student Words pages at the back of the book. How close did you come to figuring out their meanings for yourself?

1:1 Using Context

For each of the boldfaced words in this exercise, go back and read the paragraph in which the word appears, paying special attention to the sentence in which it is used. Then, in the list that follows the vocabulary word, circle the word that has the same or almost the same meaning. Be prepared to support your choices.

1. **disdained**   popular   ignored   scorned   unknown

2. **meager**   numerous   exotic   ancient   sparse

3. **prowess**   height   youth   ability   appearance

4. **melancholy**   gloomy   distant   famous   luxurious

5. **subsequent**   earlier   spectacular   national   following

1:2 Making Connections

Listed below are the five vocabulary words you worked with in the last exercise, followed by sixteen words and phrases that are related to them in some way. They may be synonyms, antonyms or definitions. On the line next to each word or phrase, write the vocabulary word that is related to it.

disdained   meager   prowess   melancholy   subsequent

1. skill _____
2. abundant _____
3. valued _____
4. admired _____
5. somber _____
6. sad _____
7. following _____
8. minimal _____
9. held in contempt _____
10. clumsiness _____
11. plentiful _____
12. preceding _____
13. ability _____
14. cheerful _____
15. next _____
16. despised _____

1:3 Using Context

Below are five vocabulary words from the reading passage. Write them next to their meanings. Try to figure out the meaning of each word from the way in which it is used in the passage.

revered   rubble   pilgrimage   moratorium   rituals

1. Which word means "broken fragments"? _____

2. Which word means "ceremonies"? _____

3. Which word means "delay"? _____

4. Which word means "long journey"? _____

5. Which word means "highly respected"? _____

1:4 Making Connections

Complete each sentence with the correct vocabulary word.

revered   rubble   pilgrimage   moratorium   rituals

1. After the earthquake, rescuers searched through the _____, hoping to find survivors.

2. In Chaucer's *Canterbury Tales*, a motley assortment of characters travels for days, making a _____ to Canterbury.

3. Members of the Islamic faith observe religious _____ unfamiliar to most Americans.

4. Rock stars are among the most _____ heroes of American youth.

5. The bank issued a _____ on check-cashing during a temporary shortage of funds.

16   UNIT ONE

2: The Roots of Our Language

mono- *Mono-* is probably a familiar root to you. It means one, single, or alone. When used as part of a word, it indicates one of something. A monorail is a train that runs on one rail, and a monoplane is an airplane with one wing. You can see that by knowing the meaning of *mono-* and the meaning of *rail* and of *plane*, you are close to knowing the meanings of the words, even if you have never encountered them before.

chroma Knowing the meaning of *mono-*, you can make an educated guess at the meaning of *monochromatic* if you know that the root *chroma* refers to color. You could guess that a monochromatic picture is all of one color.

ocul- *Ocul-* is a root meaning eye. Combining *ocul-* with *mono-* gives us *monocular*. Something that is monocular affects or involves only one eye. Monocular vision is vision with only one eye. In times past, it was fashionable to wear a monocle, which was an eyeglass for just one eye.

-gram The root *-gram*, which means written or drawn, combines with *mono-* to create *monogram*. A monogram is several letters, usually initials, combined to form a single design.

tele- *-Gram* also appears in the word *telegram*. *Tele-* means far. So a telegram is a message sent a long distance. *Tele-* is part of many words that are frequently used today. All involve something done over a distance, or from afar.

-graph Simple roots combine with other roots to create networks of interrelated words. For example, *tele-* combined with *-graph* makes *telegraph*. *-Graph* is a root related to *-gram*, and means to write. So a telegraph is a device for communicating over a distance. And just to complete the circle, a monograph is a written document on one subject. It is a book or an article, usually a scholarly one.

This is a good point at which to suggest a word of caution. Knowing roots will help you to figure out the meanings of unfamiliar words, but will not provide you with precise definitions. Knowing the meanings of *tele-*, *-gram*, and *-graph*, for example, will not tell you whether *telegram* is the message or the means of sending it.

-gamos *Mono-* forms a part of many commonly used words. In the word *monogamy*, **-tonous** the root *-gamos* refers to marriage. Monogamy is the state of being married to only one person at a time. Do you know anyone who is monotonous? This word is related to *monotone*, which means all in the same tone or at the same pitch. Hence, a monotonous person is one who tends to get on one subject and who is therefore dull and boring.

Mono- is also a frequent root in the specialized vocabulary of the sciences. A monochloride, for example, is a substance whose molecules contain a single chloride atom.

-arch When *mono-* comes right before a part of a word beginning with a vowel, it is shortened to *mon-*, as in *monarch*. *-Arch* means rule, so a monarch is one who rules alone. A king is a monarch. Likewise, a monarchy is a state having a single ruler. Sociologists refer to a family or group that is ruled or dominated **matri-** by a woman as a matriarchy. Male dominated families or groups are called **patri-** patriarchies. *Matri-* means mother, and *patri-* means father.

UNIT ONE 17

2:1 Write each word or root listed on the left beside its meaning on the right.

monochromatic 1. _____ eye

monogamy 2. _____ one color

ocul- 3. _____ marriage to one person

chroma 4. _____ color

monotone 5. _____ on one note

2:2 Mark each statement as either true or false.

_____ 1. The root *tele-* means many.

_____ 2. A group or family ruled by a woman is a monarchy.

_____ 3. To improve vision in one eye, a person might use a monocle.

_____ 4. Monograms would help to keep your sweaters from getting mixed up with your roommate's.

_____ 5. If a person tells the same story three times, he is becoming monotonous.

2:3 Answer the following questions.

1. How many atoms of sodium would you find in monosodium glutamate? _____

2. If you know that *kinesis* means movement, what might *telekinesis* mean? _____

3. If polytheism is the worship of multiple gods, how many gods does a monotheist pray to? _____

4. How many sound tracks does a monophonic, or monaural, recording have? _____

5. If *bi-* means two, what does *bigamy* mean? _____

3: Meeting Words in Context

The Contests

In the sixth century B.C., the Ancient Olympic Games reached the **pinnacle** of their splendor. Athletes **vied** in about twenty events.

The pentathlon **comprised** the five most important events. The first was the long jump. The athletes carried weights known as halteres (hal-TEER-eez). They were released in midair, propelling the jumper forward. Modern jumpers have yet to discover how to use them to **augment** their distance. Legend says that one athlete leaped fifty feet using halteres. Today, a triple jump is necessary to **traverse** such a distance.

The second event was the discus throw. The ancient discus was a circular plate of metal or stone. It was two to three times the weight of the modern discus, which is two kilograms (about 4.4 pounds).

Next, the pentathletes competed in the javelin throw. A leather strap was wound around the shaft, rotating the javelin upon release. The strap increased stability and provided greater distance. Accuracy, as well as distance, was a **factor** in determining the winner.

The fourth event was the one-stade run. The stade was a unit of length equal to 190 feet—the length of the Olympic stadium.

The first four events were designed to narrow the field to two finalists. Those **contenders** would compete in the ultimate challenge of the pentathlon—the wrestling bout.

Several foot races were held at Olympia. The one-stade sprint was the most glamorous, and determined the swiftest runner. Longer races used a turning post. Contestants ran up and down the stadium as many as twenty-four times, a distance of about 2.75 miles. There were no marathon races at Olympia.

Most of the events were held in the main stadium. Crowds of spectators numbered up to fifty thousand. They sat on grassy slopes. The judges, because of the **prestige** of their role, sat on stone seats. Competitors performed naked, and no women were permitted inside the stadium.

Outside the stadium, in the hippodrome, horse and chariot races were held. Together, ten four-horse chariots might race, steering around the tight turns **simultaneously**. Accidents were the chief thrill for the crowd. Women were allowed in the hippodrome. In fact they won some equestrian events, because the prize was awarded to the owner of the horse or team.

The great ambition of the Greek athlete was to win at each festival. Many athletes became professionals, living off the rewards **bestowed** by their states.

Choose from the story two words that are unfamiliar to you or whose meanings you are not completely sure of. (Do not choose words that appear in boldfaced type.) Write the words on the lines provided below. Then, beside each word, write what you think it means, based on how it was used in the story.

1. _____ : _____

2. _____ : _____

When you have finished the exercises in this lesson, go to your dictionary and find the definitions for the words you entered above. If a word has more than one meaning, look for the one that defines the word as it is used in the story. Then write the words and their dictionary definitions in the Student Words pages at the back of the book. How close did you come to figuring out their meanings for yourself?

3:1 Using Context
Put an *x* in the box beside each correct answer. For clues to the meanings of the words, reread the parts of the passage in which they appear.

1. The sentence in which *simultaneously* appears gives you a clue that **simultaneously** means
   - ☐ a. hazardously.
   - ☐ b. at top speed.
   - ☐ c. occasionally.
   - ☐ d. at the same time.

2. Since the verb *vied* tells you what athletes did in sports events, you can guess that **vied** has to do with
   - ☐ a. cooperation.   ☐ c. training.
   - ☐ b. competition.   ☐ d. speed.

3. Since you are told that modern athletes have not been able to learn to use halteres and that they cannot jump as far as the ancient athletes who did use them, you can guess that **augment** means
   - ☐ a. record.   ☐ c. leap.
   - ☐ b. increase.   ☐ d. maintain.

4. From the information about what they did in the Olympics, you can figure out that **contenders** are
   - ☐ a. wrestlers.
   - ☐ b. losers.
   - ☐ c. contestants.
   - ☐ d. spectators.

5. In the story's final sentence, **bestowed** clearly means
   - ☐ a. taxed.
   - ☐ b. honored.
   - ☐ c. begrudged.
   - ☐ d. awarded.

3:2 Making Connections
Complete the following analogies by inserting one of the five vocabulary words in the blank at the end of each one. In an analogy, the last two words or phrases must be related to each other in the same way that the first two are related. The colon in an analogy is read "is to," and the symbol ∷ is read "as." So "high:low∷wide:narrow" would be read "high is to low as wide is to narrow."

simultaneously   vied   augment   contenders   bestowed

1. apart:separately∷together: _____

2. existed:lived∷granted: _____

3. selection:applicants∷elimination: _____

4. increase:lessen∷decrease: _____

5. failed:attempted∷lost: _____

3:3 Using Context

Listed below are five boldfaced words from the reading passage. The list is followed by definitions of the words as they are used in the passage. Write each word in front of its definition.

To figure out what each word means, go back to the passage and read the sentence that contains the word. If you can't discover the meaning from the way the word is used in the sentence, read the sentences that come before and after it for clues.

factor   traverse   comprised   pinnacle   prestige

1. _____ : highest point of development or achievement

2. _____ : something that tends to produce a result

3. _____ : contained

4. _____ : commanding position in people's minds

5. _____ : go across; span

3:4 Making Connections

The boldfaced words in the following sentences are short definitions of or synonyms for the five vocabulary words you worked with in the last exercise. On the line in front of each sentence, write the vocabulary word that has the same meaning as the boldfaced word or words.

1. _____ The author reached the **peak** of her success at the age of thirty-two. After that she could never recapture the magic that had made best-sellers of her early books.

2. _____ The exam **was made up of** questions on material covered during the entire semester.

3. _____ Because the bridge had been badly damaged by the hurricane, it was dangerous to **cross** the river at that point.

4. _____ A substantial salary increase was the biggest **influence** in my decision to accept the job.

5. _____ The fact that Emily Harrison was asked to be keynote speaker at the fiftieth international conference of the museum association is evidence of her **high standing** in the curatorial field.

4: The Roots of Our Language

uni-

cycle

The Latin root meaning one or single is *uni-*. It is the basis of such common words as *unicycle*, *unique* and *unit*. A unicycle is a one-wheeled vehicle that is often ridden by clowns at the circus. *Cycle*, of course, means wheel. *Unique* is an adjective that means one of a kind or having no equal. A *unit* is a single thing or a group of things considered as one. *Unit* is a noun. When we want a verb form, we use *unite*, which means to bring a number of things or people together to form a unit.

Union and *unify* are another closely related noun-verb pair. Union is the uniting of a group of things or people. For example, an organization of working people who have banded together to bargain for higher wages and improved working conditions is called a union. To unify means to unite or bring together as one.

Uni- also appears in the word *unicameral*, which means one chamber or one room. *Unicameral* is most frequently used to refer to a system of government that has one legislative chamber or body of elected officials. The United States has a *bicameral* legislature—the House of Representatives and the Senate.

Recognizing a root in a word is only a clue to the meaning of the word, of course. Let's look at *unisex* as an example. It is often seen on signs in hair salons and clothing stores. It doesn't mean that those establishments cut hair or sell clothes for only one sex. It means that they provide the same styles in hair and clothing for both men and women, giving everyone a somewhat uniform appearance.

Uniform means all the same, or all in one form. It can be a noun, referring to clothes that look just alike, or it can be an adjective, as in the following sentence: The bowls were of a uniform size and shape. Adding suffixes to many of the words we have mentioned so far creates other forms of those words. For example, *uniformity* and *uniformness* refer to the state or quality of being uniform.

Be careful not to confuse words containing the *uni-* prefix with words beginning with *i* to which the prefix *un-*, meaning not, has been affixed, as in *unintelligent* and *uninhibited*.

prime

prima

While we are talking about words that mean one, it's a good time to consider a root with a similar meaning—*prime*. *Prime* and the variation *prima* mean first. A prime minister is the first or most important minister in a government body. Prime beef is of the first quality. In an opera, the *prima donna* is the first lady or featured female singer. Over the years, a person who is temperamental and who expects special treatment has come to be referred to as a prima donna. A primer is the first reading textbook in school. Watch out for the difference in pronunciation between *primer* (PRIM-er), the beginning reader, and *primer* (PRY-mer), which is a first coat of paint.

genus

gener

Prime combines with the root *genus* or *gener*, meaning birth, to produce such words as *primogenitor*, a term for primitive human beings, literally "first to give birth." Don't confuse *primogenitor* with *primogeniture*, which means first to be born. Primogeniture refers to a system of inheritance whereby the first-born son inherits the parents' entire estate.

4:1 Write each word or root listed on the left beside its meaning on the right.

unify	1. _____	single
bicameral	2. _____	bring together
uniformity	3. _____	first
prime	4. _____	sameness
uni-	5. _____	two chambers or rooms

4:2 Mark each statement as either true or false.

_____ 1. Something that is unique is an almost exact match for something else.

_____ 2. A prima donna is a primitive human ancestor.

_____ 3. The first coat of paint is called prima.

_____ 4. The United States has a bicameral form of government.

_____ 5. A unisex barber serves both men and women.

4:3 Put an *x* in front of the answer choice you think is correct.

1. A first reading textbook is called a
   - ☐ a. prima.
   - ☐ b. primer.
   - ☐ c. primitive.

2. Things that are the same could be called
   - ☐ a. unified.
   - ☐ b. uniform.
   - ☐ c. unicameral.

3. If you were to invent a new kind of musical instrument, and you made just one, that instrument would be
   - ☐ a. prime.
   - ☐ b. unique.
   - ☐ c. primary.

4. The root *genus* refers to
   - ☐ a. intelligence.
   - ☐ b. sex.
   - ☐ c. birth.

5. A united group of people is called a
   - ☐ a. unit.
   - ☐ b. unicameral.
   - ☐ c. union.

5: Extending Your Word Power

5:1 Multiple Meanings

Some of the vocabulary words you encountered in this unit have meanings other than those they held in the reading passages. Below, two or three meanings are shown for each of the words *contend, factor* and *pinnacle*. On the line before each sentence, write the letter of the definition appropriate to the way in which the vocabulary word is used in the sentence.

contend

a. (v.) to compete

b. (v.) to state as a fact

_____ 1. Although she was in top physical condition, Margo did not feel ready to **contend** against the reigning champion.

_____ 2. We knew he was mistaken when we heard Alex **contend** that the state's unemployment rate had dropped.

_____ 3. I won the debate, in which I **contended** that participation in sports should be a requirement for students.

factor

a. (n.) something that contributes to a result or process

b. (n.) a number that is multiplied with another to produce a product

_____ 4. Because 2 x 3 = 6, both 2 and 3 are **factors** of six.

_____ 5. Improved nutrition is just one **factor** in the nation's longer average life span.

_____ 6. There are many sets of **factors** for some numbers.

pinnacle

a. (n.) a small turret or steeple attached to a building

b. (n.) a peak, as of a pointed form or structure

c. (n.) the highest point of development or achievement

_____ 7. Just as they reached the **pinnacle** of their popularity, the band stopped doing concert tours.

_____ 8. **Pinnacled** houses were typical of the Victorian period in architecture.

_____ 9. At the beach, Max takes pleasure in knocking the **pinnacles** off children's sand castles.

_____ 10. The Christmas tree had a star decorating its **pinnacle**.

5:2 Roots Review

The incomplete sentences below contain words that you learned in the two roots lessons in this unit. Complete each sentence so that it makes sense and shows the meaning of the boldfaced vocabulary word.

1. The highways in the Midwest are so **monotonous** that _____.

2. The teacher asked the first graders to open their **primers** so that they could _____.

3. One thing that makes elephants **unique** is that _____.

4. Marilyn's assignment for art was to create a **monochromatic** picture, so she decided to paint _____.

5. The babysitter was careful to cut **uniform** slices of cake for the children so that they _____.

6. The head of a **patriarchal** society is always _____.

7. According to the rules of **primogeniture**, the firstborn son _____.

8. The speaker delivered his speech in such a **monotone** that _____.

9. Although **monogamy** is the rule in many cultures, there are societies in which _____.

10. Ellen showed that she considered herself a real **prima donna** when she _____.

5:3 Choosing Just the Right Word

As you have seen in the exercises in lessons one and three of this unit, many of the words you have worked with have a number of synonyms. In some cases the synonyms convey different shades of meaning. It is up to you to choose the words that express your ideas as vividly and accurately as possible.

In this exercise, synonym studies are provided for three of your vocabulary words. Use either the vocabulary words or their synonyms to complete the sentences in the exercise. Refer to the synonym studies as you decide which choice carries the best meaning for the specific context of each sentence.

revere   reverence

Both the verbs *revere* and *reverence* indicate deep respect for something or someone. *Revere* means to feel deep respect mixed with love. *The troops revered their leader.* *Reverence* implies respect and love, but also awe and wonder. *Reverence* usually applies to things, rather than people. *Some newcomers to America reverence the Statue of Liberty, which to them symbolizes this country's opportunities.*

1. In some societies, young people are taught to _____ elderly citizens for their wisdom and experience.

2. Many modern feminists _____ Susan B. Anthony and others who helped win women the right to vote.

3. In anthropology, we learned about a tribe of Indians who _____ the moon, for they believed that it held mystical powers.

delay   postponement   moratorium

Delay means the general fact of being put off to another time or being caused to be late. *Our train is behind schedule. We expect a two-hour delay.* *Postponement* implies putting something off until a definite time. *The wedding will take place May 30 rather than April 10; we have informed the guests about the postponement.* In the case of a *moratorium*, action stops temporarily because of an official or legal authorization. *The police chief declared a moratorium on issuing parking tickets downtown during the busy shopping season.*

4. I couldn't phone you until now; I apologize for the _____ .

5. There was a brief _____ between acts as the stagehands arranged the props on the set.

6. At first it seemed that the meeting would have to be rescheduled for the following Tuesday, but a _____ turned out to be unnecessary.

7. Since there was a budget surplus, citizens petitioned for a _____ on city taxes, but the mayor denied their request.

8. When Mrs. Burlingame was called for jury duty, she was unable to attend. A _____ was granted, and she fulfilled her obligation two weeks later than originally planned.

journey   voyage   pilgrimage

> *Journey, voyage* and *pilgrimage* are nouns having to do with travel over a long distance. A journey is a long or tiring trip, usually on land and with a specific destination. *They loaded up the wagon train and set off on their journey to the West. Voyage* usually implies a long trip by water. It is also used in speaking of space travel. *Seasickness plagued him during the voyage to Europe. Pilgrimage* is sometimes used to mean a long journey, but usually it suggests that the journey is made to some sacred place, or any place that is to be reverenced. *Each year, thousands make a pilgrimage to Shakespeare's birthplace, Stratford-upon-Avon.*

9. Christopher Columbus's _____ to the New World was sponsored by the Queen of Portugal.

10. Ancient Greeks, on a _____ to honor the goddess Athena, made their way to the Parthenon in Athens.

11. Our _____ to Mexico was interrupted when the car broke down.

12. Apollo 11 carried the first lunar astronauts on their _____ to the moon.

13. "You must be tired from your _____," said our host. "Come in and rest. Let the servants tend to your horses."

5:4 Recognizing Word Forms

The words listed below are other forms of the vocabulary words you have worked with in this unit. Fill in the blank in each sentence with the appropriate vocabulary word. Use what you have learned in this unit to help you figure out what the words mean.

comprises   contender   simultaneous   prestigious   reverent   disdain   augmented

factors   traversed   meagerness   ritualistic   vying   subsequently

1. Marlie gave me a look of _____ when I suggested that she spend Saturday morning cleaning her room.

2. The Nobel Prize is a particularly _____ award.

3. Because of the _____ of his salary as a public defender, Alan rarely purchased luxury items.

4. A large supply of natural resources has been one of the primary _____ in the nation's economic growth.

5. The _____ worshipers made offerings at the religious service.

6. The graduate student _____ her income by delivering mail.

7. The two basketball players made a _____ leap for the ball and collided under the backboard.

8. The _____ commencement exercises always included a procession of graduates, remarks by a guest speaker, and the singing of the school song.

9. Starting from New York, with San Francisco as their destination, Marty and Chris _____ the country by car.

10. Because he didn't meet the tournament's eligibility requirements, Eric was not allowed to be a _____.

11. This new album _____ the group's greatest hits.

12. Today, the supervisor will train and assist you. _____, you'll be on your own.

13. _____ for their parents' praise, the two children tried to outdo each other in every activity they were involved in.

5:5 Putting Your Vocabulary to Use

This word-search puzzle conceals fifteen vocabulary words from this unit. They are printed horizontally, vertically, diagonally, backward and upside down.

Begin by listing the vocabulary words next to their clues below. Then find the words in the puzzle, circling them as you locate them.

1. _____ following
2. _____ one-wheeled vehicle
3. _____ holy journey
4. _____ peak
5. _____ king or queen
6. _____ broken fragments
7. _____ scorned
8. _____ temperamental person
9. _____ respected
10. _____ to join
11. _____ sad
12. _____ tiresomely repetitive
13. _____ one-winged plane
14. _____ increase
15. _____ one of a kind

```
a b p i l g r i m a g e o g j i
a g r k h l i i k n g l g d p s
p k j m f s m o n a r c h e r k
i s u o n o t o n o m y w w i i
n y l o h c n a l e m c i r m h
n a d z k l a d o b t i v n a g
a k m i t c n h g p u n s h d e
c m h c s w m c l t e u q e o n
l t n o l d b a a b b s g n n a
e n o r n d a d m s l s e a n l
p e q u i p s i e s o u v l a p
n m o e z d l q n r y f k p r o
i g n g s a u p n e e q p i r n
r u b b l e y s x s d v w b u o
n a c e n u n i q u e n e t o m
t h e t i n u r a o n b e r c s
```

UNIT ONE 29

UNIT 2

1: Meeting Words in Context

    Reading Selection   Subterranean Spectacles

    Words Introduced   abyss allure apprehension exhilaration
                                  fissures impel misgivings scrutinizing
                                  subterranean thrive

2: The Roots of Our Language

    Roots Introduced   du- dual plex plic bi- annual cent-
                                  -ennial -ped -ary

3: Meeting Words in Context

    Reading Selection   Caving Equipment

    Words Introduced   abrasion afford banter capacious ensure
                                    labyrinth paraphernalia profusion
                                  provocative prudent

4: The Roots of Our Language

    Roots Introduced   di- -plo -opia pteron -sauros pod-
                                  ped- manus

5: Extending Your Word Power

Multiple Meanings
Roots Review
Using Words Precisely
Recognizing Word Forms
Putting Your Vocabulary to Use

1: Meeting Words in Context

Subterranean Spectacles

In a magical realm beneath the surface of the earth, passageways twist for mile upon mile. They alternate between tunnels as wide as superhighways and **fissures** so thin that a body can barely squeeze through. Caverns offer dramatic scenery that has attracted adventurous spirits for hundreds of years.

The **subterranean** landscape holds fantastic geological formations created by the slow passage of water through massive layers of limestone. Over many thousands of years, natural chemical processes have formed stalactites and stalagmites. Those spears of rock decorate the floors and ceilings of underground rooms. Delicate mineral crystals shimmer in pools and streams. Sheets of flowstone form graceful draperies.

By **scrutinizing** such formations, geologists have found clues to events that took place in the earth a billion years ago. Other scientists have studied the unique life forms that **thrive** in the cold, dark, wet world of caves. Their observations have shed light on the incredible adaptability of living things.

Caves have given a great deal to science. But it is amateur explorers who most frequently probe their dark mysteries. A keen sense of adventure and a strong desire to experience the **exhilaration** of discovery **impel** them to seek out new passages and chambers. Cavers must be well prepared and cautious, for caverns hold great peril as well as great beauty. Vertical shafts, often hidden in shadow, extend hundreds of feet down into the earth. A fall into such an **abyss** would mean death. Because of such dangers, many cavers set forth on their explorations with a healthy mix of **apprehension** and excitement. Despite any **misgivings** they might have, thousands of cavers venture underground every year. For them, the **allure** of the caverns outweighs the risks.

Choose from the story two words that are unfamiliar to you or whose meanings you are not completely sure of. (Do not choose words that appear in boldfaced type.) Write the words on the lines provided below. Then, beside each word, write what you think it means, based on how it was used in the story.

1. _____ : _____

_____

2. _____ : _____

_____

When you have finished the exercises in this lesson, go to your dictionary and find the definitions for the words you entered above. If a word has more than one meaning, look for the one that defines the word as it is used in the story. Then write the words and their dictionary definitions in the Student Words pages at the back of the book. How close did you come to figuring out their meanings for yourself?

1:1 Using Context

Put an *x* in the box beside each correct answer. For clues to the meanings of the words, reread the parts of the passage in which they appear.

1. As used in the passage, **subterranean** means
   - ☐ a. ancient.
   - ☐ b. treacherous.
   - ☐ c. bizarre.
   - ☐ d. underground.

2. In the last paragraph, **apprehension** means
   - ☐ a. fiction.
   - ☐ b. fear.
   - ☐ c. darkness.
   - ☐ d. joy.

3. The word *such* in the phrase "such an abyss" tells you that an abyss was described in the previous sentence. That context tells you that an **abyss** is
   - ☐ a. an adventure.   ☐ c. a pit.
   - ☐ b. a gallery.   ☐ d. a risk.

4. Since cavers weigh the allure of caverns against the risks of exploring them, **allure** must mean
   - ☐ a. danger.
   - ☐ b. attraction.
   - ☐ c. beauty.
   - ☐ d. mystery.

5. Look at the sentence in which the word *impel* appears. All the ideas that come before the verb tell you that **impel** must mean
   - ☐ a. require.
   - ☐ b. discourage.
   - ☐ c. allow.
   - ☐ d. drive.

1:2 Making Connections

Complete each sentence with the correct vocabulary word.

subterranean   apprehension   abyss   allure   impel

1. Jason's _____ about starting school disappeared when his kindergarten teacher greeted him warmly.

2. Since the volcano is no longer active, one can climb to the top and peer into the _____ that once spewed destruction over the surrounding countryside.

3. In Montreal, _____ malls allow shoppers to escape winter's cruel elements while they complete their errands.

4. I know that her strong sense of professional ambition will _____ her to seek a promotion.

5. The _____ of the exotic and delicious foods drew hundreds of diners to the restaurant.

1:3 Using Context
Write each vocabulary word beside its correct meaning. Try to figure out what the word means from the way it is used in the story.

1. **thrive**

_____ swim   _____ flourish

_____ freeze   _____ hibernate

2. **scrutinizing**

_____ digging   _____ removing

_____ examining   _____ climbing

3. **fissures**

_____ canyons   _____ openings

_____ roadways   _____ streams

4. **misgivings**

_____ doubts   _____ mistakes

_____ solitude   _____ dizziness

5. **exhilaration**

_____ reward   _____ challenge

_____ thrill   _____ conquest

1:4 Making Connections
Listed below are the five vocabulary words you worked with in the last exercise, followed by twelve words and phrases that are related to them in some way. They may be synonyms, antonyms or definitions. On the line next to each word or phrase, write the vocabulary word that is related to it. Consult a dictionary for the definition of any word whose meaning you are unsure of.

thrive   scrutinizing   fissures   misgivings   exhilaration

1. cracks _____   7. confidence _____

2. worries _____   8. inspecting _____

3. fail _____   9. high spirits _____

4. boredom _____   10. grow vigorously _____

5. studying _____   11. schisms _____

6. joy _____   12. prosper _____

34   UNIT TWO

2: The Roots of Our Language

du-   In words that mean two of something, the Latin prefix *du-* is often present. For example, a duet is a piece of music composed for two voices or instruments, and two singers or musicians who perform together are called a duo.

dual   A duo is a pair of people or things. The word *dual* means *two*. It is often used to refer to two things that are alike. A dual-tired truck, for instance, has tires that are mounted on the axles in pairs, creating double tires. (The word *double* comes from *duo*.) People sometimes speak of a thing as having a dual purpose, meaning that it has two uses. You have to be careful when writing the word *dual*, because the English language has another word that is pronounced the same but is spelled differently and has a different meaning. A du*e*l is a fight between two people.

-plex   Something that is duplex has two main elements or parts. A duplex house is a two-family house. *-Plex* means fold, so *duplex* means two-fold. *-Plex* is a

-plic   form of the root *-plic*, which appears in the noun *duplicate* (DOO-plih-kut), meaning one of two things that are alike. Duplicates are usually copies or reproductions. The verb form of the word means to make an exact copy. When we photocopy a document, we are duplicating it. The copy itself is a duplicate of the original.

A closely related word is *duplicity* (doo-PLIS-ut-ee), which means doubleness of thought, speech or action. Duplicity is a form of dishonesty whereby a person talks or acts in a manner that contradicts what he or she really thinks or intends to do.

bi-   Another Latin root that means two is *bi-*. It appears, for instance, in the words *bicycle* (two-wheeled) and *bicameral* (bye-KAM-uh-rul) (two-chambered).

Bi- is, without a doubt, a useful prefix, but it is known to cause confusion in certain instances. Because of *bi-*, it can be hard to know for sure when

annual   something is going to take place. *Biannual* means twice a year. (*Annual* means yearly.) But *bimonthly* can mean either twice a month or every two months! Likewise, *biweekly* means twice a week or every two weeks. *Bicentennial*, thank goodness, has only one meaning. It refers to a two-hundredth anniver-

cent-   sary. *Cent-* means hundred, and *-ennial* is a form of *-annual*. An event that

-ennial   occurs biennially takes places every two years. *Biennial* should not be confused with *biannual*.

Another common word that uses the prefix *bi-* is *binocular*, meaning for two eyes, or using two eyes. Binoculars are double telescopes that are joined to be used with both eyes. *Bifocal* means having two focal lengths. In eyeglasses, a bifocal lens is ground so that half the lens corrects for near vision, and half for vision at a distance.

Bimanual, biped and *bicuspid* all relate to parts of the body. *Bimanual* means done with or needing two hands. A *biped* is a two-footed creature.

-ped   (-*Ped* means foot.) A bicuspid is a tooth that has two cusps, or points. Your bicuspids are the fourth and fifth teeth from the middle, on both your top and bottom rows of teeth.

Bi- is also used in mathematics. *Binary* (BYE-nuh-ree) means made up of two parts. The binary number system is based on the number 2. The root

-ary   *-ary* means pertaining to. Digital computers are based on the binary system.

2:1 Write each word or root listed on the left beside its meaning on the right.

duplicity   1. _____ double

-ennial   2. _____ twice a year

binocular   3. _____ annual

biannual   4. _____ saying one thing but meaning another

dual   5. _____ for two eyes

2:2 Mark each statement as either true or false.

_____ 1. A horse is a biped.

_____ 2. A statue that is made to look just like a famous sculpture is a duplicate.

_____ 3. A bicentennial is celebrated twice every hundred years.

_____ 4. A person has two bicuspids.

_____ 5. A binary number system uses only two numbers.

2:3 Put an *x* in front of the answer choice you think is correct.

1. Eyeglasses that help a person see better both near and far are called
   ☐ a. bimanual.   ☐ b. bifocals.   ☐ c. binoculars.

2. A machine whose operation requires the use of two hands is
   ☐ a. bimanual.   ☐ b. bilateral.   ☐ c. bicuspid.

3. A song for two voices is a
   ☐ a. duel.   ☐ b. duet.   ☐ c. duo.

4. A tooth having two points is called a
   ☐ a. biped.   ☐ b. binary.   ☐ c. bicuspid.

5. A reproduction is a
   ☐ a. dual.   ☐ b. duplicate.   ☐ c. bimanual.

3: Meeting Words in Context

Caving Equipment

Cavers require a great deal of specialized equipment in order to safely and successfully maneuver through the unique terrain of caverns. The very first cavers entered those mysterious underground landscapes equipped with nothing but intense curiosity. They soon discovered that though their curiosity led them to wondrous discoveries, they needed bodily protection and some kind of equipment to help them in their precarious explorations.

The sturdy clothes of today's caver include high boots, kneepads and a helmet. These **afford** warmth and prevent **abrasion** from rubbing against rough walls. A speleologist (SPEE-lee-AHL-uh-jist), or caver, also carries a pack that is small enough to fit through tight spots but **capacious** enough to hold basic supplies. It may contain high energy food, a first aid kit, a super-insulating blanket, water and tools to repair the helmet light. **Prudent** cavers also carry a flashlight, waterproof matches and candles. They take a compass, notepad and pencil to record their winding route through the **labyrinth** of passageways.

In the 1890s, maverick caver Édouard-Alfred Martel and some companions were on their way to explore a French cave. Martel recalled that a puzzled policeman stopped to question them. Taking note of the enormous amount of baggage that the men were carrying, the officer asked if they were a traveling circus, and if so, if they had a license. Martel tolerated such **banter** cheerfully, for he was fully aware that his life depended on his **profusion** of equipment.

Modern speleologists have improved many of Martel's methods and devices. They have also developed a wide array of caving hardware. But they still share his belief in thorough preparation and reliable gear.

Harnesses, nylon ropes, and other mountaineering gear are needed for exploring caves. A small steel-cable ladder is good for short climbs. Longer climbs require mechanical ascenders. A rappel rack eases rope stress and allows a controlled drop. A carabiner—an oblong metal ring that clips to a rope harness that goes around the caver's chest—attaches securely to other gear and to ropes used for climbing and descending. It is used to **ensure** safe harness connections.

Martel was the first to use traditional mountain climbers' **paraphernalia** in caves. In the ups and downs of caving, he found this gear most useful. He knew many mountaineers loved dramatic adventure. So he made a **provocative** challenge to the daring mountaineers of his day. He said, "Try mountaineering reversed for once."

Choose from the story two words that are unfamiliar to you or whose meanings you are not completely sure of. (Do not choose words that appear in boldfaced type.) Write the words on the lines provided below. Then, beside each word, write what you think it means, based on how it was used in the story.

1. _____ : _____

2. _____ : _____

When you have finished the exercises in this lesson, go to your dictionary and find the definitions for the words you entered above. If a word has more than one meaning, look for the one that defines the word as it is used in the story. Then write the words and their dictionary definitions in the Student Words pages at the back of the book. How close did you come to figuring out their meanings for yourself?

3:1 Using Context
For each of the boldfaced words in this exercise, go back and read the paragraph in which the word appears, paying special attention to the sentence in which it is used. Then, in the list that follows the vocabulary word, circle the word or words that have the same or almost the same meaning. Be prepared to support your choices.

1. **profusion**   type   purchase   large amount   knowledge   abundance

2. **prudent**   careful   nervous   tired   wise   novice

3. **afford**   require   decrease   change   provide   prevent

4. **abrasion**   illness   fear   irritation   scraping   damage to instruments

5. **capacious**   convenient   roomy   useful   organized   strong

3:2 Making Connections
Complete the following analogies by inserting one of the five vocabulary words in the blank at the end of each one. Remember that in an analogy the last two words or phrases must be related to each other in the same way that the first two are related. The colon in an analogy is read "is to," and the symbol :: is read "as." So "high:low::wide:narrow" would be read "high is to low as wide is to narrow."

profusion   prudent   afford   abrasion   capacious

1. take away:give::withhold: _____

2. small:compact::spacious: _____

3. poverty:wealth::scarcity: _____

4. bone:fracture::skin: _____

5. rash:cautious::reckless: _____

38   UNIT TWO

3:3 Using Context

Listed below are five boldfaced words from the reading passage. The list is followed by definitions of the words as they are used in the passage. Write each word in front of its definition.

To figure out what each word means, go back to the passage and read the sentence that contains the word. If you can't discover the meaning from the way the word is used in the sentence, read the sentences that come before and after it for clues.

labyrinth   provocative   ensure   banter   paraphernalia

1. _____ : tending to call forth action or thought

2. _____ : make certain; guarantee

3. _____ : equipment; apparatus

4. _____ : playful teasing

5. _____ : confusing or complicated arrangement

3:4 Making Connections

The boldfaced words in the following sentences are short definitions of or synonyms for the five vocabulary words you worked with in the last exercise. On the line in front of each sentence, write the vocabulary word that has the same meaning as the boldfaced word or words.

labyrinth   paraphernalia   provocative   banter   ensure

1. _____ The department manager frowned upon the **joking** that went on among the employees.

2. _____ New nurses at Memorial Hospital frequently lose their way in the **complicated layout** of the corridors.

3. _____ The instructor could be counted on to open the discussion with a **compelling** and interesting comment.

4. _____ Regular exercise can't **make certain** that you'll live to be one hundred years old, but it can improve your health and lengthen your life.

5. _____ Mrs. Reardon built a special enclosure in the backyard to store her gardening **tools and equipment**.

4: The Roots of Our Language

di-

The prefixes *du-* and *bi-* are the Latin way of saying two. The Greek prefix for two is *di-*. It is used in a lot of scientific words. An example is *dioxide*, a compound in which each molecule has two atoms of oxygen. Carbon dioxide, for instance, is the gas in beer, champagne and most soft drinks. *Di-* also appears in *dipole* (DYE-pole), meaning two poles. A dipole is a pair of magnetic poles of equal strength and opposite sign. A dipole is also a kind of radio or television antenna that has two horizontal conducting rods that are parallel and separated slightly.

-plo

As a student, you might be interested in acquiring one or more diplomas. The most common meaning of *diploma* today is a document granted by a university or college, testifying to a degree taken by a person. The word comes to us from a Greek word meaning to double, or to bend or fold double. The *-plo* part comes from our old friend *-ply* or *-plex*, meaning fold. Hence, a diploma was originally a piece of paper or parchment that had been folded in two. The original Greek meaning of *diploma* was a letter of recommendation, or a letter of license or privilege. Its first English meaning was a state paper, or an official document. So a diplomat is a person who carries and uses official documents. Diplomats conduct relations between their own country and a foreign country. They practice the art, or skill, of diplomacy. Diplomatic documents are official documents related to international relations. The earliest diplomats were required to carry their "diplomas" with them. To this day, diplomats present their credentials to the head of state when they arrive at a foreign post.

-opia

A word with a similar root is *diplopia*, meaning double vision. *-Opia* means eyes or vision.

A *dichotomy* is a division into two parts, especially a division into opposing groups. It is often used when speaking of a division in thought, as in the ideas of two opposing political groups.

In art we have *diptych* (DIP-tick), which refers to a two-fold, or two-part, picture. A diptych is a work of art consisting of a picture or series of pictures painted or carved on two hinged tablets. Historically, diptychs were used to decorate altars.

pteron

-sauros

Dipterous (DIP-tuh-rus) means having two wings. Flies, mosquitoes and gnats are dipterous. The *pterous* part of the word is from the root *pteron*, meaning wing. A pterosaur (also known as the pterodactyl) is the so-called flying dinosaur. *-Sauros* is the Greek word for lizard. Most of the dinosaurs were earthbound, however, and belonged to a class called sauropods (*pod* meaning feet).

pod-
ped-

manus

Pod-, a Greek root, and *ped-*, a Latin root, both mean foot. *Ped-* occurs in such common words as *pedestrian* (someone who travels on foot) and *pedal* (a lever pushed by the foot). A pedicure is the care and treatment of the feet, toes and nails. It is related, of course, to manicure (*manus* meaning hand), the care of hands and fingernails, especially the trimming and polishing of the fingernails.

4:1 Write each word or root listed on the left beside its meaning on the right.

diplomacy 1. _____ hand

-sauros 2. _____ the art of international negotiation

manus 3. _____ wing

dichotomy 4. _____ lizard

pteron 5. _____ a division into two

4:2 Mark each statement as either true or false.

_____ 1. Most creatures that are dipterous can fly.

_____ 2. When there is a dichotomy there is disagreement.

_____ 3. Diplomats are expected to be friendly and good communicators.

_____ 4. Sauropods had two wings.

_____ 5. A diptych might be found in a museum.

4:3 Answer the following questions.

1. Manacles are restraints. What part of the body are they meant to restrain? _____

2. If *bronto* means thunder, what does *brontosaurus* mean? _____

3. How many colors does a dichromatic illustration have? _____

4. With what part of the body is the condition called myopia concerned? _____

5. If a pedometer measures distance, in what activity would you expect it to be useful?

_____

5: Extending Your Word Power

5:1 Multiple Meanings
Below are several words you have met in this unit. Each of these words has more than one meaning. In this exercise, the boldfaced word or phrase in each sentence corresponds to one of the listed words. In the blank before each sentence, write the appropriate vocabulary word. Turn to your glossary for the alternate meanings of any words you are unsure of.

    apprehension   allure   banter   thrive   afford

1. _____ Following the **arrest** of the suspect, the police held a press conference to announce that the search had ended.

2. _____ You have a fine **understanding** of the basic concepts of physics, but you need to work on learning some of the specific terminology associated with the subject.

3. _____ You may think that Jamie is "just a country boy," but I predict that he will **be very successful** in Chicago.

4. _____ He couldn't **spare the money for** a new car so he bought a used one.

5. _____ I wish you wouldn't **joke around** with the trainees. They might be inclined to forget how serious this orientation session really is.

6. _____ "Do you actually think that perfume is going to **attract** any admirers?" asked Phoebe as she wrinkled her nose.

7. _____ At a job interview, you can't **safely manage** to be impolite if you want to be hired.

5:2 Roots Review
The incomplete sentences below contain words that you learned in the two roots lessons in this unit. Complete each sentence so that it makes sense and shows the meaning of the boldfaced vocabulary word.

1. A **pterosaur** was a dinosaur that _____ _____ .

2. George's **duplicity** became evident when it was discovered that he _____ _____ _____ .

3. The **bimonthly** journal that Eric writes for is published _____ _____ .

42   UNIT TWO

4. Since Angela had to write a report on a **dipterous** creature, she decided to do research on the _____.

5. Rick knew that the label **"biped"** under the picture of the deer was wrong because _____.

6. Martha explained that the **dual** purpose of her invention was to _____.

7. The debate was essentially an attempt to examine the **dichotomy** between _____.

8. The fact that Harry's science project was a **duplicate** of Terry's proved that _____.

9. Mr. Harrison's skill in **diplomacy** was evidenced by his _____.

10. Ellen's **diplopia** caused her _____.

5:3 Choosing Just the Right Word

Many of the words you have worked with in this unit have a number of synonyms. In some cases the synonyms convey different shades of meaning. When you write and speak, it is up to you to choose words that express your ideas as accurately as possible.

Following are synonym studies for three of your vocabulary words. Use either the vocabulary words or their synonyms to complete the sentences in the exercise that follows. Refer to the synonym studies as you decide which word carries the best meaning for the specific context of each sentence.

wise   prudent

Wise and *prudent* both mean having and showing good judgment. *Wise* implies that one has knowledge and understanding of people and of what is right or true in conduct or in life. *The wise judge was respected for his fair and compassionate decisions.* *Prudent* suggests good judgment with respect to practical matters, and usually includes a sense of avoiding negative consequences. *It is prudent to keep candles and flashlight batteries on hand in case of a power failure.*

ensure   insure

Although *ensure* and *insure* are often used interchangeably, they do have slight differences in meaning. *Ensure* means to make sure or certain. *Just taking vitamins won't ensure good health.* *Insure* is used to mean to arrange for money to be paid in case of loss, accident or death. *In some states it is illegal to drive a car that is not insured.*

fear   alarm   apprehension

Fear, alarm and *apprehension* all relate to the feeling experienced when harm or danger threatens. *Fear* means any feeling of being afraid. *The pilot felt no fear as he made a difficult emergency landing.* *Alarm* suggests fright brought on by the awareness of danger. *The smell of smoke caused alarm among the residents of the apartment building.* *Apprehension* implies that one fears something that he or she expects may happen. *Many cavers experience a feeling of apprehension before entering a shaft.*

1. Because of his _____ about the next day's interview, Morris could hardly sleep.

2. Madeleine has gained much knowledge and skill in her years of experience, and young editors frequently seek her _____ advice.

3. Keep the temperature of your refrigerator at forty degrees or colder to _____ that the food will remain fresh.

4. _____ tourists carry travelers' checks instead of large amounts of cash.

5. Mikey likes to have a night light on in his room to dispel his _____ of the dark.

6. If you _____ your home against theft, you will be able to replace any items that might be stolen.

7. Don't you think it would have been more _____ to have winterized your car before the cold weather hit?

8. A look of _____ crossed her face as her tires skidded on the wet pavement.

9. People who suffer from claustrophobia have an intense _____ of enclosed places.

10. _____ parents know where to draw the line between treating their children well and spoiling them.

5:4 Recognizing Word Forms

The sentences below require you to use some other forms of the words you have worked with in this unit. The words you will need to fill in the blanks are among the words listed below. Each sentence has two blanks. If you are unsure of the meaning of a word, refer to the glossary.

apprehension apprehensive   **capacious** capaciousness capacity

scrutinizing scrutinized scrutiny   **provocative** provocation provoked provoking

exhilaration exhilarated exhilarating **banter** bantering bantered

profusion profuse profusely   **ensures** ensure ensured ensuring

abrasion abrasive abrade   **impel** impelling impulse

1. The auditorium has an extremely large _____, _____ that a crowd of ten thousand could easily be accommodated.

2. Greg was _____ before making his sky dive, but the experience turned out to be so _____ that he was eager to try it again.

3. After testing several products, we found that Gleemo _____ the strongest cleaning power, but it was so _____ that it scratched the surfaces of most appliances.

4. Ellen's _____ humor _____ smiles from some and irritation in others.

5. Seized by a sudden _____, Michelle threw her arms around Derek and kissed him. He blushed _____, but I don't think he was offended.

6. The inspectors _____ the garments closely to _____ that the clothing shipped would be of the highest quality.

5:5 Putting Your Vocabulary to Use

In solving this word puzzle, you will be using some of the vocabulary words introduced in this unit and in the previous unit. Below is a list of definitions and synonyms for those words. For each definition or synonym, think of a vocabulary word that has the same meaning. Write the word in the puzzle space with the corresponding number. One letter of the word, together with the number of lines in each answer space, provide clues to the word. Notice that the letters that are given form a phrase related to caving.

1. having two wings
2. outstanding skill
3. gave ceremoniously
4. competed
5. article on one subject
6. flourish
7. examining
8. thrill
9. happening twice a year
10. happening once every two years
11. cautious
12. scorn
13. two-footed
14. tending to stir someone to action
15. long distance message
16. underground
17. music for two to play or sing
18. increase
19. teasing
20. copy

1. _ _ _ _ _ r _ _ _
2. _ _ _ _ e _ _
3. _ _ s _ _ _ _ _
4. _ _ e _
5. _ _ _ _ _ a _ _
6. _ _ r _ _ _
7. _ c _ _ _ _ _ _ _ _
8. _ _ h _ _ _ _ _ _ _
9. _ _ _ _ _ a _
10. _ _ _ n _ _ _ _
11. _ _ _ d _ _ _
12. _ _ _ _ a _ _
13. _ _ _ _ d
14. _ _ _ v _ _ _ _ _
15. _ _ _ e _ _ _ _
16. _ _ _ _ _ _ n _ _ _
17. _ _ _ t
18. _ u _ _ _ _
19. _ _ _ _ _ r
20. _ _ _ _ _ _ _ e

Mrs. Malaprop's Contribution to the Language

When accused of trying to show off by filling her ordinary conversation with difficult words whose meaning she clearly didn't know, Mrs. Malaprop replied, "Sure, if I *reprehend* anything in this world, it is the use of my *oracular* tongue, & a nice *derangement* of *epitaphs*." The words she was reaching for, but couldn't quite catch, were *apprehend, vernacular, arrangement* and *epithets*. Mrs. Malaprop was a humorous character in R. B. Sheridan's play *The Rivals,* written in 1775. Mrs. Malaprop's outrageous misuse of the English language gave rise to a couple of new words: *malaprop* (MAL-uh-PROP) and *malapropism* (MAL-uh-PROP-iz-um). They both refer to the humorous misuse of a word, especially to the erroneous use of a word that sounds somewhat like the right one but that is ludicrous in the context.

Though it would be difficult to find a person who uttered as many malapropisms as Mrs. Malaprop, most of us let them fall now and then. We might confuse *instill* with *inspire,* or *afflict* with *inflict,* for instance. Such slips are quite common.

Mr. Sheridan derived Mrs. Malaprop's name from the word *malapropos* (MAL-AP-ruh-POH), meaning not suited to the purpose, or inappropriate. That word, in turn, was derived from the French phrase *mal a propos, mal* meaning poor or unsuitable, and *a propos* meaning to the purpose or object.

Do you find this explanation reprehensible, or is it difficult to understand?

"You're welcome to share my umbrella, Professor. I'm expecting a bit of perspiration."

UNIT 3

1: Meeting Words in Context

Reading Selection   By Sun and Stars

Words Introduced   advocates attribute elude impede misconception orient replenish subtle surmised velocity

2: The Roots of Our Language

Roots Introduced   tri- dent-

3: Meeting Words in Context

Reading Selection   Where Do All the Wild Birds Go?

Words Introduced   adequate imminent imperiled initiated myriad optimal paramount perceived restored substantially

4: The Roots of Our Language

Roots Introduced   quad- quatr- quadri- poly- -gon twi- twe-

5: Extending Your Word Power

Multiple Meanings
Roots Review
Using Words Precisely
Recognizing Word Forms
Putting Your Vocabulary to Use

1: Meeting Words in Context

By Sun and Stars

Migratory birds do not travel as fast as some people once believed. A German scientist in 1895, for example, sought to **attribute** speeds in excess of 200 miles an hour to some migrating birds. But later research showed this estimate was much too high. The peregrine falcon reaches a **velocity** of 165 to 180 miles per hour while chasing food, but very few birds can fly that fast. Birds have two speeds. One is for normal flying, and a faster one allows them to **elude** enemies or pursue food. Most songbirds have cruising speeds of between 25 and 50 miles per hour during migration.

Scientists have found that migration often consists of a series of single, long flights, followed by feeding for several days to **replenish** fat needed for the next stage of the journey.

At one time it was **surmised** by many that migrating birds traveled at heights above 15,000 feet, because flying was easier high up. Lack of oxygen and of buoyancy in the thin air, however, would **impede** such high-altitude flying for all but the largest species. Observation from towers and by radar and airplanes proves that most birds travel below 5,000 feet above the earth during migration.

A particularly strange aspect of bird migration is navigation. The old **misconception** that birds have a mysterious sense of direction or some sort of built-in compass has been discarded by most modern scientists. In place of this theory are a host of others, with **advocates** and evidence to support them.

Some scientists believe that many birds travel by the sun and stars. That would account for amazing flights across the ocean. Other scientists believe that birds use familiar landmarks to guide them. Veteran fliers that have made the trek before educate young followers on the journey to nesting or wintering homes. Still other scientists say that birds can navigate by way of **subtle** differences in the earth's magnetic field. This theory assumes that young birds can detect differences in field strength.

One of the most amazing things about migration is that some birds raised without adult guidance or experience in actual migration can **orient** themselves to the proper direction and navigate accurately across vast stretches of water.

Choose from the story two words that are unfamiliar to you or whose meanings you are not completely sure of. (Do not choose words that appear in boldfaced type.) Write the words on the lines provided below. Then, beside each word, write what you think it means, based on how it was used in the story.

1. _____ : _____
   _____

2. _____ : _____
   _____

When you have finished the exercises in this lesson, go to your dictionary and find the definitions for the words you entered above. If a word has more than one meaning, look for the one that defines the word as it is used in the story. Then write the words and their dictionary definitions in the Student Words pages at the back of the book. How close did you come to figuring out their meanings for yourself?

1:1 Using Context

Write each vocabulary word beside its correct meaning. Try to figure out what the word means from the way the word is used in the story.

1. **advocates**

_____ critics   _____ information

_____ supporters   _____ research

2. **orient**

_____ adjust   _____ keep

_____ agree   _____ fly

3. **replenish**

_____ consume   _____ eliminate

_____ restore   _____ locate

4. **subtle**

_____ gravitational   _____ slight

_____ dramatic   _____ natural

5. **attribute**

_____ credit   _____ prove

_____ measure   _____ doubt

1:2 Making Connections

The boldfaced words in the following sentences are short definitions of or synonyms for the five vocabulary words you worked with in the last exercise. On the line in front of each sentence, write the vocabulary word that has the same meaning as the boldfaced word or words.

        advocates   orient   replenish   subtle   attribute

1. _____ At camp we learned how to use a compass to **face** toward a certain direction.

2. _____ We need to **refill** our reserves of fuel oil so we won't be caught short.

3. _____ The taste of the mustard was **not very noticeable**, but it made an important difference in the flavor of the sauce.

4. _____ **Supporters** of the bill spoke at the meeting today. Opponents will be heard tomorrow.

5. _____ Dave wanted to **give credit for** the story to Marcia, although she hadn't really written it.

1:3 Using Context
For each of the boldfaced words in this exercise, go back and read the paragraph in which the word appears, paying special attention to the sentence in which it is used. Then, in the list that follows the vocabulary word, circle the word that has the same or almost the same meaning. Be prepared to support your choices.

1. **impede**   increase   encourage   hinder   elevate

2. **velocity**   speed   height   record   average

3. **misconception**   fact   superstition   error   miracle

4. **elude**   hide from   attack   pursue   escape

5. **surmised**   shown   traveled   guessed   studied

1:4 Making Connections
Complete the following analogies by inserting one of the five vocabulary words in the blank at the end of each one. Remember that in an analogy the last two words or phrases must be related in the same way that the first two are related.

impede   velocity   misconception   elude   surmised

1. proved : theorized : : knew : _____

2. encourage : promote : : prevent : _____

3. sneakiness : deceive : : speed : _____

4. action : mistake : : thought : _____

5. degrees : temperature : : miles per hour : _____

2: The Roots of Our Language

tri-
The root *tri-* means three. As a number prefix, it can be used with many of the roots you encountered in the last two units, in place of the prefixes *bi-* and *du-,* meaning two. For instance, you can have a tricycle instead of a bicycle, and you may copy something in triplicate rather than in duplicate (make three copies instead of two). You remember that *-plic* is a form of *-plex,* which means "fold," or "times." That root also appears in *triplex,* which means a three-unit apartment building. A tripod (*-pod,* like *-ped,* means foot) is a three-legged stand or stool. To triple something is to make three times as much. You can publish a newsletter trimonthly (every three months) rather than bimonthly, and a triennial publication would come out every three years. With the addition of a third musician, a duo becomes a trio.

You can see that by knowing the meanings of a few roots, you can figure out the approximate meanings of many words that use those roots. That is the very purpose of learning roots.

Though many roots that take the prefix *tri-* can also take the prefixes *bi-* or *du-,* this is not always the case. There are some things that have to have three parts. A triangle is a good example. A triangle is a flat geometric figure having three sides and three angles. You cannot have a biangle. The branch of mathematics that is based on the use of triangles is trigonometry. Surveyors use trigonometry to measure distances and heights. They do this through a measurement process called triangulation, which calls for the use of three points (which, if you join them, form a triangle, of course.)

A *tri-* word with which you are undoubtedly familiar is *tribe.* In ancient Rome, the population was divided into three political subdivisions called tribes. Each tribe was one-third of the population. Today a tribe is a group of people united by common customs and traditions and following the same leaders. Since the tribal leaders who dispensed justice or settled arguments were known as the tribunal, *tribunal* took on the meaning of the seat of a judge. In modern times it is a synonym for *court.*

In ancient Rome, a tax paid to the central government by a tribe was called a tribute. When given voluntarily, the tribute was an honor bestowed on the leaders. Such voluntary offerings gave us the meaning we usually associate with the word *tribute* today: a gift or service showing respect or gratitude.

A Roman tributary was the leader of a tribe or state who paid tribute to a conqueror. A more frequent modern meaning of *tributary* is a stream or small river that feeds into a larger river. You might say that the stream contributes its water to the river. *Contribute* means to give something.

dent-
A trident is a fork with three teeth. An example is the three-pronged spear that King Neptune, the mythical god of the sea, carries. *Dent-,* of course, means tooth as in dentist and dental hygiene.

To wind this discussion up with something really big, let's look at the word *trillion.* This huge number gets its name from the fact that it is written with three sets of three zeros after 1,000. So one trillion is written 1,000,000,000,000. This huge number represents a million millions.

UNIT THREE 53

2:1 Write each word or root listed on the left beside its meaning on the right.

trimonthly   1. _____ tooth

tribunal   2. _____ every three months

tributary   3. _____ court of law

-dent   4. _____ stream or river

triangulation 5. _____ measurement process used in surveying

2:2 Mark each statement as either true or false.

_____ 1. Trident was originally the name of a dinosaur that had only three teeth.

_____ 2. A tridimensional object has length, width and height.

_____ 3. The folksingers Peter, Paul and Mary are a trio.

_____ 4. Ancient Roman tribunals were groups of people united by common customs.

_____ 5. If you begin your canoe trip on a tributary, you'll eventually find yourself on a larger river.

2:3 Put an *x* in front of the answer choice you think is correct.

1. The number of units in a trio of triplexes is
   - ☐ a. three.
   - ☐ b. six.
   - ☐ c. nine.

2. If a magazine hits the newsstands every three months, it is published
   - ☐ a. triennially.
   - ☐ b. trimonthly.
   - ☐ c. trilaterally.

3. The French flag, which is blue, white and red, is often referred to as the
   - ☐ a. tricolor.
   - ☐ b. triplex.
   - ☐ c. trifocal.

4. When you fill out a form in triplicate, you are making
   - ☐ a. two copies.
   - ☐ b. three copies.
   - ☐ c. one copy.

5. A painting that consists of three panels side by side is a
   - ☐ a. triptych.
   - ☐ b. tripod.
   - ☐ c. tribute.

3: Meeting Words in Context

Where Do All the Wild Birds Go?

The National Wildlife Refuge System has grown. Still, safe habitat for many kinds of wildlife is far from **adequate**. Many acres of wetlands, marshes, swamps, lakes and streams must be added. New lands are needed to save **imperiled** birds and other animals threatened with extinction.

Refuges protect many types of wildlife. But their role in saving waterfowl is of **paramount** importance. Three-fourths of all refuges were **initiated** just for water birds. Since 1934, most of the funds used to buy waterfowl refuges have come from the sale of migratory bird stamps.

There are also numerous waterfowl breeding areas in the Wildlife Refuge System. These small marshes in the prairie states can produce large numbers of ducks. Emphasis has been placed on acquiring such areas to prevent their **imminent** destruction. If not protected, the marshes would be drained and converted to non-wildlife uses, leaving many birds without a place to breed. More than a million acres of these lands have been bought or leased and set aside for the birds.

At refuges, one can find **myriad** types of wildlife. Few other sites afford a chance to see such great concentrations of waterfowl and other birds. Over twenty-five refuges can claim gatherings of more than fifty thousand wild geese. Refuges do not harbor only birds, however. They also provide protection for species of plants, insects, amphibians and reptiles that each year become harder to find in other places. Many refuges have fine scenic and historical values that are preserved along with the wildlife.

Refuges are often **perceived** as being self-operating paradises from the time they are begun. More often than not, though, they start as lands that have been exploited by drainage, lumbering, burning and overgrazing. To become **optimal** wildlife habitat, they need to be **restored**. This is done with dams, dikes and fences. Also, farming programs produce special wildlife foods. Irrigation systems, soil conservation practices, or forestry programs may also be used.

As a bonus, refuges can add **substantially** to local revenues. By law, local governments share in the proceeds from grazing, haying, sale of timber, and other practices necessary for the best management of wildlife habitats.

Choose from the story two words that are unfamiliar to you or whose meanings you are not completely sure of. (Do not choose words that appear in boldfaced type.) Write the words on the lines provided below. Then, beside each word, write what you think it means, based on how it was used in the story.

1. _____ : _____
   _____

2. _____ : _____
   _____

When you have finished the exercises in this lesson, go to your dictionary and find the definitions for the words you entered above. If a word has more than one meaning, look for the one that defines the word as it is used in the story. Then write the words and their dictionary definitions in the Student Words pages at the back of the book. How close did you come to figuring out their meanings for yourself?

3:1 Using Context
Below are five vocabulary words from the reading passage. Write them next to their meanings. Try to figure out the meaning of each word from the way in which it is used in the story.

restored   adequate   paramount   imperiled   optimal

1. Which word means "enough" or "satisfactory"? _____

2. Which word means "best"? _____

3. Which word means "threatened"? _____

4. Which word means "most important"? _____

5. Which word means "renewed"? _____

3:2 Making Connections
The boldfaced vocabulary words in the sentences below are taken from the story. For each vocabulary word, select a synonym and an antonym from the list that follows. Write the synonyms and antonyms in the blanks.

best   demolish   enough   worst   trivial   endangered

renovate   insufficient   most important   unjeopardized

1. The historical society will not approve the plan to **restore** the house unless it is faithful to the original design.

    synonym: _____ **antonym:** _____

2. There is no need to buy more paper. Our present supply is **adequate**.

    synonym: _____ **antonym:** _____

3. Your point about improving safety conditions was **paramount**. Make sure to include it in your report.

    synonym: _____ **antonym:** _____

4. The students knew that athletics in the schools would be **imperiled** by budget cuts.

    synonym: _____ **antonym:** _____

5. All the proposals have merit, but this one would make **optimal** use of the available funds.

    synonym: _____ **antonym:** _____

3:3 Using Context
Circle the word or phrase that most nearly matches the meaning of the boldfaced vocabulary word in the sentence.

1. Often, refuges are **perceived** as paradises.

   thought of   known   visited   advertised

2. Income from refuge management can **substantially** increase revenues of some towns.

   slightly   monetarily   occasionally   significantly

3. The destruction of some areas is **imminent**.

   unavoidable   tragic   acceptable   near

4. **Myriad** species of wildlife can be observed at some sanctuaries.

   well-protected   a vast amount   endangered   wild

5. Most refuges were **initiated** for migratory waterfowl.

   perfect   insufficient   protected   established

3:4 Making Connections
Complete each sentence with the correct vocabulary word.

perceived   substantially   imminent   myriad   initiated

1. An encyclopedia provides information about _____ subjects.

2. Many casualties were caused by the flood. People had not been warned of the danger until disaster was _____ .

3. Some foods, such as cottage cheese, are _____ as diet foods but are actually quite high in calories.

4. When the art program was _____ , we had no idea it would attain the popularity that it now has.

5. The reference book's new edition is _____ different from the last one; we will have to replace our copy.

4: The Roots of Our Language

quad-

quatr-
quadri-

Quad- is a Latin root meaning four, which we see in such common words as *quadrangle,* meaning a flat geometric figure with four angles and four sides. Actually, the root is usually seen as *quatr-* or *quadri-,* but if you remember that *quad* means four, that is usually enough to help you understand the meaning of a word with that root.

poly-
-gon

As we have said, a quadrangle is a four-angled geometric figure. Any plane (flat), closed figure made up of straight sides is called a polygon. *Poly-* means many, and *-gon* means angle. So a polygon is a many-angled flat figure. A square and a triangle are polygons. A quadrangle is also a four-sided area of land surrounded by buildings. Such quadrangles are often found on college campuses. Quadrilateral is another word for quadrangle. Both mean a four-sided, four-angled flat figure.

A *quadrant* is a quarter of a circle, or a quarter of any plane figure that is divided by intersecting lines that meet to form a 90-degree angle. It is also an instrument for measuring altitudes. The instrument consists of a 90-degree arc (a quarter of a circle), and is commonly used in astronomy and navigation.

You'll remember that a biped is a two-footed creature, and a tripod is a three-legged stand or stool. Well, now we have *quadruped,* which means four-footed. All creatures with four legs are quadrupeds. In multiplying things, we go from double to triple to *quadruple,* meaning fourfold, or four times. Similarly, multiple copies go from duplicate to triplicate to quadruplicate, or fourfold. A form in quadruplicate exists in four identical copies.

Remember biennial and triennial? Well now we have *quadrennial,* which means every four years. Quadrennial may also be used to mean continuing for four years, but when we wish to speak about a four-year period we usually use the word *quadrennium.* How long does it take to get through college? A quadrennium, if you complete your work in the usual time span.

A triplet is one of three children all born at the same time to the same mother. In some instances, a mother gives birth to *quadruplets,* four babies. The *ple* in the word is related to *-plex,* meaning, as we have learned, fold or times. So *quadruplet* means multiplied by four, or fourfold.

twi-

twe-

Two babies born at the same time are, of course, twins. *Twin* comes from a different root system—Old English. In Old English, *twi-* meant two. *Twine* is a strong cord made up of two or more strands. *Twice* means two times. Twilight is the light from the sky between sunset and full night, or between full night and sunrise, when the sun is just below the horizon. *Twilight* is related to *between,* meaning in the space or time separating, or in the middle. In *between,* the Old English root has become *twe-.* It also appears that way in the word *twenty,* meaning two tens.

4:1 Write each word or root listed on the left beside its meaning on the right.

poly-

-gon

quadrennium

twi-

twilight

1. _____ four-year period

2. _____ two

3. _____ between sunset and full night

4. _____ angle

5. _____ many

4:2 Mark each statement as either true or false.

_____ 1. The president of the United States serves a term that is a quadrennium.

_____ 2. Twilight is twice as bright as daylight.

_____ 3. The extravagantly designed automobiles of the 1960s often featured quad headlights, which meant they had four headlights, all told.

_____ 4. In baseball, if a batter swings and misses twice, he or she is called out on strikes.

_____ 5. Twine is a strong synthetic fiber that consists of one machine-produced strand.

4:3 Answer the following questions.

1. Monotheistic cultures worship one god. Polytheistic cultures worship _____
   _____ .

2. A polygon is a many-angled flat figure. *Deca* means ten. What, therefore, is a decagon? _____
   _____

3. A quadrille is a square dance designed for a specific number of couples. How many couples dance the quadrille? _____

4. If you are one of a set of quadruplets, how many brothers or sisters do you have? _____

5. How many speakers will you need to complete your quadraphonic sound system? _____

5: Extending Your Word Power

5:1 Multiple Meanings

The meanings given in this exercise are alternate meanings for the vocabulary words listed below. Write each word in front of its meaning. Consult the glossary if necessary. A word may be used more than once.

restore   perceived   adequate   initiated   orient

attribute   elude   advocates   Orient

1. _____ When used as a noun, this word refers to a trait or characteristic of a person.

2. _____ Which word can mean "baffle"?

3. _____ This word, when used in reference to a person, means competent or suitable.

4. _____ One definition for this word is "give back" or "put back."

5. _____ This word is synonymous with the Far East.

6. _____ One meaning for this word is "admitted with formal ceremonies to a group."

7. _____ In one usage, this word pertains to the senses rather than to the mind.

8. _____ An additional meaning for this word is "bring back or establish again."

9. _____ "Introduced into the knowledge of an art or subject" is one definition of this word.

10. _____ A person who speaks or writes in favor of something does this.

11. _____ Which word can mean "adjust to a new situation or condition of affairs"?

5:2 Roots Review

The incomplete sentences below contain words that you learned in the two roots lessons in this unit. Complete each sentence so that it makes sense and shows the meaning of the boldfaced vocabulary word.

1. Though Alison was unfamiliar with the campus, she knew that she had arrived at the **quadrangle** when she saw _____ .

2. When asked to create a **polygon,** Jeffrey proceeded to _____ .

3. Wilbur explained that the **triennial** event took place _____ .

4. The **quadrilateral** that the geometry teacher drew on the chalkboard had equal sides, making it a _____ .

5. The **tribunal** gathered to _____ .

6. As a **tribute** to Ms. Stevens, who had provided guidance and encouragement to many aspiring artists, _____ .

7. In a storm, the **tributary** often _____ .

8. Using **triangulation**, the surveyors were able to _____ .

9. One **quadrant** of the field was being used by the soccer team, which left _____ .

10. Two fascinating **quadrupeds** that were shown in the documentary were the _____ .

UNIT THREE

5:3 Choosing Just the Right Word

Many of the words you have worked with in Unit 3 have a number of synonyms. In some cases, the synonyms convey different shades of meaning.

Listed below are five of the words and some of their synonyms. Turn to the glossary for the precise definition of each word. Look for the slight differences in meaning between synonyms. One of the vocabulary words, *imminent,* is often confused with a similar-sounding word, *eminent,* which has an entirely different meaning. *Eminent* has been included here to help you distinguish it from *imminent*.

Complete the story that follows, using the words listed below. For each blank, try to choose the word that is just right for the context.

restore / renovate / renew **impending / imminent (eminent)**

dominant / paramount **impede / prevent** **escape / elude**

At Nutzenbolz, Inc., the strike was launched after a prolonged attempt to resolve contract disputes resulted in a deadlock. The union demanded a minor salary increase. In addition, they wanted management to _____ the benefits that had been withdrawn when the company was near bankruptcy. They also asked that the company _____ several of the older buildings of the plant, contending that they held many safety hazards.

Throughout the talks with the union, management steadfastly refused to give in to any of the demands, preferring to _____ the existing contract. _____ among the company directors' considerations was the happiness of the stockholders, who had seen the value of their stock plummet during the three preceding unprofitable years.

The union charged that management was attempting to _____ the progress of the negotiations in order to deplete the union's strike fund. The company accused the workers of trying to _____ their share of responsibility for Nutzenbolz's success or failure.

The adverse publicity that accompanied the strike was embarrassing for the _____ company. So Nutzenbolz, Inc., had enlisted the services of Drivel, Ayer and Flack, the _____ firm in the public relations industry, to try to enhance the company's image in the media. Still, Nutzenbolz could not _____ the inevitable front-page accusations that were leveled against it.

62 UNIT THREE

After thirty-six hours of silence on both sides, the press began to hear word that a settlement was _____10_____ . Resolution had been _____11_____ for a week, but each time agreement seemed certain, one side or the other had managed to _____12_____ it. This time, however, reporters _____13_____ that their sources were more confident that an agreement was about to be reached.

5:4 Recognizing Word Forms

The sentences below require you to use some other forms of the words you have worked with in this unit. The words you will need to fill in the blanks are among the words listed below. If you are unsure of the meaning of a word, refer to the glossary.

restored restoration restorative

perceived imperceptible

adequate adequately inadequate

substantially substantial

initiated initiative

attribute attributes attributed

elude eluding eludes

replenish replenished

advocates advocating

orient Oriental oriented

1. Although Ponce de Leon was certain he had found the Fountain of Youth, the spring in question turned out not to have any _____ powers.

2. Bo was afraid the amount of food would be _____ for his guests, so he ordered a few more pizzas.

3. Sue Ellen moved to Wisconsin as a child. Now her southern accent is almost _____ .

4. Do you prefer to follow someone else's lead, or to take the _____ yourself?

5. Verne's sense of humor is one of his finest _____ .

6. Speakers _____ arms control addressed the Senate.

7. When she went to China, Elaine bought two _____ rugs.

8. The _____ plans for the one-room schoolhouse called for inkwells and old-fashioned slate blackboards.

9. The secret of success still _____ Charles, who has always failed in his business ventures.

10. A _____ amount of work awaits us; we've completed only about one-fourth of the investigation.

11. If you have studied _____, you should have no trouble passing the exam.

12. Because the windows are _____ toward the east, this room is very sunny in the morning.

13. Just as the well was about to run dry, a heavy rain _____ the water supply.

14. Joan's physician _____ her headaches to fatigue, and insisted that she get more sleep.

15. James Bond is skilled at _____ enemy agents who attack him in every imaginable way.

5:5 Putting Your Vocabulary to Use
Use vocabulary words from this unit and the previous unit to complete the crossword puzzle.

ACROSS
1. fear
4. second light of the day
7. avoid or escape
8. group of three people
13. three-wheeled vehicle
15. face a particular direction
16. about to happen
17. person born at the same time as one other to the same mother
18. two-family house
19. face-off between two people

DOWN
2. many-sided figure
3. hinder
5. three copies
6. attraction
9. pit
10. thought of
11. group with common customs
12. speed
14. best
16. drive

The Moon and the Mind

Today the word *lunacy* is synonymous with *insane*. When the word was coined, however, it referred to insanity brought about by the regular changes of the moon. The Latin word *luna* means moon. Our English word *lunar* means "of the moon." The Romans believed that the mind was affected by the moon, and that some people suffered a mental disorder that caused them to grow more and more frenzied as the moon increased in fullness. Those people were called lunatics. *Lunacy* and *lunatic* are now commonly applied to any form of insanity. Though the idea that the phases of the moon affect people's minds is no longer accepted, some folks still insist that people and animals tend to carry on in strange ways when the moon is full. Do dogs really howl at a full moon? Do people get weird and frenzied? Watch for yourself for signs of lunar effects.

UNIT THREE

UNIT 4

1: Meeting Words in Context

    Reading Selection   The Voyage of the Ra-2

    Words Introduced   artifacts concur credible dispute formidable imply intrigued speculate spurious thwarted

2: The Roots of Our Language

    Roots Introduced   tetra hedra meter andro- gyn- hydra hydro quart

3: Meeting Words in Context

    Reading Selection   The Aztecs

    Words Introduced   allies amassed chronicled incarcerated instituted integral proficient subjugation tributes vestiges

4: The Roots of Our Language

    Roots Introduced   quint quinque folium de-

5: Extending Your Word Power

Multiple Meanings
Roots Review
Using Words Precisely
Recognizing Word Forms
Putting Your Vocabulary to Use

1: Meeting Words in Context

The Voyage of the Ra-2

It is said that Spanish explorers "discovered" Central and South America, but when they landed there in the fifteenth and sixteenth centuries, they found advanced peoples. **Artifacts** and traditions in Aztec, Mayan and Incan cultures suggested that white people had been there centuries before.

Thor Heyerdahl, an archaeologist from Norway, began to **speculate** about that. Had the Indians of long ago had Eastern visitors? Archaeologists had already noted linguistic clues. Also, figures in Mayan picture writing were much like some Egyptian hieroglyphs. Other researchers had seen that some faces on ancient Central American statues looked more like Egyptians than like Indians of Peru. Many other mysteries were also deemed proof of a link across the Atlantic. Some notions were clearly **spurious** and were best ignored. The more **credible** theories aroused Heyerdahl's interest.

One idea **intrigued** him more than the rest. Heyerdahl compared boats painted on pots in Peru with some depicted on tombs in Egypt. No one could **dispute** the similarities between them, for they were nearly identical.

Could they have evolved independently of each other? Some researchers said yes. Heyerdahl did not **concur**. He thought the boats and many other things had been imported. That would **imply** that Egyptians or their neighbors had crossed the South Atlantic. Their boats for such a **formidable** voyage would have been made of reeds that grew along the Nile. Could such seemingly fragile crafts have survived the trip?

Heyerdahl had already crossed the Pacific by raft to prove another point. Now he wanted to build a reed boat and cross the South Atlantic to South America. In a vessel that he named the Ra-2, he set off. Twice his attempts were **thwarted**. The third time, he finished the voyage. He proved that someone *could* have done it centuries before. Had ancient people made such a crossing? And if so, who were they? The Norwegian archaeologist left those questions unanswered.

Choose from the story two words that are unfamiliar to you or whose meanings you are not completely sure of. (Do not choose words that appear in boldfaced type.) Write the words on the lines provided below. Then, beside each word, write what you think it means, based on how it was used in the story.

1. _____ : _____

_____

2. _____ : _____

_____

When you have finished the exercises in this lesson, go to your dictionary and find the definitions for the words you entered above. If a word has more than one meaning, look for the one that defines the word as it is used in the story. Then write the words and their dictionary definitions in the Student Words pages at the back of the book. How close did you come to figuring out their meanings for yourself?

1:1 Using Context

Put an *x* in the box beside each correct answer. For clues to the meanings of the words, reread the parts of the passage in which they appear.

1. In the first paragraph, **artifacts** are
   - ☐ a. stories.
   - ☐ b. facts.
   - ☐ c. objects.
   - ☐ d. lies.

2. The sentence in which *spurious* appears, together with the sentence that follows it, tells you that **spurious** means
   - ☐ a. forgotten.
   - ☐ b. false.
   - ☐ c. dangerous.
   - ☐ d. unimportant.

3. In the sentence "No one could dispute the similarities in the paintings," **dispute** means
   - ☐ a. argue about.   ☐ c. see.
   - ☐ b. compare.   ☐ d. copy.

4. The sentences before and after the one in which *concur* appears indicate that **concur** means
   - ☐ a. care.
   - ☐ b. know.
   - ☐ c. waste time.
   - ☐ d. agree.

5. In the sentence "One idea intrigued Heyerdahl enough that he followed up on it," **intrigued** means
   - ☐ a. fascinated.
   - ☐ b. angered.
   - ☐ c. bored.
   - ☐ d. amused.

1:2 Making Connections

Complete each sentence with the correct vocabulary word.

artifacts   spurious   dispute   concur   intrigued

1. These _____ documents enabled the smuggler to pass through customs without having his baggage inspected.

2. Do you _____ with the view that the school year should be lengthened or do you think that 180 days is sufficient?

3. Archaeologists estimated the age of the buried city after examining the _____ found in the ruins.

4. Kate is so quarrelsome that she will _____ any claim made by anyone at any time.

5. The pictures of prehistoric animals so _____ Heather that she begged to be taken to the Museum of Natural History to see the dinosaur exhibit.

UNIT FOUR 69

1:3 Using Context

Write each vocabulary word beside its correct meaning. Try to figure out what the word means from the way it is used in the story.

1. **credible**

_____ amazing   _____ common

_____ believable   _____ rare

2. **thwarted**

_____ rewarded   _____ accompanied

_____ ridiculed   _____ prevented

3. **formidable**

_____ difficult   _____ long

_____ foreign   _____ tiresome

4. **imply**

_____ prove   _____ explain

_____ suggest   _____ contradict

5. **speculate**

_____ wonder   _____ write

_____ study   _____ disagree

1:4 Making Connections

The boldfaced words in the following sentences are short definitions of or synonyms for the five vocabulary words you worked with in the last exercise. On the line in front of each sentence, write the vocabulary word that has the same meaning as the boldfaced word or words.

    credible   thwarted   formidable   imply   speculate

1. _____ Greg trembled as he rose to address the **intimidating** judge.

2. _____ Isabel closed her eyes and began to **muse**: "What if I had been born into royalty?"

3. _____ "Thomas Malloy!" bellowed the algebra teacher, "Unless you can come up with a more **plausible** excuse for yesterday's absence, you may proceed to the principal's office!"

4. _____ When you volunteered the name of your hairdresser, did you mean to **suggest** that there is something wrong with my hairstyle?

5. _____ While I was baby-sitting, those boisterous children **defeated** all my efforts to do my homework.

2: The Roots of Our Language

tetra *Tetra* is the Greek root for four. It is used to form words in a wide variety of subjects.

hedra In mathematics, we find *tetra* in *tetrahedron*, which is a solid figure having four faces. *Hedron* is from the Greek *hedra*, meaning face. The four faces of a tetrahedron are triangles. The pyramids of Egypt are tetrahedrons. Geologists and chemists who study crystalography speak of tetrahedral crystals—mineral crystals in the shape of tetrahedrons. Polyhedrons are solids formed by plane (flat) faces. (You'll remember that *poly-* means many.) Also in geometry, we have *tetragon*, which means a four-angled polygon. A square and a diamond are both tetragons, because they each have four angles. Remember that *-gon* means angle.

In literature we encounter *tetralogy*, which is a series of four works, such as novels or plays, that go together, or form a whole. (A work comprising three individual parts is called a trilogy.) Poetry teachers also speak of *tetrameter*,

meter which means verse with four feet, or beats per line. *Meter* is a root that means measure. This root is found in many common words. A speedometer is an instrument for measuring speed, and a telemeter is an instrument for measuring the distance of an object from the observer. (You'll remember from the first Roots lesson that *tele-* means far or over a distance.)

Biology introduces us to *tetrapetalous* (TEH-truh-PET-ul-lus) flowers. You guessed it, they have four petals. Some flowers are also *tetrandrous*, meaning that they have four stamens, or male reproductive parts. The second part of

andro- that word is formed from the root *andro-*, meaning man. It appears in the word *androgynous*, meaning having characteristics of both male and female.

gyn- The second part of *that* word is from the Greek root *gyn-*, meaning woman.

Tetrarchy is a political word meaning rule by four people. A *tetrarch*, however, is not one of those four persons, but rather a ruler of one-fourth of a state. The *-arch* root, as you no doubt recall, means rule.

Chemistry uses many *tetra* words, frequently to describe the composition of molecules. A *tetrahydrate*, for instance, is a chemical compound having four molecules of water. *Hydrate* means water. The word *dehydrate* means to remove the water from.

hydra The root *hydra* or *hydro* appears in the names of many words, from the
hydro common fire *hydrant*, a water source for the fire department, to *hydraulic* brake systems, which transmit force by using water (or some other liquid) pressure. A hydrophone is an instrument for listening to sounds transmitted through water. A hydroplane is both a seaplane, which is an airplane that can land and take off on water, and a kind of boat that has planes (winglike surfaces) on the bottom, which lift the hull partly or completely out of the water for greater speed. Hydrotherapy is the use of water in the treatment of diseases. Soaking in warm water to relax sore muscles is a form of hydrotherapy.

Before we finish with four, we should look at the Latin root for that

quart number—*quart*. It makes an appearance in a number of commonly used English words. A quart is one-fourth of a gallon. A quarter is one-fourth of anything. When it is one-fourth of a dollar, it is the name of a coin. And to end on a harmonious note, a quartet is a group of four, especially a musical group.

2:1 Write each word or root listed on the left beside its meaning on the right.

tetralogy   1. _____ water

andro-   2. _____ having both male and female characteristics

gyn-   3. _____ man

androgynous 4. _____ a work comprising four parts

hydro   5. _____ woman

2:2 Mark each statement as either true or false.

_____ 1. A hydrophone is an airplane that lands and takes off on water.

_____ 2. A pianist, a drummer, a guitarist, a French horn player and a violinist make up a quartet.

_____ 3. A tetralogist studies the number 4 in its relation to science and technology.

_____ 4. A gynecologist specializes in the diseases and hygiene of women.

_____ 5. Since *-oid* means resembling, a robot could be classified as an android.

2:3 Put an *x* in front of the answer choice you think is correct.

1. Considering performers such as David Bowie, Boy George and Annie Lennox of Eurythmics, it would seem that England tends to produce pop stars who are
   - ☐ a. androgynous.
   - ☐ b. anonymous.
   - ☐ c. antisocial.

2. An author wrote three related books but died before she could write the fourth, thereby leaving incomplete her planned
   - ☐ a. tetrachord.
   - ☐ b. tetracycline.
   - ☐ c. tetralogy.

3. Someone tracking a submarine by listening to the noise of its engines might use a
   - ☐ a. hydrometer.
   - ☐ b. hydrophone.
   - ☐ c. hydrograph.

4. A misogynist is a person who hates
   - ☐ a. doctors.
   - ☐ b. women.
   - ☐ c. work.

5. The man who has just stumbled into the oasis after being lost in the searing desert for three days needs desperately to be
   - ☐ a. hydrated.
   - ☐ b. dehydrated.
   - ☐ c. detoxified.

3: Meeting Words in Context

The Aztecs

Long before the Spaniards migrated to Central America, the Aztecs had attained a high cultural level. Their civilization, established in the high valley that is now Mexico City, equaled that of some nations in Europe. Some of their history was **chronicled** in stone. But much of our knowledge of the Aztecs was derived from artifacts discovered by archaeologists.

At first the Aztecs supported themselves by fishing and trading. For farming, they needed more territory. Over time they **amassed** farm land by conquering neighboring tribes.

By about 1500, the Aztecs ruled a united group of tribes. They demanded that the tribes pay them large **tributes.** With the resulting wealth, the Aztecs made their capital city a center of commerce and culture.

There is much evidence that the Aztec culture was highly advanced. The Indians built comfortable houses and lavish temples and palaces. They had botanical gardens, which were unknown in Europe at that time. To improve irrigation and travel, they built a canal system. They kept records by means of picture writing. Their schools and medical facilities equaled some in Europe. They were **proficient** in law and government, and their knowledge of astronomy is still impressive today.

In 1519, the Aztec capital dazzled the Spanish explorer Hernando Cortés and his troops. Cortés plotted to capture the city.

Many of the tribes controlled by the Aztecs hated their conquerors. Cortés made those tribes his **allies.** Also in Cortés's favor was a legend that told that a white god would one day rule the Aztecs. The Indians belief in the legend helped Cortés greatly in his **subjugation** of them.

When the Spaniards reached the capital, the emperor Montezuma received them. Cortés did not trust Montezuma, so he invited him to his camp and held him prisoner. The emperor died while he was **incarcerated**.

Upon defeat of the Indians, Spanish rule was **instituted**. The Aztec country became an **integral** part of the Spanish Empire. It was given the name New Spain. Priests established Christianity there, and the Aztecs' treasures were shipped to Spain.

Today, over four centuries later, many Mexican Indians still speak the Aztec language. They are proud of their ancestry. Many customs have been preserved, and Mexican life shows **vestiges** of Aztec culture. Many Aztec words have been added to the Spanish spoken in that country. In fact some, such as *tomato, coyote* and *avocado,* are now part of the English language.

Choose from the story two words that are unfamiliar to you or whose meanings you are not completely sure of. (Do not choose words that appear in boldfaced type.) Write the words on the lines provided below. Then, beside each word, write what you think it means, based on how it was used in the story.

1. _____ : _____
   _____

2. _____ : _____
   _____

When you have finished the exercises in this lesson, go to your dictionary and find the definitions for the words you entered above. If a word has more than one meaning, look for the one that defines the word as it is used in the story. Then write the words and their dictionary definitions in the Student Words pages at the back of the book. How close did you come to figuring out their meanings for yourself?

3:1 Using Context
For each of the boldfaced words in this exercise, go back and read the paragraph in which the word appears, paying special attention to the sentence in which it is used. Then, in the list that follows the vocabulary word, circle the word that has the same or almost the same meaning. Be prepared to support your choices.

1. **proficient**   imitated   skilled   avoided   aspired

2. **instituted**   welcomed   conquered   installed   supreme

3. **incarcerated**   dishonored   imprisoned   tortured   humiliated

4. **amassed**   stripped   cultivated   devastated   acquired

5. **integral**   important   minor   distant   unique

3:2 Making Connections
Write each vocabulary word on the line between the appropriate synonym and antonym.

proficient   instituted   incarcerated   amassed   integral

1. jailed _____ liberated

2. essential _____ inconsequential

3. established _____ abolished

4. expert _____ inept

5. accumulated _____ squandered

6. vital _____ insignificant

7. gathered _____ distributed

3:3 Using Context

Below are five vocabulary words from the reading passage. Write them next to their meanings. Try to figure out the meaning of each word from the way in which it is used in the passage.

vestiges   subjugation   chronicled   tributes   allies

1. _____ Which word means "written down" or "recorded"?
2. _____ Which word means "persons or groups united for a special purpose"?
3. _____ Which word means "traces" or "remnants"?
4. _____ Which word means "a bringing under complete control"?
5. _____ Which word means "taxes" or "forced payments"?

3:4 Making Connections

Complete each sentence with the correct vocabulary word.

vestiges   subjugation   chronicled   tributes   allies

1. Because Samuel Pepys _____ important events in his diaries, we have vivid accounts of London's great plague and fire of 1665 and 1666.

2. England and the United States were _____ during World War II.

3. The Feldizrians resented their _____ by the Gromundines and refused to adopt their language and customs.

4. Do you know if Alexander the Great exacted _____ from the peoples he conquered?

5. After the thaw, a carrot, a scarf and a corncob pipe were the only _____ of the snowman we'd made.

UNIT FOUR   75

4: The Roots of Our Language

quint If you were a super bureaucrat, you might like forms and letters in *quintuplicate*—five copies. The root *quint* means five. Having quintuplicate copies on hand means, of course, that you have quintuple, or five times, the number of pieces of paper to stamp, shuffle, file and lose.

Every once in a great while, a woman gives birth to quintuplets—five babies at once. Remember the musical duos and trios? Well, with five musicians, you have a quintet. A quintet isn't necessarily made up of musicians, however. The word refers to any group of five. Sports writers sometimes refer to a basketball team as a quintet.

An impressive *quint* word is *quintessence*. It means the essence of a thing—its purest, highest form. That meaning comes from the original meaning of the word, which is related to the number five. *Quintessence* originally referred to the fifth and highest element, or essence, in ancient and medieval philosophy. The first four elements, which the philosophers believed made up all matter on earth, were air, fire, earth and water. The fifth essence, ether, was believed to permeate all of nature and to make up all the heavenly bodies. (The adjective *ethereal* relates to the regions beyond the earth. It is often used to mean heavenly or spiritual.) Something that is *quintessential* is the most typical or representative example of something. For instance, a small village in Vermont, with a white clapboard church and a village green, might be referred to as "quintessential New England," because it is a perfect representation of what most people think New England is like.

quinque- The root *quint* sometimes assumes the form *quinque-*, as in *quinquennium* (kwin-KWEN-ee-um), meaning a period of five years. A quinquennial, therefore, means lasting for five years, or taking place every five years. The meaning of this word is a cinch to figure out because you have learned the meaning of the root *-ennial*.

folium The formidable word *quinquefoliolate* (KWIN-kwa-FO-lee-uh-late) has a simple meaning. It refers to plants that have clusters of five leaflets. The Latin root *folium* means leaf—the leaf of a tree, or a leaf of paper. The pages of a book are often referred to as leaves. This meaning comes from the fact that before paper was invented writing was often done on the leaves of certain plants. Hence, if we flip through the pages of a book to get an idea of its contents, we say that we are "leafing" through it. When someone decides to "turn over a new leaf," they are determining to start afresh, on a blank page, so to speak. The numbers on the pages of a book or manuscript are called folios. Oversized books are also sometimes referred to as folios.

de- The word *foliage* refers to the leaves on trees. In autumn, the foliage of deciduous trees in many areas changes from green to brilliant colors. To foliate is to decorate with leaves, or to put forth leaves. So an artist might foliate a fancy picture frame, and trees foliate in the springtime. The reverse, to *de*foliate, is to remove the leaves from, especially prematurely. For instance, gypsy moths, which eat leaves, sometimes defoliate trees in the summer, leaving them bare. (The prefix *de-* means the reverse, or to remove.)

4:1 Write each word or root listed on the left beside its meaning on the right.

quintessence 1. _____ to remove

ethereal 2. _____ to remove leaves

foliage 3. _____ leaves on trees

defoliate 4. _____ the highest or purest form of a thing

de- 5. _____ heavenly, spiritual

4:2 Mark each statement as either true or false.

_____ 1. Many people drive long distances to admire the beauty of the colorful autumn foliage in northern New England.

_____ 2. The quintet, having lost the three members who stormed out after the argument, suddenly became a duo.

_____ 3. An ethereal person is a down-to-earth type of person.

_____ 4. A flamethrower would probably do a good job of defoliating a tree.

_____ 5. If someone describes you as "the quintessential loser," you should be quite flattered.

4:3 Put an *x* in front of the answer choice you think is correct.

1. Read this sentence: "With his outstanding passing and running abilities, Doug was the finest quarterback." With what word below could you replace the word *finest?*

   ☐ a. quintessential ☐ b. essential ☐ c. ethereal

2. If in a vision you were visited by St. Francis of Assisi, he would probably seem

   ☐ a. ethnic. ☐ b. ethereal. ☐ c. quintessential.

3. If a person were slandered and libeled, you could say that he had been

   ☐ a. dethroned. ☐ b. described. ☐ c. defamed.

4. If you wanted to lose some bad habits and start fresh, you might say that you wanted to turn over a new

   ☐ a. foliate. ☐ b. folium. ☐ c. folly.

5. New parents might be a bit worried about their finances and the size of their house if they'd just been blessed with

   ☐ a. quintessence. ☐ b. quadrangles. ☐ c. quintuplets.

5: Extending Your Word Power

5:1 Multiple Meanings

Some of the vocabulary words you encountered in this unit have meanings other than those they held in the reading passages. Below, two meanings are shown for each of the words *concur, allies, tributes* and *speculate*. On the line before each sentence, write the letter of the definition appropriate to the way in which the vocabulary word is used in the sentence.

concur

a. (v.) to agree

b. (v.) to happen at the same time

_____ 1. Do you **concur** with this author's view that a four-day work week would increase efficiency in most industries?

_____ 2. If our vacations **concur**, we can go to Martha's Vineyard together.

allies

a. (n.) persons or groups united for a specific reason

b. (v.) joins another person or group

_____ 3. People who once were my **allies** are now opposing me.

_____ 4. If Parker **allies** himself with Andrews, the two of them will make a formidable team.

tributes

a. (n.) taxes or forced payments

b. (n.) compliments; acknowledgments of thanks or respect

_____ 5. The **tributes** that the gang demanded of neighborhood shopkeepers were actually protection payments.

_____ 6. The retiring star received many **tributes** including an academy award.

speculate

a. (v.) to wonder or ponder

b. (v.) to buy or sell when there is large risk, hoping to profit from future price changes

_____ 7. If you **speculate** successfully, you could become a millionaire almost overnight. If not, you could lose your shirt.

_____ 8. I don't care to **speculate** about the outcome of the election. Let's just wait until the results are in.

5:2 Roots Review

The incomplete sentences below contain words that you learned in the two roots lessons in this unit. Complete each sentence so that it makes sense and shows the meaning of the boldfaced vocabulary word.

1. The **ethereal** aura that surrounded her made her seem _____.

2. Mr. Harrigan pointed out that the **folios** _____.

3. The fashion editor described the new look for spring as **"androgynous"** because _____.

4. Andy's heart beat with excitement as the **hydroplane** _____.

5. Last summer the area was almost entirely **defoliated**, making it appear _____.

6. Finnigan was finishing the last part of a **tetralogy** that consisted of _____.

7. In his keen admiration of Karen, Luke believed her face to be the **quintessence** of _____.

8. Helen enjoyed the **hydrotherapy** sessions because _____.

9. As the fern gradually **dehydrated**, it _____.

10. As it began to **foliate**, _____.

UNIT FOUR

5:3 Using Words Precisely

Amassed, vestiges and **dispute** are three words from this unit that have synonyms that convey different shades of meaning. **Imply** and **credible** are sometimes confused with similar-sounding words whose meanings are entirely different. Complete the story that follows, using the words listed below. Consult the glossary for help in selecting the correct word for each blank.

accumulated / amassed   implied / inferred   vestiges / traces

credible / credulous   dispute / debate

If Heyerdahl's claims that Egyptians sailed across the Pacific in reed boats were less than _____(1)_____ to some of his colleagues, the theories of Erich von Daniken seemed absolutely insane to scientists in the 1970s.

Von Daniken's *Chariots of the Gods* topped best-seller lists for weeks. In that work, the author stated that the abundant evidence he had _____(2)_____ in years of research _____(3)_____ that the ancient Egyptian and Aztec civilizations were started by visitors from outer space. That was the only way, he said, that the Egyptians and the Aztecs would have been able to attain the technological skills they possessed millenia ago.

In his book, von Daniken held that hundreds of ancient objects and writings proved that interplanetary travelers had once settled on Earth. From cave paintings and hieroglyphics depicting men with large round heads, he _____(4)_____ that the ancient civilizations had been familiar with space helmets. He claimed that the stone astronomical charts and calendars preserved in museums today were _____(5)_____ of artifacts left by visitors from afar. He even cited deep lines carved in the desert as _____(6)_____ of an ancient airport.

Von Daniken's argument was hard to _____(7)_____, for while few scientists concurred with his findings (or even recognized his work as scientific), little evidence was available to discredit his theory. Scientists had long been engaged in a _____(8)_____ over possible explanations for the similarities between the ancient Aztec and Egyptian cultures, but there had never been a consensus. Von Daniken's theory was generally considered outrageous.

After writing a second book, von Daniken slid into oblivion. In his brief stint at the top of the charts with his first book, however, he had _____(9)_____ a fortune in royalties from sales to a _____(10)_____ public.

5:4 Recognizing Word Forms

The words listed below are other forms of the vocabulary words you have worked with in this unit. Fill in the blank in each sentence with the appropriate word. If you are unsure of the meaning of a word, refer to the glossary.

speculation   speculator   incredible   intriguing   concurred

disputatious   indisputable   integer   incarceration   vestigial

credibility   implying   implicit   implication   alliance

1. The appendix is called a _____ organ because it is no longer fully developed or useful.

2. The three countries formed an _____ against their common enemy.

3. Senator Foster believes that _____ is too mild a penalty for murder, so she advocates capital punishment for that crime.

4. An _____ is any positive whole number, or zero.

5. That _____ young man will find a way to contradict even the most self-evident points in your argument.

6. Advertisers sacrifice _____ when they make exaggerated claims for the products they promote.

7. "At least *my* hair is naturally blond," sniffed Margaret, _____ that Terry's tresses had not always been golden.

8. A _____ bought five acres of land, expecting to reap a handsome profit by selling them after real estate prices rise.

9. The risks associated with the use of Baxadine are _____. This drug must be taken off the market at once.

10. "What an _____ gentleman! You simply *must* introduce us!" bubbled Mindy.

11. The Supreme Court justices _____ with the decision of the lower court and upheld the verdict.

12. There has been a great deal of _____ about who will succeed Helen as chairwoman.

13. Henry said nothing when informed that the vacation plans had been canceled, but the expression of sadness on his face was a clear _____ of his disappointment.

14. You say your cat Ziggy can open the door by pressing the latch with his paw? That's _____!

15. By not opposing the plan, Walker gave it his _____ support.

5:5 Putting Your Vocabulary to Use

In solving this word puzzle, you will be using some of the vocabulary words introduced in this unit and in the previous unit. Below is a list of definitions and synonyms for those words. For each definition or synonym, think of a vocabulary word that has the same meaning. Write the word in the puzzle space with the corresponding number. One letter of the word, together with the number of lines in each answer space, provide clues to the word. Notice that the letters that are given form a phrase related to caving.

1. give a share to
2. mistaken idea
3. wonder
4. intimidating
5. traces
6. four-person group
7. believable
8. guessed
9. a four-year period
10. having male and female characteristics
11. not obvious
12. remove the water from
13. enough
14. false
15. man-made objects
16. renewed
17. significantly

1. _ _ _ _ _ _ _ u _ _ _
2. _ _ _ _ _ _ n _ _ _ _ _ _
3. _ _ _ _ c _ _ _ _ _
4. _ o _ _ _ _ _ _ _ _
5. v _ _ _ _ _
6. _ _ _ _ _ e _
7. _ r _ _ _ _ _
8. _ _ _ _ i _ _ _
9. _ _ _ _ _ _ _ n _ _ _
10. _ _ _ _ _ g _ _ _
11. _ _ _ t _ _
12. _ _ h _ _ _ _ _
13. _ _ e _ _ _ _ _
14. _ p _ _ _ _ _
15. a _ _ _ _ _ _ _ _
16. _ _ s _ _ _ _
17. _ _ _ _ t _ _ _ _ _ _ _

Have You Got a Clue?

A clew is a ball of thread. A clue, as you probably know, is something that points the way or indicates the solution to a problem. What does one have to do with the other? *Clue* got its meaning from *clew,* and both were derived from the Old English *cliwen,* which meant a ball. That doesn't make much sense, you say? Well, the paths by which words develop and acquire their meanings are not always obvious. A dip into the history of a word often turns up some surprising and entertaining information. Just what does a ball of thread have to do with a possible solution to

a problem? The key is a Greek myth. In medieval England, some writers retold the popular Greek myth of Theseus and the Minotaur. In that myth, the Greek hero Theseus journeyed to the island of Crete to kill the Minotaur, a fierce beast with the body of a man and the head of a bull.

The Minotaur was kept in a labyrinth—a huge and hopelessly confusing maze. No one who was forced to enter the labyrinth had ever been able to find his way out. But Theseus was clever. He entered the labyrinth with a ball of thread that he gradually unwound as he wove his way through the passageways. The medieval writers referred to Theseus's "clew" of thread. After finding and killing the Minotaur, Theseus simply followed the trail of thread to the entrance of the labyrinth. His clew, or clue, showed him the way out of the puzzling enclosure.

UNIT FOUR 83

UNIT 5

1: Meeting Words in Context

Reading Selection — The Birth of Spacelab

Words Introduced — concepts crucial disciplines drastic exorbitant liaison scope stringent technology versatile

2: The Roots of Our Language

Roots Introduced — penta- -oid anthrop- -morphic -athlon homo-

3: Meeting Words in Context

Reading Selection — Spacelab in Action

Words Introduced — aft apparatus bay components configuration console dissipated elapsed remotely serenely

4: The Roots of Our Language

Roots Introduced — sex- sexi- syn- thetic sym- pathos bios -onym anti- sepsis

5: Extending Your Word Power

Multiple Meanings
Roots Review
Using Words Precisely
Recognizing Word Forms
Putting Your Vocabulary to Use

1: Meeting Words in Context

The Birth of Spacelab

In the early 1970s, decisions for the future of America's space program reached a **crucial** phase. Until then, scientific research in space had been extremely expensive. That was partly because space vehicles could be used only once, requiring new research equipment to be built for every flight. Also, experiments had had to meet **stringent** limitations of weight, size, electric power and environmental conditions. But new developments promised to ease those constraints.

The Space Shuttle was to enter full service in the 1980s. That reusable heavylift space transportation system would carry satellites into space and launch them into orbit. Most one-time-use rockets would disappear.

The changes in scientific research would be even more **drastic**. Research could be vastly increased because the Shuttle could take heavy loads into space. It could also bring heavy cargoes back to Earth.

A versatile research facility was needed to take advantage of the Shuttle's many capabilities. Scientists had already made enormous advances in space. Officials now envisioned a facility that would enable them to go beyond the existing **scope** of NASA's research.

At that time Western European countries were seeking to become involved in manned space flight. The Americans invited the European Space Agency (ESA) to join in the NASA program. The ESA agreed to design, build and finance the needed research facility, to be named Spacelab. Ten European nations would take part in the project. NASA would assist with design **concepts** and provide ground facilities and crew training.

NASA's funds were strained by Shuttle development costs. The European partnership promised a much-sought contribution to the American space transportation system. And the **liaison** would allow the ESA to do research in space but avoid the **exorbitant** costs of starting its own program.

Ten years and one billion dollars later, the ESA completed Spacelab. NASA's expense was half a billion dollars. Spacelab's first flight, late in 1983, came soon after the 25th anniversary of NASA's founding.

Spacelab is the result of steady **evolution** in space **technology**. It permits scientists from many nations and in many scientific **disciplines** to go into space. They may now undertake in-orbit research themselves, with instruments they have designed and built.

Choose from the story two words that are unfamiliar to you or whose meanings you are not completely sure of. (Do not choose words that appear in boldfaced type.) Write the words on the lines provided below. Then, beside each word, write what you think it means, based on how it was used in the story.

1. _____ : _____

   _____

2. _____ : _____

   _____

When you have finished the exercises in this lesson, go to your dictionary and find the definitions for the words you entered above. If a word has more than one meaning, look for the one that defines the word as it is used in the story. Then write the words and their dictionary definitions in the Student Words pages at the back of the book. How close did you come to figuring out their meanings for yourself?

1:1 Using Context

Below are five vocabulary words from the reading passage. Write them next to their meanings. Try to figure out the meaning of each word from the way in which it is used in the passage.

discipline   scope   technology   concept   liaison

1. _____ Which word means "idea"?

2. _____ Which word means "the science of the industrial and mechanical arts"?

3. _____ Which word means "field of study"?

4. _____ Which word means "the area over which an activity extends"?

5. _____ Which word means "connection or communication to improve cooperation"?

1:2 Making Connections

Complete each sentence with the correct vocabulary word.

disciplines   scope   technology   concepts   liaison

1. The uneasy _____ between the United States and the U.S.S.R. was further strained by the defection last week of a high-ranking Soviet official.

2. Improvements in _____ have resulted in sophisticated computers that are easy to use.

3. So far, Mr. Cosgrove, your response to every question has been, "That matter was beyond the _____ of our investigation." Would you mind telling the committee exactly what your inquiry *did* cover?

4. The instructor's clear explanations illuminated even the most difficult _____.

5. At this college more students major in biology than in all other _____ combined.

UNIT FIVE

1:3 Using Context

For each of the boldfaced words in this exercise, go back and read the paragraph in which the word appears, paying special attention to the sentence in which it is used. Then, in the list that follows the vocabulary word, circle the word that has the same or almost the same meaning. Be prepared to support your choices.

1. **evolution**   increase   cooperation   research   development

2. **exorbitant**   countless   usual   prohibitive   possible

3. **drastic**   extreme   sudden   expensive   amazing

4. **stringent**   official   strict   various   flight

5. **crucial**   inactive   new   slow   important

1:4 Making Connections

Listed below are the five vocabulary words you worked with in the last exercise, followed by thirteen words and phrases that are related to them in some way. They may be synonyms, antonyms or definitions. On the line next to each word or phrase, write the vocabulary word that is related to it.

evolution   exorbitant   drastic   stringent   crucial

1. radical _____
2. rigorous _____
3. lax _____
4. liberal _____
5. decisive _____
6. cheap _____
7. slight _____
8. unimportant _____
9. process of change _____
10. critical _____
11. expensive _____
12. progress _____
13. affordable _____

2: The Roots of Our Language

penta-   *Penta-* is a Greek root meaning five. Hence, a pentagon is a plane figure with five sides and five angles. Something that is in the shape of a pentagon is *pentagonal*. Something that resembles a pentagon may be referred to as

-oid   pentagonoid (pen-TAG-un-oyd). The root *-oid* means appearance or form. So *pentagonoid* means like a pentagon in form.

anthrop-   *Anthrop-,* or *anthropo-,* means human being. You might deduce, therefore, that *anthropoid* (AN-thruh-poyd) means like a human being in form or appearance. And that's very close to the dictionary meaning of the word. As a noun, *anthropoid* means any of the large, tailless or short-tailed apes, such as chimpanzees, gorillas and orangutans. As an adjective, *anthropoid* may mean either resembling a person, especially in shape, or resembling an ape, especially in action. Referring to a person as anthropoid is, as you can imagine, an insult. It's like calling someone a big ape—subhuman. In literature, nonhuman characters are sometimes anthropomorphized (AN-thruh-

-morphic   puh-MOR-fized)—given human characteristics. The root *-morphic* means form. So nonhumans that are described or thought of as having human form or human traits are said to be anthropomorphic.

     The pentathlon is a contest in the Olympic Games consisting of five events.

-athlon   The Greek root *-athlon* means contest, as in *athletics,* which are sports or games engaged in by athletes—people who are trained and skilled in sports or games requiring physical skill or strength. A triathlon, as you might guess, is an athletic contest consisting of three events.

     A pentagram is a five-pointed star made with alternate points connected by straight lines. As we saw in the first lesson, *-gram* means written or drawn. It also means line. A parallelogram, therefore, is a quadrilateral (a four-sided plane figure, as you'll remember) whose opposite sides are parallel (extending in the same direction and an equal distance apart at all points) and of equal length. A square and a rectangle, for instance, are parallelograms.

     You'll recall that *-graph,* like *-gram,* is derived from the Greek *graphos,*

homo-   meaning written or writing. Combining that root with the Greek root *homo-,* meaning same, we get *homograph.* Homographs are words that are spelled the same but differ in meaning or pronunciation. Two examples are *fair* and *lead. Fair* can mean an exhibition or market, or it can mean beautiful. *Lead* means to conduct, but with a different pronunciation it names a kind of metal. Homonyms are words that are spelled and pronounced the same, but have different meanings. Homonyms are sometimes called homophones (*phone* meaning sound). Things that are homogeneous (HO-muh-JEE-nee-us) have the same nature or a uniform structure. To homogenize, therefore, is to blend into a uniform mixture.

     In some words, the prefix *homo-* has a different meaning. That is because those words were derived from Latin, rather than Greek. The Latin root *homo-* means man. From this root we get the name of our species—*Homo sapiens. Sapiens* comes from the Latin *sapient,* meaning wise.

2:1 Write each word or root listed on the left beside its meaning on the right.

anthrop-   1. _____ form

-morphic   2. _____ human being

homo-   3. _____ describe as having human form or characteristics

anthropomorphize 4. _____ wise

sapient   5. _____ same

2:2 Mark each statement as either true or false.

_____ 1. A person who is anthropomorphized is immortalized, or given permanent fame.

_____ 2. Anthropoid may mean either resembling an ape or resembling a person.

_____ 3. Two objects that are homomorphic are alike in form or size.

_____ 4. One who possesses sapience possesses wisdom.

_____ 5. Mickey Mouse is anthropomorphized.

2:3 Put an *x* in front of the answer you think is correct.

1. The Greek root *homo-* means same, but the Latin root *homo-* means
   - ☐ a. man.
   - ☐ b. animal.
   - ☐ c. different.

2. Anthropology is the study of the relationships, origins, classifications and distribution of
   - ☐ a. animals.
   - ☐ b. humans.
   - ☐ c. anthropoids.

3. Something that occurs in many forms, characters or styles is
   - ☐ a. homomorphic.
   - ☐ b. monophonic.
   - ☐ c. polymorphous.

4. A synonym for monochromatic is
   - ☐ a. polychromatic.
   - ☐ b. homochromatic.
   - ☐ c. anthrochromatic.

5. To make a decision sapiently is to do so
   - ☐ a. foolishly.
   - ☐ b. impatiently.
   - ☐ c. wisely.

3: Meeting Words in Context

Spacelab in Action

Since the flame and thunder of liftoff, one hour has **elapsed**. At the Kennedy Space Center in Florida, the puffs of exhaust have **dissipated**. The Space Shuttle now floats **serenely** in weightlessness on the opposite side of the Earth. The crew of six begin preparations for the scientific work assigned to them on this nine-day flight.

A **console** faces the rear wall of the Shuttle's upper crew compartment—the **aft** flight deck. A mission specialist flips one switch among the many dials and controls. This sets off a computer-controlled sequence of latch retractions. The huge doors extending the length of the bus-size cargo bay swing open, revealing its contents.

Peering through the two aft flight-deck windows into the cargo **bay**, crew members view a strange collection of structures. The scene seems to belong in a fantasy film.

A Z-shaped tunnel one meter in diameter runs from the back wall of the lower crew compartment (mid deck) toward the middle of the cargo bay. The tunnel connects with the first of two joined cylinders near the cargo bay's center. Those linked segments are called the module. Behind it, not visible to the crew from the windows, rests a pallet. It is a U-shaped form that, like the module, fits snugly into the 18 by 4.6-meter cargo bay. Mounted on the pallet are antennas, telescopes and other sensors.

This odd-looking assemblage is one **configuration** of Spacelab. The **components** can be arranged in different ways to meet the objectives of different research missions.

Within an hour or two, two crew members float from the mid deck through the tunnel into the module. They begin working with some of the research **apparatus** installed there, operating the instruments on the pallet **remotely**. Spacelab has now come alive and is at work.

Choose from the story two words that are unfamiliar to you or whose meanings you are not completely sure of. (Do not choose words that appear in boldfaced type.) Write the words on the lines provided below. Then, beside each word, write what you think it means, based on how it was used in the story.

1. _____ : _____

2. _____ : _____

When you have finished the exercises in this lesson, go to your dictionary and find the definitions for the words you entered above. If a word has more than one meaning, look for the one that defines the word as it is used in the story. Then write the words and their dictionary definitions in the Student Words pages at the back of the book. How close did you come to figuring out their meanings for yourself?

3:1 Using Context
Listed below are five vocabulary words from the reading passage. The list is followed by definitions of the words as they are used in the passage. Write each word in front of its definition.

To figure out what each word means, go back to the passage and read the sentence that contains the word. If you can't discover the meaning from the way the word is used in the sentence, read the sentences that come before and after it for clues.

aft   dissipated   apparatus   console   serenely

1. _____ : calmly, tranquilly

2. _____ : the rear part of a ship

3. _____ : equipment for a particular purpose

4. _____ : spread out to the point of vanishing

5. _____ : a panel with dials and switches to control mechanical or electrical devices

3:2 Making Connections
Complete the following analogies by inserting one of the five vocabulary words in the blank at the end of each one. Remember that in an analogy the last two words or phrases must be related to each other in the same way that the first two are related.

aft   dissipated   apparatus   console   serenely

1. car:dashboard::spaceship: _____

2. front:back::fore: _____

3. crowd:dispersed::cloud: _____

4. nightmare:fearfully::dream: _____

5. build:tools::experiment: _____

3:3 Using Context

Put an *x* in the box beside each correct answer. For clues to the meanings of the words, reread the parts of the passage in which they appear.

1. We are told that several components can be arranged according to the aims of the mission. **Components** are
   - ☐ a. crew members.
   - ☐ b. parts.
   - ☐ c. requirements.
   - ☐ d. experiments.

2. Since takeoff, an amount of time has **elapsed**, or
   - ☐ a. been wasted.
   - ☐ b. dragged on.
   - ☐ c. gone by.
   - ☐ d. stood still.

3. The crew in the module control the pallet equipment remotely. **Remotely** means
   - ☐ a. from a distance.
   - ☐ b. carefully.
   - ☐ c. constantly.
   - ☐ d. absent-mindedly.

4. One can look through the aft flight-deck windows into the cargo bay. In this instance **bay** means
   - ☐ a. harbor.
   - ☐ b. window.
   - ☐ c. laboratory.
   - ☐ d. compartment.

5. Refer to the paragraph in which *configuration* is used. The word *assemblage* and the following sentence give you clues that **configuration** means
   - ☐ a. purpose.
   - ☐ b. section.
   - ☐ c. arrangement.
   - ☐ d. advantage.

3:4 Making Connections

The boldfaced words in the following sentences are short definitions of or synonyms for the five vocabulary words you worked with in the last exercise. On the line in front of each sentence, write the vocabulary word that has the same meaning as the boldfaced word or words.

   components   elapsed   remotely   bay   configuration

1. _____ He put off answering his parents' letter until three weeks had **gone by**.

2. _____ The illegal cargo was found in one **enclosed section** of the plane.

3. _____ Some unmanned spacecraft can be controlled **distantly** with signals from the ground.

4. _____ You call that hideous **formation** *art?* It belongs in a junkyard, not a museum!

5. _____ The basic **constituents** of a stereo are a receiver, a turntable and speakers.

4: The Roots of Our Language

sex-
sexi-

Our counting roots now bring us to the number six. The Latin root for six is *sex-*. As a prefix connected to other roots, it sometimes appears as *sexi-*. To add to our musical vocabulary, therefore, a sextet may be a group of six musicians or a musical composition for six instruments or voices. In a broad sense, it can be any group or set of six. Hockey teams are sometimes referred to as sextets. *Sextuple* means sixfold, *sextuplicate* means six copies, and *sextuplets* are six babies born at one birth.

A sextant (SEK-stunt) is a measuring instrument used in celestial navigation. The captain of a sailboat might use a sextant to determine the exact location of the boat and to follow a plotted course. The instrument gets its name from the fact that the main part consists of an arc that is one-sixth of a circle.

syn-

Now let's switch to another root that begins with *s* but has nothing to do with numbers: *syn-*. You are no doubt familiar with the word *synthetic*. It means not natural, or man-made. It comes from the word *synthesis* (SIN-thuh-sus), because it is through synthesis that synthetic products are made. In the realm of science, *synthesis* means the uniting of chemical elements or compounds to form a new product. In a broader sense, *synthesis* means the combining of separate elements into a unified whole. Hence, we can speak of a synthesis of ideas—ideas that have been merged, or brought together. All this leads us to the meaning of *syn-* itself. It means with, or together with.

thetic

The *thetic* in *synthetic* means to put or lay down, or place. So *synthetic* is to place together, or to combine. The word *thesis* comes from the same root. A thesis is an idea or proposition that a person offers or puts forward.

When things are synchronized (SING-kruh-nized), they happen at the same time. In movies, for instance, the sound and the picture are synchronized, so that the sound is properly timed with the action. The sound and the picture can be said to be synchronous (SING-kruh-nus).

sym-

The prefix *sym-* has the same origin and meaning as *syn-*. *Sympathy*, for instance, means a sharing of feelings, such as feeling sorry for another's suffering, or a feeling or condition that is the same as another person's. If two people hold the same view on a subject, their ideas may be said to be in sympathy. The *-pathy* in *sympathy* comes from the Greek root *pathos*,

pathos

meaning suffering, experience or emotion. So the literal meaning of the word is "with feeling." *Symbiosis* refers to the living together in close association of

bio

two or more different kinds of organisms (*bio* meaning life).

Synonyms, as you know, are words that have the same or almost the same meaning. Therefore, such words can be said to be *synonymous* (suh-NON-uh-

-onym
anti-

mus). *-Onym* is a root that means name or word. An antonym is a word that has an opposite meaning. The *ant-* comes from *anti-*, which means against or opposite.

Someone who is antisocial is opposed to being social. A trust is a combination of big businesses, so an antitrust law is intended to break up huge business combinations. In your medicine cabinet, you may have an

sepsis

antiseptic for use on cuts. *Septic* comes from the Greek *sepsis*, meaning decay. An antiseptic helps to prevent the spread of infection, or the growth of harmful microorganisms.

4:1 Write each word or root on the left beside its meaning on the right.

syn-   1. _____ suffering, experience or emotion

synthesis   2. _____ against or opposite

thesis   3. _____ combining separate elements into a whole

pathos   4. _____ with, together with

anti-   5. _____ an idea or proposition

4:2 Mark each statement as either true or false.

_____ 1. A sextant is a navigational measuring device that gets its name from the fact that it has six moving parts.

_____ 2. An antonym is a word that defies definition, because it is, as you can see by its combination of roots, against meaning.

_____ 3. A thesis is an unquestioned universal law.

_____ 4. Synthetic products usually come into being naturally; they are not manufactured.

_____ 5. Since apartheid is a policy of racial segregation, to be antiapartheid is to oppose an official governmental policy of racial segregation.

4:3 Answer the following questions.

1. If a thesis is an idea or a proposition, what is an antithesis? _____

2. If *tax* comes from a root meaning to arrange something (words, for example), and you know the meaning of the root *syn-*, what do you think *syntax* means? _____

3. *Symphony* means many sounds interacting harmoniously, because *sym-* means _____ , and *phonos* means _____ .

4. How are you expected to respond to a story that uses pathos as a plot element? _____

5. If a revolutionary believes in revolution, what might you call someone opposed to the idea of revolution? _____

UNIT FIVE 95

5: Extending Your Word Power

5:1 Multiple Meanings

Below are several words you have met in this unit. Each of these words has more than one meaning. In this exercise, the boldfaced word or phrase in each sentence corresponds to one of the listed words. In the blank before each sentence, write the appropriate vocabulary word. Turn to your glossary for the alternate meanings of any words you are unsure of.

    liaison   discipline   dissipated   console   bay   remotely

1. _____ In yesterday's episode Blaine found out about Sheena's **affair** with Zeke. I knew she wouldn't get away with it!

2. _____ We used to go swimming in the **harbor**, but now it's too polluted.

3. _____ Mrs. Maher chooses to **punish** her children by taking privileges away temporarily.

4. _____ Sir Smedley, unable to manage his money, **squandered** his fortune soon after he inherited it.

5. _____ Why don't you see if you can **comfort** your brother. He's very upset about what happened to Joe.

6. _____ All the dog does all night is **howl** at the moon. I have a good mind to call the pound.

7. _____ Do you think you can **train** yourself to get your work done without someone standing over you?

8. _____ Pointing a toy pistol, Maria kept the intruder at **a distance** while Dan called the police.

9. _____ I can **faintly** remember my conversation with Adrian, but I don't recall any of the details that you're interested in.

5:2 Roots Review

The incomplete sentences below contain words that you learned in the two roots lessons in this unit. Complete each sentence so that it makes sense and shows the meaning of the boldfaced vocabulary word.

1. In her story, Mary Ellen **anthropomorphized** a tree by _____.

2. In the midst of a serious disagreement with his best friend, Alex showed himself to be **sapient** when he _____.

3. The substance of his **thesis** indicated that Mr. Fortunato _____.

4. At regular intervals during his journey, Harley used his **sextant** to _____.

5. Ms. O'Donnell pointed out that *delight* is **synonymous** with _____.

6. The museum guide pointed out that the tiles in the mosaic were **pentagonal** by outlining with her finger the _____.

7. Harry enjoyed the study of **anthropoids** because _____.

8. The **homogeneous** grouping of the dogs in the pet shop _____.

9. Through a **synthesis** of various cultures, the country _____.

10. Gale, Manuel, Shirley and George were in stitches over their futile attempts to **synchronize** their _____.

UNIT FIVE 97

5:3 Choosing Just the Right Word

Many of the words you have worked with in this unit have a number of synonyms. As you know, in some cases the synonyms convey different shades of meaning.

Following are synonym studies for four of your vocabulary words. Use either the vocabulary words or their synonyms to complete the sentences in the exercise that follows. In some cases you may need to use a plural or a past tense. Refer to the synonym studies as you decide which choice carries the best meaning for the specific context of each sentence.

component   ingredient

Both *component* and *ingredient* refer to the parts that make up something. A component is a part that joins with other parts to form a unit. *The components of this modular sofa can be arranged to fit the shape of the room.* An ingredient is something that loses its individual identity in a mixture or combination. *Water, lemon juice and sugar are the ingredients that make up lemonade.*

scatter   dissipate

Scatter and *dissipate* both mean to separate or break up, so that an original arrangement or form is lost. *Scatter* applies to a mass of people or individual objects that spread apart, or are scattered in many directions. *When the wind came up, the pile of leaves scattered throughout the neighborhood.* Dissipate means to disintegrate or dissolve to the point of disappearing. *By midmorning the mist had dissipated.*

range   scope

Two words that mean extent are *range* and *scope*. Range emphasizes the extent and variety that can be included or covered. *The public library offers a wide range of materials.* Scope emphasizes the limits beyond which something does not or cannot extend. *Those skills are beyond the scope of the fourth-grade curriculum.*

excessive   exorbitant

Both *excessive* and *exorbitant* mean exceeding an appropriate limit. *Excessive* means going beyond what is right or proper in amount or extent. *He spends an excessive amount of time playing video games.* Exorbitant usually applies to extremely high prices. *At first the prices of color TVs were exorbitant; now they are more reasonable.*

1. At the sound of the gunshot, the flock of birds _____.

2. That young performer has an impressive _____ of talents.

3. I know the sauce is missing some important _____, but I can't figure out what to add.

4. Lee purchased the _____ of the personal computer at different stores and then assembled them herself.

5. Steam rose steadily from the vaporizer and _____ in the dry air of the heated house.

6. That clumsy oaf knocked my term paper off the desk and _____ the pages all over the floor!

7. "Determination, luck, brains—these are just three _____ of success," boomed Jenkins as he lit a cigar.

8. The company's advertising campaign is meant to acquaint consumers with the full _____ of services that are available to clients.

9. If you think one dollar an hour is an _____ wage for a baby-sitter, you're living in the past.

10. "A VCR isn't an indispensible _____ of *my* home entertainment center," Sandra explained to the salesman. "I don't even have a television."

11. Even after the smoke had _____, its odor lingered in the kitchen.

12. It's a good idea to reward children verbally when they do well, but _____ praise can do more harm than good.

13. "Madam, kindly assure me that the washing of windows will not fall within the _____ of my duties."

5:4 Recognizing Word Forms

The words listed below are other forms of the vocabulary words you have worked with in this unit. Fill in the blank in each sentence with the appropriate word. Use what you have learned in the unit to help you figure out what the words mean.

stringently   drastically   evolved   conception   exorbitance   disciplinarian

technological   dissipating   inconsolable   consolation   remotest   remote

1. In *The Cay,* a boy and a man stranded on a _____ island struggle to survive, never giving up hope that they will be rescued.

2. Wishing to increase the city's revenues through the collection of fines, the mayor ordered the police to enforce parking regulations more _____ by ticketing all violators.

3. Higher forms of life _____ from protozoa.

4. The manufacturer is touting this heat sensor as a _____ breakthrough, but experts recognize that it is hardly an innovation.

5. When we browsed in the jewelry store we were astounded by the _____ of the prices.

6. By the time the skywriter finished forming the message, the first letters were already _____ .

7. Warren's behavior has changed _____ since he started going to school. Spending the day with other children has had a tremendous effect on him.

8. It's impossible to know just how Pompeii looked after the eruption of Mt. Vesuvius in AD 79; this picture is an artist's _____ of the scene.

9. Why are you asking *me?* You know I don't have the _____ idea!

10. Shelly was _____ when her kitten ran away.

11. I've heard that the new assistant principal is a strict _____ . I'm sure she can get these students in line.

12. Barbara didn't win any money when she appeared on the game show, but her _____ prize was a year's supply of oven cleaner.

5:5 Putting Your Vocabulary to Use

This word-search puzzle conceals seventeen vocabulary words from both this and the previous unit. They are printed horizontally, vertically, diagonally, backward and upside down.

Begin by listing the vocabulary words next to their clues below. Then find the words in the puzzle, circling them as you locate them.

1. _____ wrote down
2. _____ sports
3. _____ remove the leaves from
4. _____ extreme
5. _____ resembling a human being
6. _____ page numbers
7. _____ development
8. _____ relating to regions beyond the earth
9. _____ forced payments
10. _____ ideas
11. _____ partners
12. _____ extent
13. _____ gathered
14. _____ a control panel
15. _____ most typical example of something
16. _____ words spelled and pronounced alike but having different meanings
17. _____ imprisoned

```
s u b j q u i n t e s s e n c e
a h t d b s n s c r j d a k e l
i s d e t a r e c r a c n i h d
s o f f w s p k o o p m t q z a
m i g o c o p d n n p y h l w y
y l u l b d r m s r s e r x a c
n o i i t a g u o b u s o t h e
o f s a s a m a l e d e p r b v
m m c t c t s i e i c d o i l o
o d i e q e a l l o e n i b a l
h c t o i q u i n t i s d u e u
v n e l d e f c o c l i a t r t
o e l p r s e y l t s y n e e i
m a h r c p s e i n a r e s h o
n g t f w d t u c a r c h t n
a m a s s e d e l i t a s r e v
```

UNIT FIVE 101

UNIT 6

1: Meeting Words in Context

Reading Selection   Excerpt from the Inaugural Address of President John F. Kennedy—January 20, 1961

Words Introduced   adversary asunder civility endeavor host negotiate quest stays subject tempered

2: The Roots of Our Language

Roots Introduced   hex- -gram pod -ology bio- micro- -zo anthro- geo-

3: Meeting Words in Context

Reading Selection   Excerpt from "I Have a Dream," a speech made by Martin Luther King, Jr.

Words Introduced   appalling content discords languishing manacles momentous oppression seared self-evident withering

4: The Roots of Our Language

Roots Introduced   sept- vir hepta- path pathy

5: Extending Your Word Power

Multiple Meanings
Roots Review
Using Words Precisely
Recognizing Word Forms
Putting Your Vocabulary to Use

1: Meeting Words in Context

Excerpt from the Inaugural Address of President John F. Kennedy—January 20, 1961

We dare not forget today that we are the heirs of that first revolution. Let the word go forth from this time and place, to friend and foe alike, that the torch has been passed to a new generation of Americans—born in this century, **tempered** by war, disciplined by a hard and bitter peace, proud of our ancient heritage—and unwilling to witness or permit the slow undoing of those human rights to which this Nation has always been committed, and to which we are committed today at home and around the world.

Let every nation know, whether it wishes us well or ill, that we shall pay any price, bear any burden, meet any hardship, support any friend, oppose any foe to assure the survival and the success of liberty.

This much we pledge—and more.

To those old allies whose cultural and spiritual origins we share, we pledge the loyalty of faithful friends. United, there is little we cannot do in a **host** of cooperative ventures. Divided, there is little we can do—for we dare not meet a powerful challenge at odds and split **asunder**. . . .

Finally, to those nations who would make themselves our **adversary**, we offer not a pledge but a request: that both sides begin anew the **quest** for peace, before the dark powers of destruction unleashed by science engulf all humanity in planned or accidental self-destruction. We dare not tempt them with weakness. For only when our arms are sufficient beyond doubt can we be certain beyond doubt that they will never be employed.

But neither can two great and powerful groups of nations take comfort from our present course—both sides overburdened by the cost of modern weapons, both rightly alarmed by the steady spread of the deadly atom, yet both racing to alter that uncertain balance that **stays** the hand of mankind's final war.

So let us begin anew—remembering on both sides that **civility** is not a sign of weakness, and sincerity is always **subject** to proof. Let us never **negotiate** out of fear. But let us never fear to negotiate. . . .

And if a beachhead of cooperation may push back the jungle of suspicion, let both sides join in creating a new **endeavor**, not a new balance of power, but a new world of law, where the strong are just and the weak secure and the peace preserved.

Choose from the story two words that are unfamiliar to you or whose meanings you are not completely sure of. (Do not choose words that appear in boldfaced type.) Write the words on the lines provided below. Then, beside each word, write what you think it means, based on how it was used in the story.

1. _____ : _____

    _____

2. _____ : _____

    _____

When you have finished the exercises in this lesson, go to your dictionary and find the definitions for the words you entered above. If a word has more than one meaning, look for the one that defines the word as it is used in the story. Then write the words and their dictionary definitions in the Student Words pages at the back of the book. How close did you come to figuring out their meanings for yourself?

1:1 Using Context

Put an *x* in the box beside each correct answer. For clues to the meanings of the words, reread the parts of the passage in which the words appear.

1. The word *split* gives you a clue that **asunder** means
   - [ ] a. together.
   - [ ] b. apart.
   - [ ] c. forever.
   - [ ] d. defenselessly.

2. The phrase "both sides" suggests that **adversary** means
   - [ ] a. victim.
   - [ ] b. ally.
   - [ ] c. enemy.
   - [ ] d. oppressor.

3. As used in the passage, **host** means
   - [ ] a. venture.
   - [ ] b. one who receives guests.
   - [ ] c. prevention.
   - [ ] d. great number.

4. In the opening paragraph, **tempered** means
   - [ ] a. trained.
   - [ ] b. battered.
   - [ ] c. intimidated.
   - [ ] d. hardened.

5. **Civility** toward an opponent is
   - [ ] a. distrust.
   - [ ] b. generosity.
   - [ ] c. politeness.
   - [ ] d. defense.

1:2 Making Connections

Listed below are the five vocabulary words you worked with in the last exercise, followed by fifteen words and phrases that are related to them in some way. They may be synonyms, antonyms or definitions. On the line next to each word or phrase, write the vocabulary word that is related to it.

        asunder   adversary   host   tempered   civility

1. multitude _____
2. into parts _____
3. as one _____
4. foe _____
5. small number _____
6. friend _____
7. partner _____
8. tact _____
9. rudeness _____
10. antagonist _____
11. courtesy _____
12. toughened _____
13. in fragments _____
14. mellowed _____
15. steeled _____

UNIT SIX 105

1:3 Using Context

For each of the boldfaced words in this exercise, go back and read the paragraph in which the word appears, paying special attention to the sentence in which it is used. Then, in the list that follows the vocabulary word, circle the word that has the same or almost the same meaning. Be prepared to support your choices.

1. **quest**   need   search   conditions   victory

2. **stays**   checks   keeps   remains   supports

3. **subject**   superior   close   agreeable   liable

4. **negotiate**   retreat   attack   confer   begin

5. **endeavor**   treaty   undertaking   nation   age

1:4 Making Connections

Complete each sentence with the correct vocabulary word.

        quest   **stays**   **subject**   **negotiate**   **endeavor**

1. Of course your appointment is _____ to approval by the director, but I see no reason that you shouldn't get the job.

2. Would-be stars need self-confidence and perseverance to sustain them in their _____ for fame.

3. It will be impossible to reach a compromise if the other side refuses to _____ .

4. Although she knew that the _____ would be long and difficult, Alicia was determined to devote the next three years to training for the Olympics.

5. Continual encouragement is the only factor that _____ Elroy's fear of failure.

2: The Roots of Our Language

hex-
-gram

The Greek prefix meaning six is *hex-*. *Hex-* can be combined with several of the roots we have encountered in other lessons. Joined to the root *-gram,* for instance, we get *hexagram*. A hexagram is a six-pointed star made by drawing an equilateral (having equal sides) triangle out from each side of a regular hexagon. A hexagon, as you can probably figure out, is a polygon having six angles and six sides. On a regular hexagon, the sides and angles are equal. If you ever find yourself in a hardware store in search of a hex nut, you should look for a nut in the shape of a regular hexagon. A hexahedron is a polyhedron having six faces—in other words, a cube. You may remember that tetrameter is a line of verse, or poetry, having four feet, or beats. It follows, therefore, that hexameter is a line of verse having six feet. Latin and Greek epic poetry is written in hexameter.

Hexaemeron (HEK-suh-EM-uh-RON) means six days. It refers to the six days of creation, or a written account of them like that contained in the Bible.

pod

You're probably thinking that *hexaemeron* is not a word that you are likely to encounter on a regular basis, and you're right. In fact, there are not many commonly used words that employ the prefix *hex-*. Most words that sport the Greek prefix for six are related to mathematics or chemistry. *Hexapod,* for instance, is another word for insect. It means, literally, six feet. You remember that *pod* means feet. A hexachloride is a chloride containing six atoms of chlorine in each molecule, and a hexadecimal number system is based on the number 16 (*hexa,* six, plus *dec,* ten). You can see that those are specialized words. If you come across words with the prefix *hex-* in your study of mathematics or science, you'll know that they refer to six of something. You'll then have a clue to their meanings.

-ology
bio-
micro-

Since we're talking about science, it would be a good idea to take a look at the root *-ology,* which means science or study of. You've no doubt already come across it many times in your school career. When we study biology, we are studying the science of living things. *Bio-* means life. Our biosphere is that part of the earth's crust, water and atmosphere in which life can exist. So, the biosphere is life supporting. A branch of biology that specializes in the study of very small living things is microbiology. The root *micro-* means small. In order to see the organisms that they study, microbiologists use microscopes— optical instruments that magnify minuscule things. Some of the tiny organisms that microbiologists study under their microscopes are called microbes—more commonly known as germs. A biography, of course, is a written account of a person's life.

zo-

In your study of biology, you may focus on the study of animals. That specialized branch of biology is called zoology (zoh-OL-uh-jee). *Zo-* comes from the Greek word for life, and refers to animals. Thus, zoos are places where animals are kept. The science of human beings, especially the study of their origins, races, environmental and social relations, and cultures is called anthropology. You'll remember that the root *anthrop-* means man. An anthropologist is a person who studies anthropology.

geo-

One other common *-ology* word is geology, the study of the history of the earth and its life, especially as recorded in rocks. *Geo-* means earth. One who works in the field of geology is called a geologist.

2:1 Write each word or root on the left beside its meaning on the right.

-ology   1. _____ study of life

biology   2. _____ earth

micro-   3. _____ life, especially animal life

zo-   4. _____ small

geo-   5. _____ the study of

2:2 Mark each statement as either true or false.

_____ 1. Biology is the study of very small living things.

_____ 2. A micrometer is used to measure very short distances.

_____ 3. A zoologist is a person engaged in the study of animals.

_____ 4. In music, a hexachord would be made up of six notes.

_____ 5. Hexaemeron means six days, especially the six days of the creation of the world as recounted in the Bible.

2:3 Put an *x* in front of the answer choice you think is correct.

1. The tiny organisms we call germs are
   - ☐ a. microscopes.
   - ☐ b. microbes.
   - ☐ c. micrometers.

2. A hexahedron is formed in the shape of a
   - ☐ a. square.
   - ☐ b. rectangle.
   - ☐ c. cube.

3. Zoology is a specialized branch of
   - ☐ a. tautology.
   - ☐ b. biology.
   - ☐ c. geology.

4. The lines of *The Odyssey,* the epic poem by the ancient Greek poet Homer, are written in the meter known as
   - ☐ a. tetrameter.
   - ☐ b. hexameter.
   - ☐ c. octometer.

5. A comparatively short electromagnetic wave is called a
   - ☐ a. megawave.
   - ☐ b. macrowave.
   - ☐ c. microwave.

3: Meeting Words in Context

Excerpt from "I Have a Dream,"
a speech made by Martin Luther King, Jr.

Five score years ago, a great American, in whose symbolic shadow we stand, signed the Emancipation Proclamation. This **momentous** decree came as a great beacon light of hope to millions of Negro slaves who had been **seared** in the flames of **withering** injustice. It came as a joyous daybreak to end the long night of captivity.

But one hundred years later, we must face the tragic fact that the Negro is still not free. One hundred years later, the life of the Negro is still sadly crippled by the **manacles** of segregation and the chains of discrimination. One hundred years later, the Negro lives on a lonely island of poverty in the midst of a vast ocean of prosperity. One hundred years later, the Negro is still **languishing** in the corners of American society and finds himself an exile in his own land. So we have come here today to dramatize an **appalling** condition. . . .

I say to you today, my friends, that in spite of the difficulties and frustrations of the moment I still have a dream. It is a dream deeply rooted in the American dream.

I have a dream that one day this nation will rise up and live out the true meaning of its creed: "We hold these truths to be **self-evident**; that all men are created equal." . . .

I have a dream that one day even the state of Mississippi, a desert state sweltering with the heat of injustice and **oppression**, will be transformed into an oasis of freedom and justice.

I have a dream that my four little children will one day live in a nation where they will not be judged by the color of their skin but by the **content** of their character. . . .

This is our hope. This is the faith with which I return to the South. With this faith we will be able to hew out of the mountain of despair a stone of hope. With this faith we will be able to transform the jangling **discords** of our nation into a beautiful symphony of brotherhood. With this faith we will be able to work together, to pray together, to struggle together, to go to jail together, to stand up for freedom together, knowing that we will be free one day.

Choose from the story two words that are unfamiliar to you or whose meanings you are not completely sure of. (Do not choose words that appear in boldfaced type.) Write the words on the lines provided below. Then, beside each word, write what you think it means, based on how it was used in the story.

1. _____ : _____

2. _____ : _____

When you have finished the exercises in this lesson, go to your dictionary and find the definitions for the words you entered above. If a word has more than one meaning, look for the one that defines the word as it is used in the story. Then write the words and their dictionary definitions in the Student Words pages at the back of the book. How close did you come to figuring out their meanings for yourself?

3:1 Using Context
Write each vocabulary word beside its correct meaning. Try to figure out what the word means from the way it is used in the passage.

1. **oppression**

   _____ fire   _____ drought

   _____ unjust treatment   _____ violence

2. **content**

   _____ essence   _____ greatness

   _____ satisfaction   _____ color

3. **seared**

   _____ abandoned   _____ raised

   _____ freed   _____ burned

4. **manacles**

   _____ remnants   _____ shackles

   _____ injuries   _____ laws

5. **languishing**

   _____ hiding   _____ wilting

   _____ relaxing   _____ living powerlessly

3:2 Making Connections
The boldfaced words in the sentences below are short definitions of or synonyms for the five vocabulary words you worked with in the last exercise. On the line in front of each sentence, write the vocabulary word that has the same meaning as the boldfaced word or words.

      oppression   content   seared   manacles   languishing

1. _____ "But I am an innocent man!" cried the scoundrel as the constables clamped **handcuffs** around his wrists.

2. _____ "Murderin' Mary" spent forty years **pining away** in prison.

3. _____ This poem may resemble the other in form, but its **substance** is very different.

4. _____ **Persecution** of a people can lead to revolution.

5. _____ Robert **cooked the outside of** the steak at high heat and then lowered the flame before adding sliced onions and mushrooms to the skillet.

110 UNIT SIX

3:3 Using Context

Below are five vocabulary words from the reading passage. Write them next to their meanings. Try to figure out the meaning of each word from the way in which it is used in the passage.

momentous   withering   self-evident   appalling   discords

1. _____ Which word means "dismaying"?

2. _____ Which word means "harsh sounds"?

3. _____ Which word means "needing no proof"?

4. _____ Which word means "of great consequence"?

5. _____ Which word means "devastating"?

3:4 Making Connections

Write each vocabulary word on the line in front of the appropriate synonym and antonym.

momentous   withering   self-evident   appalling   discords

	synonym	antonym
1. _____	cacophony	harmony
2. _____	important	trifling
3. _____	obvious	unclear
4. _____	dreadful	pleasing
5. _____	discouraging	strengthening

4: The Roots of Our Language

sept-   *Sept-* is the Latin root for seven. It forms the beginning of *September,* which is the ninth month of the year. That doesn't seem very logical, but it came about because September was the seventh month of the earliest Roman calendar, from which our present Gregorian calendar was derived. That early calendar had only ten months. Each new year began on March 1. January and February were later added to the calendar, and when Julius Caesar took the throne he made some more changes and moved New Year's Day to January 1.

Ancient Rome was governed by a septemvirate (sep-TEM-ver-it)—a group of seven men who were called septemvirs (sep-TEM-vers). The literal meaning
vir   of *septemvir* is seven men. The root *vir* from that word is part of the adjective *virile,* meaning manly or masculine. So virility is masculinity, or manly vigor and energy.

A septuagenarian (SEP-tyoo-uh-juh-NER-ee-un) is a person in his or her seventies.

The word *septic* looks as though it is related to the number seven, but it isn't. It comes from a Greek word meaning infected. You may remember from a previous lesson that *antiseptic* means against infection (*anti-* meaning against). Another word with the root *septic* is *septicemia* (SEP-tih-SEE-me-uh), an illness in which the bloodstream is infected by disease-causing bacteria.
-emia   Since *-emia* means blood, *septicemia* literally means infected blood. Anemia is an unhealthy condition in which the blood is deficient in red blood cells.

hepta-   The Greek root for seven, *hepta-,* is less common in English words than is the Latin *sept-*. It does, however, combine with several of the roots we have seen before, forming words whose meanings you can undoubtedly decipher. A heptagon is a polygon with seven sides and seven angles, and a heptahedron is a solid figure, or polyhedron, having seven faces. *Heptateuch* (HEP-tuh-took) is the name of the first seven books of the Old Testament.

In the last lesson we looked at a number of words containing the suffix *-ology.* Let's talk about one more, *pathology,* meaning the study of the nature of diseases. Something that is pathological is related to disease—often changed or caused by disease. For example, a pathological liar is someone for whom lying is a disease.

pathos   You may recall from a previous lesson that the roots *pathos, path* and
path   *pathy* all come from the Greek word for suffering, experience or emotion. We
pathy   looked at the meaning of the word *sympathy*: sharing the feelings or interests of another. There are a number of closely related words. They are *empathy, antipathy* and *apathy.* The meaning of *empathy* is very close to that of *sympathy.* Empathy stresses a stronger linking of feelings, however, wherein there is such a close understanding and sensitivity between two people that the feelings, thoughts and experience of one are strongly felt by the other, without their having to be thoroughly explained. *Antipathy,* you'll notice, contains the root *anti-,* meaning against. It means a basic aversion to or dislike for someone or something. *Apathy* means indifference, or lack of feeling or emotion about something. Some people are apathetic about sports, having no feeling about them one way or the other.

A person, object or condition that makes us feel pity is said to be *pathetic.* The English word *pathos* is some element in experience or in art that evokes in us feelings of compassion or pity. A movie that would informally be termed "a real tear-jerker" might be more genteelly referred to as being "filled with pathos."

4:1 Write each word or root listed on the left beside its meaning on the right.

septemvir   1. _____ aversion to

virile   2. _____ seven

hepta-   3. _____ manly

antipathy   4. _____ indifference

apathy   5. _____ seven men

4:2 Mark each statement as either true or false.

_____ 1. Antipathy is a nerve disease that causes a person's senses to numb and deaden.

_____ 2. All the members of a septemvir could, possibly, be quite virile.

_____ 3. If you didn't care whether the answer to this question were true or false, you would be apathetic.

_____ 4. Empathy, sympathy and antipathy all mean about the same thing.

_____ 5. To be a septuagenarian, a person must be seventy-seven years old.

4:3 Put an *x* in front of the answer choice you think is correct.

1. In the seventh and eighth centuries, England is thought to have been divided into the kingdoms of Kent, Essex, Wessex, Northumbria, East Anglia, Sussex and Mercia. The confederacy of those kingdoms was called the

    ☐ a. monarchy.   ☐ b. oligarchy.   ☐ c. heptarchy.

2. There is a condition in which secondary male characteristics appear in a female; it is called

    ☐ a. virile.   ☐ b. apathy.   ☐ c. virilism.

3. An event that takes place every seven years occurs

    ☐ a. irregularly.   ☐ b. sequentially.   ☐ c. septennially.

4. Imagine two graffiti statements on a wall. The first reads "Apathy reigns." The second, in agreement, reads "Who

    ☐ a. thinks?"   ☐ b. cares?"   ☐ c. is?"

5. Pathology is the study of the nature of

    ☐ a. emotions.   ☐ b. experience.   ☐ c. diseases.

UNIT SIX   113

5: Extending Your Word Power

5:1 Multiple Meanings

Below are several words you have met in this unit. Each of these words has more than one meaning. In this exercise, consult the glossary if necessary as you decide which word correctly completes each sentence.

discords   subject   negotiate   languishing   stays

content   host   tempered   endeavor   withering

1. The manufacturer of the defective seat belts hopes to _____ an out-of-court settlement and avoid a legal battle.

2. Are you _____ with your present job, or would you prefer more responsibility?

3. The book's cover is appealing, but the _____ is unoriginal.

4. Usually one sales representative _____ in the office to answer the phones while the other goes out to solicit new business.

5. The topic sentence states the main idea, or _____, of a paragraph.

6. An effective manager, Ms. Fontaine always _____ any criticism by phrasing it as a constructive suggestion.

7. I can't believe you spend your weekends _____ at home when you could be out socializing.

8. Only a professional racer can safely _____ these tight turns at high speeds.

9. A physician must always _____ to uphold the professional standards set forth in the Hippocratic oath.

10. The _____ greeted us at the door when we arrived at the party.

11. Although the portrait was recognizable, the artist had not captured the spirit of his _____.

12. "I shall carry out the will of my queen," said the valiant knight, "as any loyal _____ would hasten to do."

13. The potter _____ the clay by mixing it with a small amount of water before he began making the bowls.

14. The masts on the earliest sailboats were freestanding; they had no _____ to support them.

15. Like any parasite, a tapeworm cannot survive without a _____.

16. If a college interviewer asks what your favorite school _____ is, don't answer, "lunch."

17. The committee members hid their _____ from the press because they wished to present an image of unity.

18. The music teacher silenced the impertinent child with a _____ look.

5:2 Roots Review
The incomplete sentences below contain words that you learned in the two roots lessons in this unit. Complete each sentence so that it makes sense and shows the meaning of the boldfaced vocabulary word.

1. Gertrude decided to become a **microbiologist** because she was fascinated by _____.

2. Albert thought he'd make himself appear more intelligent by using the term **hexapod** for _____.

3. Sarah Carlyle's research in **anthropology** focuses on _____.

4. In order to inject **pathos** into the story, the writer _____.

5. Luke tried to impress the girls with his **virility** by _____.

UNIT SIX 115

6. Myron's **apathy** toward the study of history was evident in the way he _____ .

7. When the environmentalist had finished speaking, George showed his **sympathy** for the ideas that had been expressed by _____ .

8. Scientists stress that concern for the **biosphere** is crucial because _____ .

9. Peter felt such **antipathy** for television commercials that _____ .

10. Mr. Feldman's **pathological** sweating was caused by _____ .

5:3 Choosing Just the Right Word

Many of the words you have worked with in this unit have a number of synonyms. In some cases the synonyms convey different shades of meaning.

Following are synonym studies for three of your vocabulary words. Use either the vocabulary words or their synonyms to complete the sentences in the exercise that follows. Refer to the synonym studies as you decide which word carries the best meaning for the specific context of each sentence.

adversary   opponent

Adversary and *opponent* both mean someone who is against a person or thing. *Adversary* usually suggests hostile opposition—that one person is actively blocking or openly fighting another. *Hawkins spat bitter accusations at his adversary. Opponent* refers to someone on the other side of an argument, contest or game, but does not imply personal ill will. *Before the match I shook hands with my opponent.*

civility   courtesy

Civility and *courtesy* share the basic meaning of politeness. *Civility* suggests being just polite enough to avoid rudeness. *I admired the civility with which you responded to that customer's obnoxious manner. Courtesy* implies that one is thoughtful of the feelings and wishes of others. *It's important to treat your elders with courtesy and respect.*

effort   endeavor

Both *effort* and *endeavor* mean use of mental or physical power to do something. *Effort* implies trying hard but perhaps not long or effectively. *He made an effort to finish developing the photographs this afternoon.* *Endeavor* is a more formal word that suggests sincere and serious effort over time. *Researchers were faced with one obstacle after another in their endeavor to find a cure for the devastating disease.*

1. At the press conference the president answered questions with _____, but it was clear that he would have preferred to be elsewhere.

2. I made a few attempts to reach her by phone, but my _____ was unsuccessful.

3. It is a sign of sportsmanship to praise your _____ regardless of **whether** you win or lose.

4. MacIntyre's fondest wish was to humiliate his _____.

5. Out of _____ to his guests, Rodney rescheduled the luncheon to a more convenient time.

6. In a concerted effort to overcome his self-defeating habit of procrastination, James had become his own _____.

7. It is considered poor manners to distract your _____ during a chess match.

8. When the ambitious project was completed, Tanya was satisfied with the results of her _____.

9. Please make an _____ to answer these letters promptly.

10. In some countries it is considered a sign of _____ to bow when you are introduced to someone, but most Americans shake hands instead.

UNIT SIX   117

5:4 Recognizing Word Forms

The words listed below are other forms of the vocabulary words you have worked with in this unit. Fill in the blank in each sentence with the appropriate vocabulary word. Use what you learned in this unit to help you figure out what the words mean.

discord   civil   adverse   stay   oppressive   withered   negotiating

civilities   appallingly   subjected   languidly   manacled

1. All the defense witnesses were _____ to cross-examination by the prosecutor.

2. Instead of improving the patient's condition, the medication actually had an _____ effect.

3. We are in the process of _____ with the sellers to persuade them to lower their price on the house.

4. I know you don't like your brother's friend, but please be _____ toward him when he stops by.

5. At the last minute, when it looked as though nothing could save the condemned prisoner, the governor granted a _____ of execution.

6. One August afternoon, Angelique reclined in a hammock, fanning herself _____.

7. The police officer _____ the violent suspect to a railing and called the station to request assistance.

8. I found the atmosphere _____ in the windowless room, so I stepped outside for some fresh air.

9. The legacy of their late father was an added source of _____ for Jake and Luke Hopkins, who had never gotten along well.

10. During her long illness Belinda grew _____ gaunt and frail.

11. Deprived of water and light, the plants _____ and then died.

12. The expressions "Have a good day" and "How are you?" are often spoken merely as _____ and are not necessarily motivated by sincere interest.

5:5 Putting Your Vocabulary to Use

In this exercise you will create rhyming phrases using vocabulary words from this unit and the preceding one. The phrases will complete humorous definitions of the words.

Examples: A seafood dinner is marine cuisine.
A fish doctor might be a sturgeon surgeon.

1. People who purchase expensive items to impress their friends are buying status _____.

2. A very masculine, bushy-tailed rodent is a _____ squirrel.

3. An ingenious effort is a clever _____.

4. Airplanes flying in formation create an aviation _____.

5. A search for bird homes is a nest _____.

6. A large number of supernatural beings is a _____ of ghosts.

7. A container that holds a cow's favorite meal might be called a hay _____.

8. Singed facial hair is a _____ beard.

9. A dreadful attack by a bear would be an _____ mauling.

10. A tranquil member of the armed forces is a _____ marine.

Negotiating a Good Deal

Have you ever dickered with a salesperson over the price of an item? Today the word *dicker* means to haggle over a price. As used by the Romans over two thousand years ago, it meant something quite different. *Dicker* comes from the Latin word *decuria*. To Roman merchants, *decuria* meant any set of ten articles. Merchants often bought and sold goods such as animal skins in bundles of ten. Over the centuries the practice of buying and selling in tens continued, and *decuria* changed through use to *dicker*. Europeans brought the term to the New World. They regularly swapped trinkets or hardware for a dicker of furs from the Indians. Since there was often some disagreement about the value of a dicker of pelts, the buyer and seller would argue over the terms of the trade. So *dicker* gradually became linked with the practice of haggling.

"Ok, I'll give *you* five dollars to *take* it. But that's my final offer!"

UNIT 7

1: Meeting Words in Context

Reading Selection   Excerpt from *The Mill on the Floss* by George Eliot

Words Introduced   abstain alleviating compliance depreciated entreated furtively mutual stowed tacit void

2: The Roots of Our Language

Roots Introduced   oct- gen-

3: Meeting Words in Context

Reading Selection   Excerpt from *The Metamorphosis* by Franz Kafka

Words Introduced   arbitrary breadth bulk enunciating metamorphosis plaintive reflection repose resolves tentatively

4: The Roots of Our Language

Roots Introduced   nona- nove- ennea- astro -nomy -naut cosmo

5: Extending Your Word Power

Multiple Meanings
Roots Review
Using Words Precisely
Recognizing Word Forms
Putting Your Vocabulary to Use

1: Meeting Words in Context

Excerpt from **The Mill on the Floss** by George Eliot

The only **alleviating** circumstance in a *tête-à-tête* with uncle Pullet was that he kept a variety of lozenges and peppermint drops about his person, and when at a loss for conversation, he filled up the **void** by proposing a **mutual** solace of this kind.

"Do you like peppermints, young sir?" required only a **tacit** answer when it was accompanied by a presentation of the article in question.

The appearance of the little girls suggested to uncle Pullet the further solace of small sweet-cakes of which he also kept a stock under lock and key for his own private eating on wet days; but the three children had no sooner got the tempting delicacy between their fingers than aunt Pullet desired them to **abstain** from eating it till the tray and the plates came, since with those crisp cakes they would make the floor "all over" crumbs. Lucy didn't mind that much, for the cake was so pretty, she thought it was rather a pity to eat it; but Tom, watching his opportunity while the elders were talking, hastily **stowed** it in his mouth at two bites and chewed it **furtively**. As for Maggie, becoming fascinated, as usual, by a print of Ulysses and Nausicaa, which uncle Pullet had bought as a "pretty Scripture thing," she presently let fall her cake, and in an unlucky movement crushed it beneath her foot—a source of so much agitation to aunt Pullet and conscious disgrace to Maggie, that she began to despair of hearing the musical snuff-box today, till after some reflection, it occurred to her that Lucy was in high favor enough to venture on asking for a tune. So she whispered to Lucy, and Lucy, who always did what she was desired to do, went up quietly to her uncle's knee, and, blushing all over her neck while she fingered her necklace, said, "Will you please play us a tune, uncle?"

. . . But uncle Pullet, when **entreated** to exhibit his accomplishment, never **depreciated** it by a too ready consent. "We'll see about it," was the answer he always gave, carefully abstaining from any sign of **compliance** till a suitable number of minutes had passed.

Choose from the story two words that are unfamiliar to you or whose meanings you are not completely sure of. (Do not choose words that appear in boldfaced type.) Write the words on the lines provided below. Then, beside each word, write what you think it means, based on how it was used in the story.

1. _____ : _____
   _____

2. _____ : _____
   _____

When you have finished the exercises in this lesson, go to your dictionary and find the definitions for the words you entered above. If a word has more than one meaning, look for the one that defines the word as it is used in the story. Then write the words and their dictionary definitions in the Student Words pages at the back of the book. How close did you come to figuring out their meanings for yourself?

1:1 Using Context
Write each vocabulary word beside its correct meaning. Try to figure out what the word means from the way it is used in the sentence.

1. **depreciated**

_____ devalued   _____ regretted

_____ showed   _____ played

2. **compliance**

_____ displeasure   _____ haste

_____ cooperation   _____ amusement

3. **furtively**

_____ quickly   _____ covertly

_____ hungrily   _____ noisily

4. **abstain**

_____ despair   _____ make a mess

_____ have fun   _____ refrain

5. **tacit**

_____ polite   _____ unspoken

_____ solemn   _____ enthusiastic

1:2 Making Connections
Listed below are the five vocabulary words you worked with in the last exercise, followed by fourteen words and phrases that are related to them in some way. They may be synonyms, antonyms or definitions. On the line next to each word or phrase, write the vocabulary word that is related to it.

furtively   depreciate   tacit   abstain   compliance

1. engage in _____

2. silent _____

3. vocal _____

4. openly _____

5. verbal _____

6. stealthily _____

7. implied _____

8. forbear _____

9. exalt _____

10. indulge _____

11. unobtrusively _____

12. hold back _____

13. willingness _____

14. lessen the value of _____

UNIT SEVEN 123

1:3 Using Context

Below are five vocabulary words from the reading passage. Write them next to their meanings. Try to figure out the meaning of each word from the way in which it is used in the sentence.

    entreated   stowed   mutual   alleviating   void

1. Which word means "asked" or "made a plea to"? _____
2. Which word means "shared in common"? _____
3. Which word means "making more bearable"? _____
4. Which word means "emptiness"? _____
5. Which word means "loaded" or "packed"? _____

1:4 Making Connections

Complete each sentence with the correct vocabulary word.

    entreated   stowed   mutual   alleviating   void

1. When Binky the pup ran away, we knew nothing would ever fill the _____ in our lives.

2. When Oscar and Millicent get together they talk for hours about their _____ loathing of their boss.

3. I couldn't get my neighbor to stop practicing the trumpet, but these earplugs might have an _____ effect.

4. Did you see how fast your cousin _____ away that jumbo pizza? No wonder they call him "The Vacuum Cleaner."

5. We _____ Mom and Dad to let us go swimming alone, but they insisted on supervising us.

2: The Roots of Our Language

oct- The root for the number eight, in both Latin and Greek, is *oct-*. Since you have already learned that September, the ninth month of the year, contains the root for seven, it should come as no surprise to you that October, the tenth month, contains the root for eight. It was the eighth month in the early Roman calendar. An octagon, then, is a polygon having eight sides and eight angles, and an octahedron is a solid figure bounded by eight plane faces. To continue with the other number words we have been looking at in these lessons, an octet is a group of eight, and an octogenarian is a person in his or her eighties. An octave is a span of eight notes in a musical scale, and an octopus, as you know, is a sea creature that has eight arms, or tentacles.

gen- Let's move now from words having to do with eight to words that begin with the prefix *gen-*. Many English words have grown up from the Latin word *genus* and the Greek word *genos*, both meaning birth, race or kind. One such word that you are undoubtedly familiar with is *generate*, meaning to bring into existence, or to produce. Generation is the action or process of coming or bringing into being. A generation is also a group of people constituting a single step in the line of descent from an ancestor.

Genealogy (JEE-nee-AHL-uh-jee) is the study of family ancestries or histories. A genealogy is also an account of the descent of a person or family from an ancestor. Such an account is commonly referred to as a family tree.

Genes, as you have probably learned in your study of biology, are those tiny parts of chromosomes that transmit characteristics from one generation to another. It is the genes that determine such things as the color of a person's hair and eyes, the shape of his nose, and whether or not he has freckles. Genetics, therefore, is the branch of biology that deals with the principles of heredity. A characteristic that is genetic is related to genes or to genetics. For example, genetic birth defects are physical abnormalities caused by some defect in the genes.

Genesis (JEN-uh-sus) means origin or creation. For example, the genesis of people's desire to fly probably grew from their observation of birds in flight. With a capital letter, *Genesis* refers to the first book of the Old Testament, which describes the creation of the world.

So far all the words we have looked at with the *gen-* prefix have had to do with birth or origin. But the root also means type or class. The word *genus*, for instance, means any group of similar things. It refers especially to a group—a kind or class—of related plants or animals. Plants and animals of the same genus have certain characteristics in common. Those characteristics are said to be generic (juh-NARE-ik) or applicable to all members of the genus. *Generic* also means general—not specific or special. You have probably heard of generic drugs. They are drugs that do not have a specific manufacturer's name attached to them. Aspirin, for instance, is a generic drug, although many manufacturers of aspirin products attach their own special names to that drug. Cornflakes, facial tissues and gelatin dessert are also the generic names for products that are marketed under a wide variety of specific names.

Finally, let's look at a word that is related to art, literature and music. *Genre* (ZHAN-ruh) means kind or sort, and usually refers to a category of art, music or literature that is characterized by a particular style or form. Opera, for instance, is a musical genre, and the short story is a literary genre.

2:1 Write each word or root listed on the left beside its meaning on the right.

oct- 1. _____ origin

genus 2. _____ bring into existence or produce

generate 3. _____ birth, race or kind

genesis 4. _____ eight

genre 5. _____ artistic style or form

2:2 Mark each statement as either true or false.

_____ 1. To regenerate is to produce anew.

_____ 2. An octopod has eight feet.

_____ 3. The proper noun *Genesis* is the name of the first chapter of any book.

_____ 4. A literary genre is a group of people who get together to talk about books.

_____ 5. Genealogy is the study of genetic characteristics.

2:3 Answer the following questions.

1. If generation is the process of bringing into being, and the prefix *de-* means to undo, what might you call the process that brings about a living thing's deterioration?

   _____

2. Genesis, the first book of the Bible, provides a definition of its own title in the opening line, which reads, "In the _____ ."

3. Some well-known brand names have become so familiar to people that they are used as _____ terms.

4. If everyone in an octet took a turn playing all the notes in an octave, how many times would those notes be sounded? _____

5. If you wanted to trace your family's history, what kind of an expert would you consult?

   _____

3: Meeting Words in Context

Excerpt from **The Metamorphosis** by Franz Kafka

As Gregor Samsa awoke one morning from uneasy dreams he found himself transformed in his bed into a gigantic insect. He was lying on his hard, as it were armor-plated, back and when he lifted his head a little he could see his dome-like brown belly divided into stiff arched segments on top of which the bed quilt could hardly keep in position and was about to slide off completely. His numerous legs, which were pitifully thin compared to the rest of his **bulk**, waved helplessly before his eyes.

What has happened to me? he thought. It was no dream. . . .

. . . "Gregor! Gregor!" At the . . . door his sister was saying in a low, **plaintive** tone: "Gregor? Aren't you well? Are you needing anything?" He answered . . . "I'm just ready," and did his best to make his voice sound as normal as possible by **enunciating** the words very clearly and leaving long pauses between them. . . . But his sister whispered: "Gregor, open the door, do." However, he was not thinking of opening the door, and felt thankful for the prudent habit he had acquired in traveling of locking all doors during the night, even at home.

His immediate intention was to get up quietly without being disturbed . . .

He thought that he might get out of bed with the lower part of his body first, but this lower part, which he had not yet seen and of which he could form no clear conception, proved too difficult to move; it shifted so slowly. . . .

So he tried to get the top part of himself out first, and **tentatively** moved his head towards the edge of the bed. That proved easy enough, and despite its **breadth** and mass the bulk of his body at last slowly followed the movement of his head. . . .

But when after a repetition of the same efforts he lay in his former position again, sighing, and watched his little legs struggling against each other more wildly than ever, if that were possible, and saw no way of bringing any order into this **arbitrary** confusion, he told himself again that it was impossible to stay in bed and that the most sensible course was to risk everything for the smallest hope of getting away from it. At the same time he did not forget meanwhile to remind himself that cool **reflection**, the coolest possible, was much better than desperate **resolves**. . . . And for a little while he lay quiet, breathing lightly, as if perhaps expecting such complete **repose** to restore all things to their real and normal condition.

Choose from the story two words that are unfamiliar to you or whose meanings you are not completely sure of. (Do not choose words that appear in boldfaced type.) Write the words on the lines provided below. Then, beside each word, write what you think it means, based on how it was used in the story.

1. _____ : _____

2. _____ : _____

When you have finished the exercises in this lesson, go to your dictionary and find the definitions for the words you entered above. If a word has more than one meaning, look for the one that defines the word as it is used in the story. Then write the words and their dictionary definitions in the Student Words pages at the back of the book. How close did you come to figuring out their meanings for yourself?

3:1 Using Context

Listed below are five boldfaced words from the reading passage. The list is followed by definitions of the words as they are used in the reading passage. Write each word in front of its definition.

To figure out what each word means, go back to the passage and read the sentence that contains the word. If you can't discover the meaning from the way the word is used in the sentence, read the sentences that come before and after it for clues.

plaintive   enunciating   tentatively   breadth   arbitrary

1. _____ : hesitantly
2. _____ : not based on sense or reason
3. _____ : speaking clearly and distinctly
4. _____ : melancholy
5. _____ : width

3:2 Making Connections

Write each vocabulary word on the line in front of the appropriate synonym and antonym.

plaintive   enunciating   tentatively   breadth   arbitrary

	synonym	antonym
1. _____	articulating	mumbling
2. _____	girth	slenderness
3. _____	mournful	cheerful
4. _____	senseless	logical
5. _____	uncertainly	confidently

3:3 Using Context

For each of the boldfaced words in this exercise, go back and read the part of the passage in which the word appears, paying special attention to the sentence in which the word is used. You'll notice that the word *metamorphosis* appears only in the title. The first sentence holds a clue to its meaning. In the list that follows each vocabulary word, circle the word that has the same or almost the same meaning. Be prepared to support your choices.

1. **metamorphosis**   insect   change   ordeal   victim

2. **resolves**   decisions   fears   actions   efforts

3. **bulk**   limbs   features   mass   experience

4. **repose**   silence   solitude   laziness   rest

5. **reflection**   contemplation   relaxation   attitude   memory

3:4 Making Connections

The boldfaced words in the sentences below are short definitions of or synonyms for the five vocabulary words you worked with in the last exercise. On the line in front of each sentence, write the vocabulary word that has the same meaning as the boldfaced word or words.

metamorphosis   resolves   bulk   repose   reflection

1. _____ The jangling of the alarm clock interrupted my **tranquility**.

2. _____ After I took one look at the buffet table, all my **vows** to diet went right out the window.

3. _____ Seeing the film about the caterpillar's **transformation** into a butterfly helped us to better understand the process.

4. _____ The trained elephant settled its **huge body** onto a three-legged stool.

5. _____ Morris seemed lost in **meditation** as he stared out the window.

4: The Roots of Our Language

nona-
nove-
The Latin root for nine has two forms: *nona-* and *nove-*. There are few English words that carry these prefixes. November is probably the most familiar. The month got its name from the fact that it was the ninth month in the early Roman calendar. A novena (no-VEE-nuh) is a Roman Catholic devotion that lasts for nine days, and a nonagenarian (NO-nuh-juh-NARE-ee-un) is a person in his or her nineties. Novemdecillion (NO-vum-dih-SIL-yun) is a huge number that is written as 1,000 followed by nineteen (nine, *novem*, plus ten, *dec*) sets of three zeros.

ennea-
The Greek root for nine, *ennea-* (EN-ee-uh), is even less common than the Latin. You may, however, at some point in your life, encounter an enneagon (EN-ee-uh-gon) (also called a nonagon), which is a polygon with nine angles, or an enneahedron (EN-ee-uh-HEE-drun), a polyhedron with nine faces.

astro
Moving away from nines, let's take a look at words related to the stars. Since the root *astro* means star, you might expect that the word *astrology* would mean the science or study of the stars. Well, although that was the original meaning of the word, today astrology is the study of the various aspects and positions of stars and planets in order to try to determine their supposed influences on human affairs. Astrology is not taken seriously by astronomers—scientists who study astronomy, which is the science of the celestial bodies.

-nomy
The root *-nomy* means system of laws or arrangement. Thus, *astronomy* literally means the system of laws governing the stars.

Astronomical means related to astronomy. However, this adjective also means enormously large or great. Novemdecillion, for instance, is an astronomical number.

-naut
We all know that an astronaut is a person who travels into outer space, but did you realize that the word means, literally, star sailor? The root *-naut* means sailor. The word *nautical* means pertaining to sailors, navigation or ships.

Asteroids are small bodies that revolve about the sun. As we saw in a previous lesson, *-oid* means like or similar to. Asteroids get their name because their appearance is starlike. An asterisk is a small star symbol (∗) used in writing and printing. The word *asterisk* means little star.

cosmo
Another root related to things that are otherworldly is *cosmo*, meaning order or universe. The cosmos, then, is an orderly, harmonious universe. Cosmology is a branch of astronomy that deals with the origin and structure of the universe. *Cosmic* is an adjective that means related to or characteristic of the cosmos. The disintegration of a star would be a cosmic event.

Cosmo is also found in combination with other roots. Just as an astronaut is a star sailor, a cosmonaut is a sailor of the universe. This word was coined by the Russians, which is why Soviet space travelers are called cosmonauts rather than astronauts.

A person who is cosmopolitan is worldly and sophisticated. He or she has a worldwide rather than a limited perspective on events. *Cosmopolitan* means, literally, citizen of the world.

4:1 Write each word or root listed on the left beside its meaning on the right.

nona-   1. _____ relating to the universe

astro   2. _____ sailor

-naut   3. _____ order or universe

cosmo   4. _____ nine

cosmic   5. _____ star

4:2 Mark each statement as either true or false.

_____ 1. A microcosm is a little world, especially one that is representative of a larger world.

_____ 2. Since *-polis* means city, a cosmopolis is a cosmopolitan city.

_____ 3. *Asterisk* means little star because *aster* means little.

_____ 4. Plotting one's course through the skies, as in outer space, is called astronavigation.

_____ 5. Cosmology is the study of the origin, structure and space-time relationships of the universe.

4:3 Answer the following questions.

1. Given the average life span of human beings, what is one major reason that the word *nonagenarian* is not used a lot? _____

2. If you know that *astral* is an adjective that means of or related to the stars, do you think there would be a heavy cloud cover on an astral night? Explain your answer. _____

3. Very fine particles of solid matter, called dust, are found in all parts of the universe. What do you think the dust in outer space is called? _____

4. One of the first sports stadiums to have a clear, dome-shaped roof was called an astrodome. Why is that an appropriate name? _____

5. Nautical miles are units of distance used for navigation in the air and on _____ .

5: Extending Your Word Power

5:1 Multiple Meanings

Some of the vocabulary words you encountered in this unit have meanings other than those they held in the reading passages. Below, two to four definitions are shown for each of the words *void, resolve, abstain, depreciated* and *tentatively*. On the line before each sentence, write the letter of the definition appropriate to the way in which the vocabulary word is used in the sentence.

void

a. (n.) empty space

b. (adj.) not valid

c. (v.) to invalidate

_____ 1. Unless you pay the premiums on time, your insurance policy will become **void**.

_____ 2. You made an error in ringing up that sale. Please **void** it and enter the numbers again.

_____ 3. A meteorite crashed to earth and left the gaping **void** that you see before you.

resolve

a. (n.) a firm decision

b. (v.) to settle or find an answer to

c. (v.) to reach a firm decision

d. (n.) determination

_____ 4. I **resolved** to get more exercise.

_____ 5. When Hans quit smoking, it was a difficult test of his **resolve**.

_____ 6. Let's **resolve** this dispute before it gets out of hand.

_____ 7. Andrew made a **resolve** to spend more time with his family.

depreciated

a. (v.) lessened the value or price of

b. (v.) lessened in value

_____ 8. The Pinkeys **depreciated** their property when they chopped down the shade trees in the backyard.

_____ 9. Because the stock has **depreciated** since I bought it, I will not make a profit on it.

tentatively

a. (adv.) not definitely, not completely worked out

b. (adv.) uncertainly, hesitantly

_____ 10. The festival has been **tentatively** scheduled for the first week in August.

_____ 11. Someone opened the door **tentatively**, peeked in, and then retreated.

5:2 Roots Review

The incomplete sentences below contain words that you learned in the two roots lessons in this unit. Complete each sentence so that it makes sense and shows the meaning of the boldfaced vocabulary word.

1. The literary **genre** that Harold most enjoys is _____.

2. Emma reminded the group that the **genesis** of the idea that the school should offer some student-run courses _____.

3. Alexandra's **cosmopolitan** perspective is the result of _____.

4. Micky's **nautical** costume made him look _____.

5. Marcia decided to investigate her **genealogy** because _____.

6. In order to **generate** new business, the health spa _____.

7. Mr. Pedigrew captivated the audience with his imaginative vision of a **cosmos** that _____.

8. Elsie is a firm believer that **generic** soap _____.

9. Ted and Norma were impressed by the **astronomical** _____ _____.

10. Susan's **genetic** link to her great-grandmother was evident in _____ _____.

5:3 Choosing Just the Right Word

Many of the words you have worked with in this unit have a number of synonyms. In some cases the synonyms convey different shades of meaning.

Following are synonym studies for three of your vocabulary words. Use either the vocabulary words or their synonyms to complete the sentences in the exercise that follows. Refer to the synonym studies as you decide which word carries the best meaning for the specific context of each sentence.

alleviate   allay

Both *alleviate* and *allay* mean to make more tolerable. To allay is to lay to rest, to quiet or soothe that which is excited. *The surgeon's explanation was enough to allay my misgivings about the operation.* To alleviate is to lighten a burden, make it more bearable. *This medication will alleviate your pain, but will not completely eliminate it.*

repose   rest

Repose is complete freedom from mental or physical activity. *The aroma of bacon penetrated Ben's repose.* Rest is a temporary break in activity, and it implies recuperation from mental or physical fatigue. *Get some rest—you look exhausted.*

resolve   decision

Resolve and *decision* both involve coming to a conclusion. *Decision* implies previous consideration of a matter causing doubt, wavering, debate or controversy. *After a long discussion, we came to a decision. Resolve* implies an expressed or clear determination to do or refrain from doing something. *Have you made a resolve to wash the dishes at least once a week?*

1. We had trouble reaching a _____ about which movie to see, so we flipped a coin.

2. Let's take a little _____ before we climb this next hill.

3. I'm glad you were able to _____ Mac's fear of airplanes. He actually enjoyed the flight.

4. Sammy wasn't able to keep his _____ to watch less television.

5. If you burn your hand while cooking, running cold water over the burn will _____ the discomfort.

6. Scotte, Woody needs to know what you want him to buy at the supermarket. Please stop wavering and make a _____ .

7. Though I hadn't slept soundly all week, last night I enjoyed complete _____ .

8. You can tell Herb about your _____ to get to work on time every day, but he probably won't believe you can do it.

9. This decongestant will _____ your symptoms, but it won't cure your cold.

10. I was savoring complete relaxation and tranquility on the beach until a careless seagull disturbed my _____ .

5:4 Recognizing Word Forms

The words listed below are other forms of the vocabulary words you have worked with in this unit. Fill in the two blanks in each sentence with the appropriate vocabulary words. Use what you have learned in this unit to help you figure out what the words mean.

plaintively   abstained   mutually   bulky   tacitly

resolve   arbitration   entreaty   furtive   reflects   alleviate

stowing   abstaining   comply   enunciation   voided

1. You can _____ your allergy symptoms by _____ from the foods you are sensitive to.

2. His _____ behavior _____ betrayed his guilt.

3. All week Harry had stuck to his diet and _____ from sweets, but by Saturday his _____ was weakening.

UNIT SEVEN   135

4. Your lease is a contract with your landlord. By failing to _____ with the terms therein, you have _____ the agreement and can be evicted.

5. Bella's clear _____ on stage _____ years of speech lessons.

6. During the _____ session, the mediator proposed to the opposing parties a solution that was _____ acceptable.

7. On the news last night, a distraught mother spoke _____ as she made a public _____ for the return of her missing daughter.

8. The security guard caught the shoplifter, whom she had observed _____ merchandise under his _____ down parka.

5:5 Putting Your Vocabulary to Use

This word-search puzzle conceals twenty-two vocabulary words from both this and the previous unit. They are printed horizontally, vertically, diagonally, backward and upside down.

Begin by listing the vocabulary words next to their clues below. Then find the words in the puzzle, circling them as you locate them.

1. _____ a feeling of close understanding
2. _____ lessening pain or discomfort
3. _____ emptiness
4. _____ shared in common
5. _____ eight-sided plane figure
6. _____ horrifying
7. _____ singed, burned
8. _____ harsh sounds, cacophony
9. _____ begged
10. _____ any group of similar things
11. _____ packed or stored
12. _____ something that evokes feelings of compassion or pity

13. _____ to produce, make

14. _____ silent, implied

15. _____ devastating, destructive

16. _____ a group of people constituting a single step in the line of descent from an ancestor

17. _____ handcuffs

18. _____ study of family ancestries or histories

19. _____ substance, essence

20. _____ refrain

21. _____ aversion to someone or something

22. _____ the parts of chromosomes that transmit characteristics from one generation to the next

```
a r t a n g n i r e h t i w o n
p c o n t e n t f m t l c e g i
a r c e l n a l b v c a w d h g
t e t a r e n e g m q u c x n e
h e a l d s p r d u l s t i k n
g c g y m b n e a d g e l p t e
n e o q p a t h o s y l b a j r
i z n c b a r o t d a c e g e a
t f h e e j s k l p p a m m o t
a d e r a e s n p s u n p n u i
i a t b g l t a j m p a q u t o
v n r p e v o i d s t m u w h n
e c q d n f w g p h i a m p l i
l a u t u m e g y a k r b c s d
l i j e s f d i s c o r d s m g
a n t i p a t h y n i a t s b a
```

UNIT SEVEN 137

UNIT 8

1: Meeting Words in Context

    Reading Selection   Appalachia

    Words Introduced   decline diversified earnest fledgling innovative isolation nurture prosperity secluded sever

2: The Roots of Our Language

    Roots Introduced   decem- deca- -logue epi- dia- deci- dem

3: Meeting Words in Context

    Reading Selection   Foxfire

    Words Introduced   conviction crude destined harried intense perpetuation reared semblance sober unearthed

4: The Roots of Our Language

    Roots Introduced   cent- centi- -grade retro-

5: Extending Your Word Power

Multiple Meanings
Roots Review
Using Words Precisely
Recognizing Word Forms
Putting Your Vocabulary to Use

1: Meeting Words in Context

Appalachia

Two hundred years ago, when the United States was a **fledgling** nation, Appalachia was its first frontier. It challenged the new Americans with its rugged and beautiful mountains.

When the great westward movement began in **earnest**, thousands crossed the Appalachians. Many, however, remained to make their homes in the narrow valleys and along the winding rivers. For them the growing cities and the promise of the west held little romance. They chose, instead, the **isolation** of the mountains and the right to live according to their own rules.

As the nation became increasingly mobile and sophisticated, Appalachians maintained their traditional ways. Family was more important than the broader society; freedom to live where they chose more important than the **prosperity** of the cities. Even hard times could not **sever** the bond between the people and their land.

In the early 1960s, Appalachia's economic problems became a national cause. Out of that public attention came a stereotyped image of isolation and poverty, which was, in large part, the result of a **decline** in the coal industry, the region's major resource and primary industry.

Congress devised a special development program to help Appalachia. Appalachia was defined by law, on the basis of shared heritage, problems and potentials, to include one whole state, West Virginia, and parts of Alabama, Georgia, Kentucky, Maryland, Mississippi, New York, North Carolina, Ohio, Pennsylvania, South Carolina, Tennessee and Virginia.

The Congress also wisely took into account the nature of the people in legislating the Appalachian Regional Development Program. It recognized Appalachians as a proud, independent people, bound to the land and their past by a strong sense of place and belonging. The goal has been to build a **diversified** economic base for the region through key investments in highways, human services, community facilities and housing. Care is always taken, however, to **nurture** Appalachia's uniquely American culture.

Appalachia holds an intriguing mixture of the past, the present and the future. There you can attend an opera or an old-time fiddlers contest, buy a traditional hand-sewn quilt or a piece of world-renowned crystal. You can visit an **innovative** environmental center, a nuclear power plant or an exhibition coal mine; camp out on a mountainside or pamper yourself at a historic spa; trout fish in a **secluded** stream or ski on slopes that rarely require the aid of a snow-maker.

Choose from the story two words that are unfamiliar to you or whose meanings you are not completely sure of. (Do not choose words that appear in boldfaced type.) Write the words on the lines provided below. Then, beside each word, write what you think it means, based on how it was used in the story.

1. _____ : _____

   _____

2. _____ : _____

   _____

When you have finished the exercises in this lesson, go to your dictionary and find the definitions for the words you entered above. If a word has more than one meaning, look for the one that defines the word as it is used in the story. Then write the words and their dictionary definitions in the Student Words pages at the back of the book. How close did you come to figuring out their meanings for yourself?

1:1 Using Context

Write each vocabulary word beside its correct meaning. Try to figure out what the word means from the way it is used in the passage.

1. **fledgling**

_____ smaller   _____ violent

_____ nonexistent   _____ young

2. **earnest**

_____ seriousness   _____ desperation

_____ later years   _____ uncertainty

3. **prosperity**

_____ glitter   _____ mystery

_____ economic success   _____ fast pace

4. **sever**

_____ break   _____ strengthen

_____ harm   _____ threaten

5. **decline**

_____ mine   _____ strike

_____ energy shortage   _____ slump

1:2 Making Connections

The boldfaced vocabulary words in the sentences below are the words you worked with in the last exercise. For each vocabulary word, select a synonym and an antonym from the list that follows. Write the synonyms and antonyms in the blanks.

> pretense   rise   seasoned   success   connect
>
> drop   cut   poverty   inexperienced   sincerity

1. She owes her **prosperity** to business sense and luck.

   synonym: _____   **antonym:** _____

2. The **fledgling** real estate agent was uncomfortable about discussing finances with prospective buyers.

   synonym: _____   **antonym:** _____

UNIT EIGHT

3. If you **sever** that wire you will be unable to make or receive phone calls.

   synonym: _____ antonym: _____

4. There has been a **decline** in the crime rate since we instituted the neighborhood watch.

   synonym: _____ antonym: _____

5. I hope you made your offer in **earnest**; we are all counting on you.

   synonym: _____ antonym: _____

1:3 Using Context

Below are five vocabulary words from the reading passage. Write them next to their meanings. Try to figure out the meaning of each word from the way in which it is used in the passage.

secluded   isolation   diversified   nurture   innovative

1. Which word means "characterized by variety"? _____

2. Which word means "set apart" or "sequestered"? _____

3. Which word means "cultivate" or "foster"? _____

4. Which word means "condition of being separate from others"? _____

5. Which word means "new"? _____

1:4 Making Connections

The boldfaced words in the following sentences are short definitions of or synonyms for the five vocabulary words you worked with in the last exercise. On the line in front of each sentence, write the vocabulary word that has the same meaning as the boldfaced word or words.

secluded   isolation   diversified   nurture   innovative

1. _____ The **remoteness** of this cabin makes it a perfect vacation hideaway.

2. _____ We want to **encourage the development of** Melissa's musical talent.

3. _____ The library was so crowded that I couldn't find a **private** place to study.

4. _____ The programs available at the YMCA are more **varied** than they were a decade ago.

5. _____ Your approach is **characterized by new ideas and methods**.

2: The Roots of Our Language

decem- The Latin root for the number ten is *decem-*. December got its name because it used to be the tenth month of the old Roman calendar.

deca- Many of our words related to the number ten come from the Greek root *deca-*. A decade is a period of ten years. A decapod is a mollusk, or shellfish, with ten legs. Shrimps, lobsters and crabs, for instance, are decapods.

Remember triathlon and pentathlon? Well, an athletic contest comprising ten field and track events is called a decathlon.

Deca- can also be combined with several metric terms to mean ten of each unit. A decaliter, for example, is ten liters, a decagram is ten grams, and a decameter is ten meters.

-logue Another term for the Ten Commandments is the Decalogue. The root *-logue* comes from the Greek word *logos,* meaning word or speech. With a lowercase first letter, *decalogue* means a basic set of rules that carries binding authority.

epi-
dia- There are many English words that have the root *-logue*. A monologue is a speech by one person. A prologue is an introductory speech or a preface to a piece of literature. (Remember that the prefix *pro-* means before.) An epilogue is a speech at the conclusion of a play, or a concluding section of a literary work. One of the meanings of the prefix *epi-* is after. A dialogue is a conversation or discussion between two or more people. *Dia-* means between or across. This prefix also forms the beginning of the word *diagonal,* meaning across at an angle (you remember that *-gon* means angle).

deci- The prefix *deci-* means tenth. In combination with a metric root, it indicates an amount that is one-tenth of the amount indicated by the root. A deciliter is one-tenth of a liter, a decigram is a tenth of a gram, and a decimeter is a tenth of a meter.

Decimate means to destroy a large part of something. Farmland, for instance, may be decimated by fierce storms, and famine may decimate the population of an undeveloped country. What does that have to do with ten? Well, *decimate* originally referred to the practice of selecting and killing every tenth man.

dem Let's finish up this lesson by looking at a couple of words that begin with the prefix *epi-*: *epidemic* and *epidemiology.* In these words, *epi-* means on or upon. The *dem* in the words comes from the root *demo-,* meaning people. An epidemic is the rapid spread of a disease upon the people. In a more general sense, an epidemic is the spread of anything that affects many individuals within an area. The rapid spread of an idea or a fashion, for instance, can be said to be epidemic. As an adjective, then, *epidemic* means widespread, or affecting many people at the same time. Epidemiology is a branch of medicine dealing with the causes, distribution and control of the spread of diseases in a community.

2:1 Write each word or root listed on the left beside its meaning on the right.

deca-   1. _____ speech by one person

monologue   2. _____ ten

-logue   3. _____ people

dia-   4. _____ between or across

demo-   5. _____ word or speech

2:2 Mark each statement as either true or false.

_____ 1. A monologue is a speech on one subject.

_____ 2. An epilogue is an introductory speech or a preface to a piece of literature.

_____ 3. A conversation among five people is a dialogue.

_____ 4. One who studies the spread of diseases in a community is an epidemiologist.

_____ 5. A decathlete competes in the decathlon.

2:3 Put an *x* beside the answer choice you think is correct.

1. A decimated urban neighborhood would probably have a number of destroyed or abandoned
   ☐ a. people. ☐ b. buildings. ☐ c. streetcars.

2. "Working in one" is a vaudeville phrase that describes a comedian standing onstage by himself, delivering a comic speech, or
   ☐ a. dialogue. ☐ b. monologue. ☐ c. song.

3. From your knowledge of the meanings of the roots in this exercise, you can figure out that the word meaning an identifying motto used by a business is
   ☐ a. epilogue. ☐ b. logo. ☐ c. monograph.

4. You know that *-graph* comes from a root that means to write, and that *demo-* means people. Demography, then, is the writing down of statistics concerning
   ☐ a. animals. ☐ b. people. ☐ c. machines.

5. Since *democracy* means government by the people, the *-cracy* part of the word must mean
   ☐ a. people. ☐ b. government. ☐ c. rule.

3: Meeting Words in Context

Foxfire

In 1966, Brooks Eliot Wigginton, fresh from Cornell University, came to teach at the Rabun Gap-Nacoochee School in Rabun Gap, Georgia. Born in West Virginia, **reared** in Athens, Georgia, he had drifted from pre-med to archaeology and finally settled on teaching. He arrived in Rabun Gap **destined**, he figured, to bring literature to the "backwoods."

At the entrance of the school, in stone, are these words: "Dedicated to the idea of a school where all work their way." Wigginton's first students, the school's ninth- and tenth-grade English classes, certainly tried to work their way—on him. They whittled graffiti into their desks and even tried to set fire to his lectern. Desperate, the young teacher came in one day and said: "Look, this is boring you to death. Me too. So how would you like to do something like a magazine for the rest of the year?" His sophomores yawned a yes. Thus was *Foxfire* born.

The magazine took the form of oral history. With notebooks and tape recorders under their arms, Wigginton's students fanned out into the mountains and began to interview their elders. They listened, and they began to discover marvelous things: home remedies, wild superstitions, folk legends. They **unearthed** long-kept secrets about tanning hides, raising log cabins, planting by the signs, making banjos—anything that had to do with the affairs of country living.

The rest is history. From a **crude** school literary magazine, *Foxfire* has grown to become a nationally circulated journal. Material from the magazines has also been compiled to create a series of best-selling books.

Wigginton is usually found in the cramped, cluttered *Foxfire* office, a little **harried**. Alternately **sober** and scatterbrained, humorous and **intense**, he small-talks and roughhouses with a student; talks brisk business on the phone; scribbles a note to the *Foxfire* legal counsel in New York. With a **semblance** of order imposed on the place, he drops into a chair to explain the evolution of *Foxfire*: "Everything outgrew from something else. We began a decade ago with a single idea. Now we've got books, videotape recordings—we're even thinking about a series of folklore records.

"And, of course, there's Foxfire Village—we want to have a living community where students can come and learn how the old ways worked. The older folks can use the village to teach the younger ones, and that way there'll be a **perpetuation**."

"My **conviction**," Wigginton says, "is that a community—this community—should be able to run itself. That's our underlying vision."

Choose from the story two words that are unfamiliar to you or whose meanings you are not completely sure of. (Do not choose words that appear in boldfaced type.) Write the words on the lines provided below. Then, beside each word, write what you think it means, based on how it was used in the story.

1. _____ : _____

2. _____ : _____

When you have finished the exercises in this lesson, go to your dictionary and find the definitions for the words you entered above. If a word has more than one meaning, look for the one that defines the word as it is used in the story. Then write the words and their dictionary definitions in the Student Words pages at the back of the book. How close did you come to figuring out their meanings for yourself?

3:1 Using Context
Circle the word or phrase that most nearly matches the meaning of the boldfaced vocabulary word in the sentence.

1. The students **unearthed** secrets of country life.

   found out   disproved   studied   questioned

2. *Foxfire* began as a **crude** school magazine.

   offensive   unknown   unrefined   insignificant

3. Mr. Wigginton was by turns **intense** and humorous.

   shy   pleasant   aloof   fervent

4. Sometimes his manner was **sober**; at other times, scatterbrained.

   sensible   absentminded   confused   dull

5. According to Wigginton, if the older people teach the traditions to the young people, there will be a **perpetuation**.

   education   communication   continuation   result

3:2 Making Connections
Listed below are the five vocabulary words you worked with in the last exercise, followed by nineteen words and phrases that are related to them in some way. They may be synonyms, antonyms or definitions. On the line next to each word or phrase, write the vocabulary word that is related to it.

unearthed   crude   intense   sober   perpetuation

1. apathetic _____
2. silly _____
3. extension _____
4. discovered _____
5. concealed _____
6. solemn _____
7. ardent _____
8. sophisticated _____
9. preservation _____
10. uncovered _____
11. termination _____
12. rudimentary _____
13. giddy _____
14. indifferent _____
15. learned _____
16. serious _____
17. refined _____
18. hid _____
19. cessation _____

3:3 Using Context

Listed below are five boldfaced words from the reading passage. The list is followed by definitions of the words as they are used in the passage. Write each word in front of its definition.

To figure out what each word means, go back to the passage and read the sentence that contains the word. If you can't discover the meaning from the way the word is used, read the sentences that come before and after it for clues.

semblance   harried   conviction   reared   destined

1. _____ : a strong belief

2. _____ : marked by fate

3. _____ : raised

4. _____ : beset by problems, harassed

5. _____ : outward appearance or show

3:4 Making Connections

Complete each sentence with the correct vocabulary word.

semblance   harried   conviction   reared   destined

1. The _____ host tried to hide his grimace as one guest spilled wine on the carpet and another used the aquarium as an ashtray.

2. "It is my firm _____ that children should be seen and not heard," intoned Beatrice.

3. Please try to maintain at least a _____ of competence when the district manager comes in. There's no need to let her know the truth on her first visit to this office.

4. Even though Alex was born and _____ in the city, he loves the country life.

5. Zaza set out for Hollywood, thinking she was _____ to become the next Marilyn Monroe.

4: The Roots of Our Language

cent-

With this lesson we take a big jump to the number one hundred. The Latin root for one hundred is *cent-*. You have already encountered the word *bicentennial,* which is a two-hundredth anniversary. A centennial, of course, is a one-hundredth anniversary. A period of one hundred years, as you know, is a century. A person who has lived for a hundred years is a centenarian.

centi-

Cent itself is a word, referring to a coin that is worth one-hundredth of a dollar. In the metric system, *centi-* is used to indicate one-hundredth. Thus, a centimeter is one-hundredth of a meter, a centigram is one-hundredth of a gram, and a centiliter is one-hundredth of a liter.

-grade

Centi- can also mean a hundred. The temperature scale whose name contains the prefix *centi-* is the centigrade scale. On the centigrade scale, the freezing point of water is 0 degrees, and the boiling point is 100 degrees. Since *-grade* comes from the Latin *gradus,* meaning step, *centigrade* literally means one hundred steps, referring to the one hundred degrees between the freezing and the boiling temperatures of water.

A number of English words are derived from the Latin word *gradus. Gradual,* for instance, means taking place by steps or degrees—little by little. A gradual change is a slow change. *Gradient* refers to the steepness of a slope or inclination. For example, when railroad tracks are being laid in mountainous regions, tunnels were often blasted through hills in order to avoid steep gradients that would be difficult for a train to negotiate.

To graduate is to take a big step from one level to another, whether it's from elementary school to junior high or from high school to college. Graduation is the act of graduating.

Gradation (gray-DAY-shun) refers to a series that forms connected stages, steps or degrees, each leading directly to the next. At sunset, for instance, the sky may show gradations of color, starting with red at the horizon and progressing up into lighter and lighter shades of pink. Also, the numbers indicated on a thermometer are gradations of temperature. In karate, gradations of skill are denoted by the color of the belt that is worn, with white being the lowest and black the highest.

If your position at work is upgraded, you are moved up in rank or level of importance. To be downgraded, of course, is to be moved to a lower-ranking position. To degrade someone is to bring him into dishonor, or to "put him down."

retro-

Finally, *retrograde* as an adjective or a verb refers to a backward motion. It can mean to retreat or move backward, or to deteriorate or worsen. In astronomy, it refers to a satellite that moves in the opposite direction of the body it is orbiting. As you have probably figured out, *retro-* means backward.

4:1 Write each word or root listed on the left beside its meaning on the right.

cent- 1. _____ a two-hundredth anniversary

bicentennial 2. _____ backward

-grade 3. _____ taking place by steps

gradual 4. _____ step

retro- 5. _____ one hundred

4:2 Mark each statement as either true or false.

_____ 1. When the town of Greenville was two hundred years old, it celebrated its centennial.

_____ 2. An event that takes place gradually occurs all of a sudden, usually without warning.

_____ 3. The word *retrograde* refers only to the backward motion of celestial bodies.

_____ 4. A high school graduate has completed all the steps involved in earning a diploma.

_____ 5. A retro-rocket produces thrust in a direction opposite to the motion of the main missile, causing the missile to slow down.

4:3 Put an *x* beside the answer choice you think is correct.

1. If to progress is to move forward, to retrogress is to move
   - ☐ a. sideways.
   - ☐ b. upward.
   - ☐ c. backward.

2. A newly passed law that has a retroactive effect extends its scope to
   - ☐ a. a time in the past.
   - ☐ b. the future.
   - ☐ c. a limited time.

3. The boiling point on a centigrade thermometer is
   - ☐ a. 32 degrees.
   - ☐ b. 212 degrees.
   - ☐ c. 100 degrees.

4. Roman centurions were officers who commanded divisions of the Roman army. The divisions were called centuries. How many soldiers do you think were in each division?
   - ☐ a. one hundred
   - ☐ b. two hundred
   - ☐ c. one thousand

5. If *spect* comes from a root that means to look, then an artist's retrospective exhibition takes a look at work the artist
   - ☐ a. has become famous for.
   - ☐ b. is doing in the present.
   - ☐ c. did in the past.

5: Extending Your Word Power

5:1 Multiple Meanings
The meanings given in this exercise are alternate meanings for the vocabulary words listed below. Write each word in front of its meaning. Consult the glossary if necessary. A word may be used more than once.

unearthed   sober   conviction   reared

decline   fledgling   earnest   crude

1. _____ In reference to a horse, this word can mean "rose up on hind legs."
2. _____ "Serious and eager" is one definition of this word.
3. _____ One meaning of this word is "dug up."
4. _____ A person who is rude, vulgar and completely lacking in taste can be described with this word.
5. _____ "To wane or draw toward a close" can be one definition of this word.
6. _____ This word describes a person who is not drunk.
7. _____ One meaning for this word is "the act of proving that someone committed a crime."
8. _____ This is a name for a young bird.
9. _____ This word can mean "to refuse politely."
10. _____ One meaning of this word is "to slope downward."

5:2 Roots Review
The incomplete sentences below contain words that you learned in the two roots lessons in this unit. Complete each sentence so that it makes sense and shows the meaning of the boldfaced vocabulary word.

1. Because the forest had been **decimated**, _____

_____

_____ .

150   UNIT EIGHT

2. The opening **monologue** was a failure because _____ .

3. The **gradations** between childishness and maturity show that _____ .

4. When she reached the **epilogue**, Gloria _____ .

5. The change in temperature was so **gradual** that _____ .

6. The **decalogue** for the secret society provided _____ .

7. The steepness of the **gradient** made it difficult for _____ .

8. Mr. Fox **degraded** Stanley by _____ .

9. Randal asked for a **deciliter** of vinegar, because a liter _____ .

10. The **retrograde** motion of the carousel _____ .

5:3 Choosing Just the Right Word

Many of the words you have worked with in this unit have a number of synonyms. In some cases the synonyms convey different shades of meaning.

Following are synonym studies for four of your vocabulary words. Use either the vocabulary words or their synonyms to complete the sentences in the exercise that follows. Refer to the synonym studies as you decide which word carries the best meaning for the specific context of each sentence.

decline   deterioration

Decline and *deterioration* both mean a falling from a higher to a lower level. *Decline* means a gradual decrease in size, amount, volume, intensity, etc. *After a steady decline, the inflation rate has stabilized.* *Deterioration* means a making or growing worse in quality or value. *Because of deterioration caused by salt, the road needs to be completely resurfaced.*

belief   conviction   sentiment

Belief, conviction and *sentiment* all mean a judgment that one holds to be true. Belief is the acceptance of an idea, with or without certainty. *We hope Sasha will give up her belief in the tooth fairy soon.* A conviction is a belief that is unshakable and undoubting. *It is my conviction that gambling is immoral.* A sentiment is an attitude or view prompted by feelings. *Bart feels that we must not sell the house where we grew up, but I don't share his sentiment.*

serious   sober   earnest   staid

Serious, sober, earnest and *staid* all mean not light or frivolous. *Serious* means thoughtful or subdued in appearance or manner. *Sharon's smile changed to a serious expression when she heard the news report.* *Sober* means restrained, realistic and reasonable. *We can depend on Gwen, who is sober and sensible even in difficult situations.* *Earnest* means eager, strong and firm in purpose. *We were moved by the candidate's earnest appeal for support.* *Staid* means showing prim self-restraint. *I knew I was in for an unexciting evening when I found myself seated between two staid gentlemen.*

1. You'd be surprised to hear about all the wild times that this seemingly _____ woman had in her youth.

2. Andrew expressed the _____ that there is no place like home.

3. The Maynards had confidence in the new baby-sitter, who seemed _____ and level-headed.

4. The band is hoping to stem a _____ in their popularity by releasing a new album and embarking on a nationwide tour.

5. The _____ of the neighborhood was rapid after the main street was made part of a four-lane highway.

6. Cynthia has a great sense of humor, but she also knows when to be _____.

7. The _____ young trainee was anxious to make a good impression on his boss.

8. Elias stubbornly maintained his _____ that the college of hard knocks is the best schooling there is.

9. Her firm _____ in the value of education led Bridget to study hard and earn top honors in her class.

5:4 Recognizing Word Forms

The words listed below are other forms of some of the vocabulary words you have worked with in this unit. Fill in the blank in each sentence with the appropriate vocabulary word. If you are unsure of the meaning of a word, refer to the glossary.

seclusion   resemblance   innovations   innovators   perpetuate

earnestly   prosper   severed   declined   intensified

diversity   sobriety   destiny   crudeness   convict

1. A few new businesses _____, but it is more usual for them to struggle and even to fail completely in the first few years.

2. The number of robberies in the area has _____ recently because residents are learning to protect their property.

3. In the operating room, doctors worked against time to reattach the victim's _____ hand.

4. Thomas Edison was one of this country's most famous _____.

5. The music started at a moderate volume but _____ as the concert went on, until I could hardly stand the noise.

UNIT EIGHT 153

6. At the scene of the accident, police administered a _____ test to determine if the driver had been driving while intoxicated.

7. A hermit is a person who lives in _____.

8. "I didn't do it, Auntie, honest!" said Cyril _____.

9. Many _____ introduced by the new boss are no better than the old methods.

10. Some folks believe that we control our own actions, while others think we're ruled by _____.

11. Despite the _____ of their tools, the inhabitants of the island were able to build fairly advanced boats and shelters.

12. Despite all the evidence, the prosecutor failed to _____ the defendant.

13. I see no _____ between Larry and Laura, even though they are twins.

14. Because of the _____ among students here, it's hard to generalize about any aspect of campus life.

15. Lord Hillendale, having no sons, will not _____ his family name.

5:5 Putting Your Vocabulary to Use
Use vocabulary words from this unit and the previous unit to complete the crossword puzzle.

ACROSS
1. to destroy a large part of something
4. width
8. ten-event athletic contest
10. solitude
12. speaking clearly
14. conversation, discussion
15. firm decisions
16. young, inexperienced
19. mass
20. financial success
21. rapid spread of disease
22. break, cut or separate

DOWN
1. varied
2. worldly
3. one-tenth of a liter
5. decrease
6. sincere
7. woeful
9. concluding speech or section
11. study of the supposed influence of the stars on human affairs
13. preface or introductory speech
17. rest, tranquility
18. foster

UNIT EIGHT

UNIT 9

1: Meeting Words in Context

Reading Selection   What Is Impressionism?

Words Introduced   asserted attest depict derided dissident milieu motif radical renowned representative

2: The Roots of Our Language

Roots Introduced   milli- -illion kilo- myria-

3: Meeting Words in Context

Reading Selection   Mary Cassatt

Words Introduced   conventional editorialized fusion identified justified marred presume spontaneous spurred surrogates

4: The Roots of Our Language

Roots Introduced   hemi- semi- demi-

5: Extending Your Word Power

Multiple Meanings
Roots Review
Using Words Precisely
Recognizing Word Forms
Putting Your Vocabulary to Use

1: Meeting Words in Context

What is Impressionism?

The broadest definition of the term "impressionism" provides an umbrella under which a variety of painters from several countries can be grouped. However, some of the most **renowned** impressionists painted in France during the 1870s, when impressionism was a **radical** and controversial way of painting.

Impressionism was not given a name until 1874 when Claude Monet, the most **representative** impressionist, exhibited an oil study of ships called *Impression; Sunrise*. A contemptuous critic, Louis Leroy, **derided** it as less finished than wallpaper. He called his review of the entire group exhibition, which included Renoir, Pissaro, Degas and Sisley, "Exhibition of the Impressionists." That label was immediately applied to the entire **dissident** group, whose method of painting was already both a movement and a style.

That style is now almost universally recognized by its high-keyed colors and accentuated brushwork. Light on moving water is perhaps the most revealing impressionist **motif**. The well-known scenes by Monet and Renoir of the Seine, the landscape along its banks, sailboats, and idyllic river life are among the most enchanting pictures of the nineteenth century.

It was **asserted** that the impressionists, in trying to approximate the brightness of outdoor light, applied oil pigment directly to canvas without mixing. They did use vivid colors, often mixed with white, for sunlit objects, but Monet's paintings **attest** that he fully accepted what was before his eyes. If the day was gray or overcast, he painted it as it appeared; but he also revealed for the first time the variety of delicate tints and tones of which natural grays are composed.

In one sense the impressionists were like reporters, as was once claimed. They recorded the social and the natural **milieu** in which they lived. Some of their pictures may have been completed or retouched in the studio, but most—even those including figures—were carried to completion on the site, within a human as well as a natural situation.

The impressionists strove to **depict** what they saw at the moment, not what they remembered. Monet once said he wished he had been born blind, so he could paint the world freshly with no previous knowledge of it. He realized, moreover, that the image which falls on the retina is not an arrangement of masses in space, but a filmy pattern of light.

Choose from the story two words that are unfamiliar to you or whose meanings you are not completely sure of. (Do not choose words that appear in boldfaced type.) Write the words on the lines provided below. Then, beside each word, write what you think it means, based on how it was used in the story.

1. _____ : _____

2. _____ : _____

When you have finished the exercises in this lesson, go to your dictionary and find the definitions for the words you entered above. If a word has more than one meaning, look for the one that defines the word as it is used in the story. Then write the words and their dictionary definitions in the Student Words pages at the back of the book. How close did you come to figuring out their meanings for yourself?

1:1 Using Context

Circle the word or phrase that most nearly matches the meaning of the boldfaced vocabulary word in the sentence.

1. Monet's paintings **attest** to the fact that he faithfully painted what he saw.

    confirm   deny   imply   respond

2. Louis Leroy **derided** the exhibition mercilessly.

    boycotted   praised   evaluated   ridiculed

3. Monet was the most **representative** impressionist.

    prolific   admired   typical   creative

4. Impressionism was a **radical** style in the 1870s.

    popular   new   extreme   exotic

5. The exhibition brought together the works of several **renowned** artists.

    modern   contemporary   famous   controversial

1:2 Making Connections

Listed below are the five vocabulary words you worked with in the last exercise, followed by seventeen words and phrases that are related to them in some way. They may be synonyms, antonyms or definitions. On the line next to each word or phrase, write the vocabulary word that is related to it.

attest   derided   representative   radical   renowned

1. well-known _____
2. moderate _____
3. criticized _____
4. show _____
5. deny _____
6. noted _____
7. tame _____
8. mocked _____
9. obscure _____
10. praised _____
11. unique _____
12. affirm _____
13. atypical _____
14. disprove _____
15. revolutionary _____
16. taunted _____
17. characteristic _____

1:3 Using Context
Put an *x* in the box beside the correct meaning of each vocabulary word. For clues to the meanings of the words, reread the parts of the passage in which they appear.

1. **milieu**
   - ☐ a. environment
   - ☐ b. turmoil
   - ☐ c. society
   - ☐ d. paradise

2. **asserted**
   - ☐ a. accused
   - ☐ b. stated
   - ☐ c. true
   - ☐ d. untrue

3. **motif**
   - ☐ a. painting
   - ☐ b. theme
   - ☐ c. mood
   - ☐ d. tradition

4. **dissident**
   - ☐ a. nonconformist
   - ☐ b. discredited
   - ☐ c. talented
   - ☐ d. diverse

5. **depict**
   - ☐ a. distort
   - ☐ b. preserve
   - ☐ c. show
   - ☐ d. improve

1:4 Making Connections
Complete each sentence with the correct vocabulary word.

      milieu   asserted   motif   dissident   depict

1. Throughout his campaign the governor _____ that there would be no tax hike during his term, but the new budget calls for an increase.

2. In her drawing, the child chose to _____ a space shuttle launch.

3. The principal agreed to listen to _____ views, but it was almost certain that she would not be swayed by them.

4. The conflict between nature and artifice is a common _____ in this author's works.

5. Psychologists insist that a child's development is influenced far more strongly by his or her _____ than by hereditary factors.

2: The Roots of Our Language

milli-
-illion

The prefix for thousand in Latin is *milli-*. The suffix for thousand is *-illion*. This suffix forms the end of the names of very large numbers. The name for the number that means a thousand thousands (1,000,000) uses both the prefix and the suffix, *milli-* plus *-illion,* giving us the word *million.*

A unit that represents one-thousandth of a dollar, or one-tenth of a penny, is called a mill. With one *l,* mil is a unit of measurement equal to one-thousandth of an inch. This minuscule unit of length is used especially for the diameter of wire.

A millenium is a period of a thousand years. For example, the year 2000 will be the start of a new millenium. Although *millipede* literally means a thousand legs or feet, a millipede does not necessarily have more legs than a centipede, which is a bug whose name means one hundred feet. A millipede differs from a centipede in that its body is long and cylindrical, whereas the body of a centipede is long and flat. A millipede has from twenty to more than a hundred body segments, with a pair of legs attached to each segment.

The root *milli-* is used with metric terms to indicate one-thousandth. Thus, a millimeter is one-thousandth of a meter, a milligram is one-thousandth of a gram, and a milliliter is one-thousandth of a liter.

kilo-

The Greek root for thousand is *kilo-*. It is used in metric terms to indicate a thousand units. Therefore, a kilogram is a thousand grams, a kiloliter is a thousand liters, and kilometer is a thousand meters. In countries that use the metric system, the kilogram is the unit of weight that is frequently used when buying foods such as meat, fruit and vegetables. A kilogram is equal to approximately 2.2 pounds. Kilometers are used to measure distance. A kilometer is equivalent to about two-thirds of a mile. Speed is measured in kilometers per hour. A kilowatt is a unit of electric power equal to one thousand watts.

A kilocycle is a unit used to measure the frequency of radio and television waves. One kilocycle is equal to one thousand cycles per second. In order to avoid interference with one another, stations transmit their broadcasts at different frequencies. The numbers on a radio dial indicate frequencies in kilocycles.

myria-

Let's look now at one more numerical root, *myria-,* meaning ten thousand. In metrics we encounter *myriagram,* which is ten thousand grams, *myriameter,* which is ten thousand meters, and *myrialiter,* which is ten thousand liters.

Myria- also makes up the greatest part of the word *myriad* (MEER-ee-ud), which means a great many. There are myriad leaves, for instance, on an oak tree, and in a lifetime a person is faced with myriad decisions.

2:1 Write each word or root listed on the left beside its meaning on the right.

milli-   1. _____ measure of radio-wave frequency

myria-   2. _____ Latin root meaning thousand

kilo-   3. _____ ten thousand

kilocycle 4. _____ a great many

myriad   5. _____ Greek root meaning thousand

2:2 Mark each statement as either true or false.

_____ 1. A millenium is a million years.

_____ 2. A kilocycle is a bicycle that will operate efficiently for at least one thousand miles.

_____ 3. *Myriad* means exactly one thousand.

_____ 4. A myriameter is used to measure myriads.

_____ 5. A kilogram is a unit of weight.

2:3 Answer the following questions.

1. In what year will the Christian world celebrate the second millenium since the birth of Christ? _____

2. One kilocycle, which is a measure of the frequency of radio and television waves, is equal to how many cycles per second? _____

3. Which vocabulary word might you use to describe the number of people who make up a crowd at a football game? _____

4. If a milligram is one-thousandth of a gram, what do you think a millidegree is? _____

5. *Myriapod* is another name for what bug mentioned in the lesson? _____

3: Meeting Words in Context

Mary Cassatt

Mary Cassatt was one of America's most accomplished artists. **Spurred** by a desire for technical excellence, she was determined to create art out of the world around her. Though **conventional** subjects were the most salable, she **identified** with the independent French impressionists, who found that the pleasures of sight amply **justified** the exploration of a bright new world. To them, it was important that their works suggest an immediacy of vision in order to make clear that they were fresh discoveries. As thus understood, Mary Cassatt was an impressionist.

This attitude toward art is important to bear in mind in considering Mary Cassatt's works, since the world from which she chose her motifs—the domestic life of women and children—is traditionally **marred** by sentimentality and coyness. One reason her pictures of infants and children are so appealing is that she never **editorialized** about their innocence or charm. She saw the life of the home as an infinitely varied and **spontaneous** source of compositional pleasures. Cassatt did not lack sympathy for the people she depicted. Rather, she sympathized so completely that she did not **presume** to intrude on her subjects' private feelings, to use them as **surrogates** for her own expression.

Despite the seeming spontaneity of vision and ease of execution, however, the compositional poise of Cassatt's pastels and color prints is striking. The evident stroke and broken color of the pastels suggest both a fleetness of vision and a balanced sureness of pattern. It is as if art were captured by chance through a glimpse of nature. Her color prints, reminiscent of Japanese prints, are far more formal. Yet the delicacy of the drypoint lines and the subtle, unpredictable coloring create a sense of process that draws the viewer into the intimacy of the work.

Somehow, Cassatt's works seem both intimate and monumental. The **fusion** of the momentary and the permanent is the basis upon which her remarkable achievement rests, affording a satisfaction that remains undiminished by time.

Choose from the story two words that are unfamiliar to you or whose meanings you are not completely sure of. (Do not choose words that appear in boldfaced type.) Write the words on the lines provided below. Then, beside each word, write what you think it means, based on how it was used in the story.

1. _____ : _____

2. _____ : _____

When you have finished the exercises in this lesson, go to your dictionary and find the definitions for the words you entered above. If a word has more than one meaning, look for the one that defines the word as it is used in the story. Then write the words and their dictionary definitions in the Student Words pages at the back of the book. How close did you come to figuring out their meanings for yourself?

3:1 Using Context
Write each vocabulary word beside its correct meaning. Try to figure out what the word means from the way it is used in the passage.

1. **spurred**

_____ lured   _____ distracted

_____ forced   _____ stimulated

2. **justified**

_____ warranted   _____ enhanced

_____ glorified   _____ encouraged

3. **conventional**

_____ fashionable   _____ practical

_____ accepted   _____ unusual

4. **fusion**

_____ combination   _____ impact

_____ confusion   _____ universality

5. **marred**

_____ diminished   _____ marked

_____ recognizable   _____ overshadowed

3:2 Making Connections
Write each vocabulary word on the line in front of the appropriate synonym and antonym.

spurred   justified   conventional   fusion   marred

	synonym	antonym
1. _____	defended	condemned
2. _____	traditional	innovative
3. _____	motivated	restrained
4. _____	union	separation
5. _____	spoiled	improved

164 UNIT NINE

3:3 Using Context

Listed below are five boldfaced words from the reading passage. The list is followed by definitions of the words as they are used in the passage. Write each word in front of its definition.

To figure out what each word means, go back to the passage and read the sentence that contains the word. If you can't discover the meaning from the way the word is used in the sentence, read the sentences that come before and after it for clues.

editorialized   spontaneous   surrogates   presume   identified

1. _____ : people or things that serve as substitutes

2. _____ : to undertake without permission or clear justification

3. _____ : introduced opinion into the reporting of facts

4. _____ : not apparently forced or manipulated

5. _____ : associated oneself with

3:4 Making Connections

The boldfaced words in the following sentences are short definitions of or synonyms for the five vocabulary words you worked with in the last exercise. On the line in front of each sentence, write the vocabulary word that has the same meaning as the boldfaced word or words.

editorialized   spontaneous   surrogates   presume   identified

1. _____ At the end of the news article the writer **revealed his opinion** that the punishment did not fit the severity of the crime.

2. _____ On a movie set, **stand-ins** take the places of the real stars while technicians adjust the lights and camera angles.

3. _____ Don't be so cynical; I'm sure Mary's generous offer was **a natural gesture.**

4. _____ I **felt a close association** with the main character in that novel.

5. _____ I'm surprised that your brother would **dare** to rearrange the furniture in your house while you were away.

4: The Roots of Our Language

hemi-
In this lesson we will look at three different roots that mean half. The first is the Greek prefix *hemi-*, which appears in the word *hemisphere*. Since a sphere is a round body, such as a ball or a planet, a hemisphere is half of a round body. The earth is commonly spoken of in terms of hemispheres. The northern hemisphere, for instance, is the half of the earth that lies north of the equator. *Hemisphere* is also used to refer to the two sides of the brain. The two hemispheres control different types of functions.

semi-
The Latin prefix for half is *semi-*. *Semi-* appears at the beginning of many English words. A semiannual sale, for instance, is a sale that takes place each half year, or twice a year. Stores often have semiannual sales in January and August. A semicircle is a half circle, and a semicentennial is a fiftieth anniversary.

Though in the words just mentioned *semi-* carries the meaning of half, in most instances it has the less specific meaning of almost, partly or somewhat. A semiautomatic camera, for instance, is one that is partly automatic. The user might be able to set the size of the aperture opening, but the length of exposure would set itself automatically. A person who is semiconscious is only partly conscious, and someone who is semiliterate is only partly literate, or able to read and write only to a limited extent. Semisweet chocolate is only slightly sweetened, and a museum exhibit that is semipermanent is intended to last for a long time but not permanently.

demi-
A third root meaning half is *demi-*. It comes to us from French. Like *semi-*, *demi-* often carries the meaning of somewhat or partly. A demigod, for instance is a mythological being with more power than a mortal but less than a god. *Demigod* is also used to refer to a person who is so outstanding that he seems to approach the divine.

A demitasse (DEM-ih-tas) is a smaller-than-average cup used to serve strong black coffee, often after dinner. The word is also used to refer to the small cup of coffee itself—a host serving a demitasse to a guest would be serving a cup of coffee, not just a small empty cup.

4:1 Write each word or root listed on the left beside its meaning on the right.

hemi-   1. _____ partly literate

hemisphere   2. _____ mythological being

demigod   3. _____ half of a circle

semicircle   4. _____ half

semiliterate 5. _____ half of a round body

4:2 Mark each statement as either true or false.

_____ 1. A demigod can read and write, but only to a limited extent.

_____ 2. The root *semi-* never means exactly half.

_____ 3. A person who is semiretired works only part-time.

_____ 4. The terms *semicircle* and *hemisphere* are interchangeable.

_____ 5. *Hemi-* may mean partly, almost or somewhat.

4:3 Put an *x* in front of the answer choice you think is correct.

1. A baseball player who plays for money but who does not do so full-time is known as
   ☐ a. a rookie.   ☐ b. a semiprofessional.   ☐ c. an all-star.

2. In the word *semiautomatic,* the prefix *semi-* carries the meaning of
   ☐ a. half.   ☐ b. almost.   ☐ c. partly.

3. Kareem Abdul-Jabbar's legendary status in the world of basketball has placed him among that sport's
   ☐ a. semi-gods.   ☐ b. demigods.   ☐ c. hemispheres.

4. We perceive the equator as dividing the planet into
   ☐ a. spheres.   ☐ b. hemispheres.   ☐ c. unispheres.

5. If you are a person who has more training than an unskilled laborer has, but less than a skilled laborer has, you are probably
   ☐ a. semiskilled.   ☐ b. self-employed.   ☐ c. unqualified.

5: Extending Your Word Power

5:1 Multiple Meanings
The eight vocabulary words listed below on the left have meanings other than the ones they held in the reading passages. Those alternate meanings are listed on the right. On the line beside each meaning, write the letter of the vocabulary word that holds that meaning. Consult the glossary for the meanings of any words you are unsure of.

a. spontaneous

b. radical

c. dissident

d. justified

e. conventional

f. presume

g. surrogate

h. representative

i. identified

_____ 1. person who favors, extreme change or reform

_____ 2. made (lines of type) the proper length

_____ 3. lacking originality

_____ 4. take for granted

_____ 5. agent

_____ 6. person who disagrees or dissents

_____ 7. fundamental

_____ 8. go beyond what is right or proper

_____ 9. in math, the sign √, which is placed before an expression to show that the square root is to be extracted

_____ 10. to put in the place of another

_____ 11. arising from a momentary impulse

_____ 12. recognized or established as being a particular person or thing

5:2 Roots Review
The incomplete sentences below contain words that you learned in the two roots lessons in this unit. Complete each sentence so that it makes sense and shows the meaning of the boldfaced vocabulary word.

1. In his **semiconscious** state, Phil _____

_____ .

2. Ms. Harrison explained that a **milliliter** _____

_____ .

168 UNIT NINE

3. Because the cabin was intended to be only **semipermanent**, _____.

4. Mr. Lentz pointed out that **kilometers** are _____.

5. Diane's report focused on the **hemisphere** _____.

6. Her close observation of the **millipede** told Mary that _____.

7. Faced with **myriad** possibilities, Shannon _____.

8. As a **demigod** in the world of sports, Carlos _____.

9. If there were a coin worth a **mill**, _____.

10. Glenda thought that the **demitasse** _____.

5:3 Choosing Just the Right Word

Many of the words you have worked with in this unit have a number of synonyms. In some cases the synonyms convey different shades of meaning.

Following are synonym studies for five of your vocabulary words. Use either the vocabulary words or their synonyms to complete the sentences in the exercise that follows. Refer to the synonym studies as you decide which word carries the best meaning for the specific context of each sentence.

UNIT NINE 169

justify   warrant

Justify and *warrant* both mean to provide a reason for. *Justify* implies that without the given reason or grounds, the action, remark, etc., would not be accepted or approved. *If you can't justify a change, stick to the established schedule.* *Warrant* suggests an emphasis on explanation or merit, rather than excuse. *The grand jury will decide if the evidence against the suspect warrants a trial.*

declare   assert

Both *declare* and *assert* mean to state positively. *Declare* means to state firmly and openly. *The vice president is about to declare that this session of Congress is open.* *Assert* means to state vigorously, sometimes when proof is lacking or even when it is clear that one is wrong. *Abby asserted that she hadn't gone to the party, but several people saw her there.*

formal   conventional

Formal and *conventional* mean in accordance with usual forms or rules. *Formal* implies strict attention to prescribed methods and procedures. *The judge conducted the hearing in a formal manner.* *Conventional* suggests paying attention to generally accepted patterns, and often implies unoriginality. *I was disappointed that Andrea chose such a conventional theme for her graduation address.*

famous   renowned   noted

Famous, *renowned* and *noted* all mean very well-known. *Famous* means widely and usually favorably known. *The famous author signed copies of her novel for hundreds of fans at the bookstore.* *Renowned* suggests great and enduring fame and honor. *Albert Einstein was a renowned scientist.* *Noted* implies being well-known for a particular talent or accomplishment. *Rhode Island is noted for being the smallest state.*

ridicule   deride

Both *ridicule* and *deride* mean to make fun of something or someone. *Ridicule* implies trying to make someone or something seem little or unimportant. *Nicky ridiculed his sister's piano playing.* *Deride* implies making fun of in contempt. *Many people derided the acquisition of Alaska in 1867, calling it "Seward's Folly."*

1. I can't _____ the expense of a new TV right now. That purchase will have to wait.

2. That comedian is especially _____ for his impersonation of Ed Sullivan.

3. In class today we heard Sid _____ that Iowa's seashore is its most valuable natural feature.

4. We're just plain folks in this town. Nobody _____ ever lived here.

5. Today the mayor is expected to _____ that she will run for reelection.

6. Mozart was one of the most _____ classical composers.

7. Since _____ methods have failed, it's time to try some creative solutions.

8. Stanley likes to _____ his teacher when her back is turned.

9. After deploring the current state of the economy, Fred proceeded to _____ the president's policies.

10. It's best not to use slang or colloquial language in a _____ writing assignment.

11. Don't you agree that these matters _____ further investigation?

5:4 Recognizing Word Forms

The words listed below are other forms of vocabulary words you have worked with in this unit. Use the words to complete the story that follows. Refer to the glossary if you need help selecting the correct word for each blank.

attested   depiction   dissidents   fuse   presumptuous
unidentified   assert   represent   radicals   spur   derision

Washington—Three armed _____(1), claiming to _____(2) a left-wing group opposing the government's policies in the Middle East, held government officials hostage in a six-hour siege that ended with no injuries.

The _____(3) stormed the State Department's Central American bureau at 10 A.M., brandishing automatic weapons and homemade bombs.

"No one was ever in danger," State Department spokesperson James Miller was quick to _____(4). "Since the rash of car bombings in Lebanon, we have had contingency plans for such an attack on our headquarters." In fact, a silent alarm was activated to _____(5) a fleet of military vehicles into action. The unit arrived on the scene at 10:20 A.M., and surrounded the building's perimeter.

Employee Brenda Roberts _____(6) to the overriding feeling of terror among the twelve officials trapped inside the building. "The kidnappers spoke with a heavy accent and pointed guns in our faces as we lay on the floor. One of them took my cigarette lighter and, to scare us, kept inching the flame closer and closer to the _____7_____ of an explosive, laughing hysterically all the time." An _____8_____ witness reported that another of the captors taunted the Americans with sarcastic _____9_____ of U.S. culture and foreign policy.

The attackers were initially thought to be members of the Palestine Liberation Organization. A PLO spokesman, however, strongly denied the allegation, claiming it was "_____10_____ on the part of U.S. officials to accuse us of this activity. This attempted _____11_____ of the PLO as a terrorist organization, which we never have been and never will be, is American propaganda."

5:5 Putting Your Vocabulary to Use

In solving this word puzzle, you will be using some of the vocabulary words introduced in this unit and in the previous unit. Below is a list of definitions and synonyms for those words. For each definition or synonym, think of a vocabulary word that has the same meaning. Write the word in the puzzle space with the corresponding number. One letter of the word, together with the number of lines in each answer space, provide clues to the word. Notice that the letters that are given form a phrase related to impressionism.

1. raised
2. outward appearance
3. stimulated
4. substitutes
5. damaged
6. a great number
7. unit used to measure the frequency of radio waves
8. continuation
9. firm belief
10. sensible
11. arising naturally
12. moving backward
13. warranted
14. expressed an opinion
15. one one-thousandth of an inch
16. little by little
17. discovered
18. marked by fate

1. _ _ a _ _ _ _
2. _ _ _ b _ _ _ _ _ _
3. s _ _ _ _ _ _ _
4. _ _ _ _ _ _ _ _ t _ _
5. _ _ r _ _ _
6. _ _ _ _ _ a _
7. _ _ _ c _ _ _ _
8. _ _ _ _ _ _ t _ _ _ _ _ _
9. _ _ _ _ i _ _ _ _ _
10. _ o _ _
11. _ _ _ n _ _ _ _ _ _ _ _
12. _ _ _ _ o _ _ _ _ _
13. _ _ _ _ f _ _ _
14. _ _ _ _ _ _ _ _ _ l _ _ _
15. _ i _
16. g _ _ _ _ _
17. _ _ _ _ _ _ h _ _
18. _ _ _ t _ _ _ _

ℋ*eckling*

Politicians, stand-up comics—anyone who speaks in public—hates to be heckled. To heckle, of course, is to interrupt and annoy a speaker by asking bothersome questions, jeering or making loud and uncomplimentary remarks. It is no doubt an

unpleasant and unsettling experience to be heckled. But heckling of that sort is probably preferable to being heckled according to the original meaning of the word. Five hundred years ago, *heckle* meant "to scratch with a steel brush." The thing that was scratched, however, was flax,

not people. Flax is the plant from which linen is made. A heckle was used to break down and split the strong

stalks at their weak points. In Scotland, questioning parliamentary candidates in such a way as to discover their weak points came to be called heckling. In time the meaning grew to mean outright badgering and gibes directed at any speaker.

UNIT 10

1: Meeting Words in Context

    Reading Selection   How to Use Paragraphs When Reading

    Words Introduced   amplify anecdotes brevity discriminating expository overview relegate reluctant subdivided transition

2: The Roots of Our Language

    Roots Introduced   multi- poly- glot

3: Meeting Words in Context

    Reading Selection   How to Write Effectively

    Words Introduced   concise conform disclose draft foremost imperative odious substantiate unadorned validity

4: The Roots of Our Language

    Roots Introduced   proto- prot- zoo- fin term ulti

5: Extending Your Word Power

Multiple Meanings
Roots Review
Using Words Precisely
Recognizing Word Forms
Putting Your Vocabulary to Use

1: Meeting Words in Context

How to Use Paragraphs When Reading

In **expository** writing, paragraphs perform specific functions. They introduce, define and illustrate. They provide information and present concluding thoughts. Identifying types of paragraphs can help you organize a chapter in your mind and find information efficiently.

A good introductory paragraph tells you what to expect in the paragraphs that follow. When you are previewing material, introductory paragraphs can give you an **overview** of the subject matter. A chapter that is **subdivided** into several major sections will have an introduction after every subheading.

Paragraphs of definition define essential words or ideas. To spot them in textbooks, look for such words or expressions as *this means, this might suggest that, it is defined as,* and *indicates.* Reread paragraphs of definition when you review for examinations.

Paragraphs of **transition**, often recognized by their **brevity**, are used to move on to new material. Like an introductory paragraph, they can preview material. They may also function as a concluding paragraph for the preceding material.

Paragraphs of information contain the meat of the subject and may provide names, dates, details, facts and explanations. Authors usually present information in one of these ways: state an opinion with supporting reasons; pose a problem and offer a solution; draw a conclusion and present proof; present steps in an argument; make comparisons; present facts and data.

In reading paragraphs of information, you must be **discriminating**. Evaluate everything and make note only of useful information.

Paragraphs of illustration present examples, personal experiences, case studies, or **anecdotes**. They clarify, reinforce or **amplify** the author's ideas. Paragraphs of illustration are often identified by such phrases as *for example, an example of this,* and *take the case of.*

A concluding paragraph gives the author's final thoughts on a subject. Very rarely, it might state a conclusion based on an entire chapter. But most authors are **reluctant** to **relegate** such important ideas to a brief final paragraph. More typically, wrap-up statements will be found at the end of every major and many minor chapter divisions. Important conclusions can then be repeated in a final paragraph. A concluding paragraph may also summarize facts. Summaries are valuable in previewing and reviewing.

Become proficient in recognizing and utilizing the various paragraph types and they will help you to organize your studying.

Choose from the story two words that are unfamiliar to you or whose meanings you are not completely sure of. (Do not choose words that appear in boldfaced type.) Write the words on the lines provided below. Then, beside each word, write what you think it means, based on how it was used in the story.

1. _____ : _____

2. _____ : _____

When you have finished the exercises in this lesson, go to your dictionary and find the definitions for the words you entered above. If a word has more than one meaning, look for the one that defines the word as it is used in the story. Then write the words and their dictionary definitions in the Student Words pages at the back of the book. How close did you come to figuring out their meanings for yourself?

1:1 Using Context

Below are five sentences from the reading passage. From the four answer choices that follow each sentence, choose the one that gives the best definition of the boldfaced word. Put an *x* in the box beside it. Use the context, or setting, provided by the sentence to help you discover the meaning of the word. If the sentence itself does not provide enough clues, go back to the passage and read the paragraph in which the word appears.

1. Paragraphs of illustration present examples, personal experiences, case studies or **anecdotes**.
   - ☐ a. brief stories
   - ☐ b. theories
   - ☐ c. diagrams
   - ☐ d. statistics

2. Paragraphs of transition, often recognized by their **brevity**, are used to move on to new material.
   - ☐ a. wording
   - ☐ b. tone
   - ☐ c. briefness
   - ☐ d. function

3. In **expository** writing, paragraphs perform specific functions.
   - ☐ a. effective
   - ☐ b. specialized
   - ☐ c. typical
   - ☐ d. explanatory

4. When you are previewing material, introductory paragraphs can give you an **overview** of the subject matter.
   - ☐ a. purpose
   - ☐ b. clarification
   - ☐ c. survey
   - ☐ d. example

5. But most authors are **reluctant** to relegate such important ideas to a brief final paragraph.
   - ☐ a. allowed
   - ☐ b. disinclined
   - ☐ c. content
   - ☐ d. forced

1:2 Making Connections

Complete the following analogies by inserting one of the five vocabulary words in the blank at the end of each one. Remember that, in an analogy, the last two words or phrases must be related in the same way that the first two are related.

        anecdotes   brevity   expository   overview   reluctant

1. detailed : analysis : : general : _____

2. money : frugality : : words : _____

3. persuade : reasons : : illustrate : _____

4. novel : narrative : : textbook : _____

5. question : uncertain : : hesitate : _____

1:3 Using Context

Circle the word or phrase that most nearly matches the meaning of the boldfaced vocabulary word in the sentence.

1. Many chapters are **subdivided** into several major sections.
       reduced   segmented   assembled   edited

2. An author will use a paragraph of **transition** to move from one aspect of a subject to another.
       padding   preparation   change   summation

3. Be **discriminating** when taking notes on information presented in a chapter.
       thorough   alert   informed   selective

4. Paragraphs of illustration can **amplify** a writer's ideas.
       expand   diminish   clutter   express

5. An author is unlikely to **relegate** a major conclusion to a brief closing paragraph.
       consign   relate   add   extend

1:4 Making Connections

The boldfaced words in the following sentences are short definitions of the five vocabulary words you worked with in the last exercise. On the line in front of each sentence, write the vocabulary word that has the same meaning as the boldfaced word or words.

    subdivided   transition   discriminating   amplify   relegate

1. _____ Be a **choosy** shopper—buy only the best.

2. _____ The students easily made the **shift** from junior high to high school.

3. _____ Would you please **elaborate on** that statement by citing some specific instances.

4. _____ I intend to **banish** these uncomfortable shoes to the farthest corner of my closet.

5. _____ This work is split into two volumes, which have been **sectioned** into four units each.

2: The Roots of Our Language

There are two roots meaning many that occur in numerous English words: *multi-* and *poly-*. *Multi-* is a Latin root, and *poly-* is from Greek.

In previous lessons we have seen how the same root can be combined with different number prefixes to form new words. For example, the root *-plex* with the prefix *du-* forms the word *duplex,* meaning twofold. The prefix *tri-* with the same root gives us *triplex,* or threefold. Likewise, *multi-* can be combined with *-plex* to create *multiplex,* meaning manyfold. While *duplex* and *triplex* refer to houses for two and three families respectively, *multiplex* is usually used to refer to circuits, such as telegraph and radio circuits, that can carry several distinct signals at the same time.

multi-

Two other words that are related in this way are *duplicity* and *multiplicity*. You'll remember that *duplicity* means acting and speaking one way while thinking another. *Multiplicity,* however, has an entirely different meaning. It means a great number, as in a multiplicity of possible solutions to a problem.

A gem that is multifaceted is one that has been cut so that it has many faces, or facets. A problem that is multifaceted is one that is complex, or has many aspects, or facets, that must be considered.

Something that is multifarious (MUL-tuh-FAR-ee-us) has many different parts or forms, or is many and varied. *The spectacular theatrical event was made up of multifarious elements. The possibilities for an exotic vacation are multifarious.*

Multiple, of course, means many. So to make multiple copies of a report means to make a number of copies.

poly-

Now let's look at *poly-*. A polygon, as you know from past discussions in these lessons, is a many-angled plane figure, and a polyhedron is a solid figure having many faces.

In early lessons we met *monogamy,* which means marriage to one person, and *bigamy,* which is marriage to two people at the same time. It follows, therefore, that polygamy is marriage to several people at the same time.

The machine commonly referred to as a lie detector is rightly called a polygraph. Its name was derived from the fact that the machine graphs, or records, simultaneously, changes in a number of involuntary body activities, including blood pressure, pulse, and breathing, while a person is being questioned. The idea behind the polygraph is that when a person lies his or her involuntary body functions change.

glot

A person who is polyglot (POL-ih-glot) knows several languages. Polyglot also means containing material in several languages. A sign that presents the same information in several languages, for instance, is polyglot. The root *glot* refers to language or tongue. The word *tongue* is sometimes used to mean language. If your first language was French, for example, that is your mother tongue.

The glottis is the opening at the top of the larynx, behind the tongue. It's natural, therefore, that the small valve-like piece of cartilage at the top of the glottis, which closes off the opening when we swallow, is called the epiglottis (EP-uh-GLOT-us). Remember that the prefix *epi-* means upon.

To finish our discussion with a word related to words, *polysyllabic* refers to a word that has several syllables.

2:1 Write each word or root listed on the left beside its meaning on the right.

multi- 1. _____ containing material in several languages

multiplicity 2. _____ many

multifaceted 3. _____ marriage to several people at the same time

polygamy 4. _____ a great number

polyglot 5. _____ having many parts

2:2 Mark each statement as either true or false.

_____ 1. An entertainer of many talents is sometimes said to be multifaceted.

_____ 2. A multiplicity is one of the cities that make up a megalopolis.

_____ 3. A person who is polyglot speaks several tongues.

_____ 4. A mutinational corporation has divisions of the corporation in many countries.

_____ 5. A polygamist must be a man, not a woman.

2:3 Answer the following questions.

1. *Polyrhythm,* a musical term, describes a combination of _____ .

2. What do you think might be a good word to describe something that has many layers?
   _____

3. What would be a way to describe a polychromatic painting? _____
   _____

4. Politicians tend to make statements such as, "A *multiplicity* of factors created this negative situation." How would you define the italicized word in that statement? _____

5. Someone who is polygamous probably has a complicated life. Why? _____
   _____

180 UNIT TEN

3: Meeting Words in Context

How to Write Effectively

Writing need not be an **odious** task. Organization is the key to successful writing. A step-by-step approach will help you structure your work. Editing will improve the quality and effectiveness of your writing and will **disclose** any errors.

Preparation is a **foremost** consideration. Determine your purpose before beginning to write. Think carefully and then write a **concise** statement explaining your subject and what you plan to say about it.

You should know in advance how long you want your paper to be. Define the limitations of your subject. Deal in depth with two or three points instead of simply touching on many.

Your paper must support as well as present your ideas. **Substantiate** your position with facts, details, definitions, descriptions, illustrations or arguments to make your ideas reasonable and acceptable to the reader.

It is important to differentiate between facts and opinions, so there will be no question as to the **validity** of your conclusions. Present facts clearly, and then state opinions based on those facts.

Make your organization clear to your readers. If they can see how you have moved from one idea to another, they will be able to follow your argument.

Finally, make sure your conclusion is justified by the evidence you have presented. Readers will be more inclined to accept a conclusion that is firmly supported by facts.

After you finish writing a first **draft**, you should read and edit it. At least one rewrite is **imperative**; skilled writers revise several times to polish their work.

Begin by looking for incomplete thoughts and run-on sentences. Make sure your ideas are expressed concisely. Go on to check punctuation. Check pronouns, making sure that the antecedent of each is clear. Also, see that each pronoun agrees with its antecedent in person and number.

Improve nouns and verbs by replacing mundane words with ones that are more specific and expressive. Be careful, however, to avoid artificial or over-inflated language. Add vivid adjectives where appropriate to make your sentences more colorful. Be careful, though; sometimes a simple, **unadorned** sentence is best.

Developing writers can benefit greatly by studying effective writing by published authors. Select a model paragraph and judge each sentence against the editing suggestions above. Good writing is certain to **conform** to high standards, especially in the use of image-provoking nouns and verbs and vivid adjectives.

Choose from the story two words that are unfamiliar to you or whose meanings you are not completely sure of. (Do not choose words that appear in boldfaced type.) Write the words on the lines provided below. Then, beside each word, write what you think it means, based on how it was used in the story.

1. _____ : _____

2. _____ : _____

When you have finished the exercises in this lesson, go to your dictionary and find the definitions for the words you entered above. If a word has more than one meaning, look for the one that defines the word as it is used in the story. Then write the words and their dictionary definitions in the Student Words pages at the back of the book. How close did you come to figuring out their meanings for yourself?

3:1 Using Context
Write each vocabulary word beside its correct meaning. Try to figure out what the word means from the way it is used in the sentence.

1. **odious**

_____ time-consuming _____ difficult

_____ detestable _____ confusing

2. **foremost**

_____ preliminary _____ minor

_____ possible _____ major

3. **concise**

_____ accurate _____ general

_____ brief _____ persuasive

4. **imperative**

_____ necessary _____ inadequate

_____ recommended _____ improved

5. **unadorned**

_____ short _____ understandable

_____ factual _____ plain

3:2 Making Connections
Write each vocabulary word on the line in front of the appropriate synonym and antonym.

odious   foremost   concise   imperative   unadorned

	synonym	antonym
1. _____	succinct	verbose
2. _____	required	optional
3. _____	despicable	delightful
4. _____	dominant	unessential
5. _____	simple	ornate

3:3 Using Context

Listed below are five boldfaced words from the reading passage. The list is followed by definitions of the words as they are used in the passage. Write each word in front of its definition.

To figure out what each word means, go back to the passage and read the sentence that contains the word. If you can't discover the meaning from the way the word is used in the sentence, read the sentences that come before and after it for clues.

disclose   substantiate   validity   draft   conform

1. _____ : version

2. _____ : soundness

3. _____ : be in agreement with

4. _____ : confirm or support

5. _____ : expose or reveal

3:4 Making Connections

Complete each sentence with the correct vocabulary word.

disclose   substantiate   validity   draft   conform

1. Professor Morin was once caught falsifying data, and now his colleagues tend to doubt the _____ of all his findings.

2. Let me see a _____ of your essay before you write the final version.

3. Do you expect that an audit of your tax return will _____ any major discrepancies?

4. The speaker was able to _____ her views with numerous facts.

5. The format of your term paper should _____ to the guidelines that were specified in class on Wednesday.

4: The Roots of Our Language

proto-
prot-

In this last lesson we will talk about roots that mean first and last. You have already met the Latin root for first, *prime* or *prima*. Now let's look at the Greek root *proto-*, sometimes seen as *prot-*.

A *prototype* is the first of a type of thing. For example, the modern computer has its prototype in the ancient abacus. A prototype may also be a model or the first full-scale, working example of a new invention.

A protagonist is the main character in a play, story or novel. The second part of the word, *agonist*, means actor or contestant. A *protagonist* is also a person who is an active supporter—who takes a leading part in some enterprise or movement. A person who works for nuclear disarmament, for instance, is a protagonist in the antinuclear movement.

Proteins are organic compounds that are made up of nitrogen and amino acids. They are essential to the structure and functioning of all living cells. Protein gets its name from the fact that it is the primary substance or fundamental material of the bodies of animals and plants.

zo-
zoo-

In the animal kingdom, protozoans are the simplest and smallest creatures. They are made up of only one cell each. Their name means first animal. You may remember that the Greek root *zo-* or *zoo-* means animal. We see it in *zoology*, which is the science that deals with animals.

fin

Now let's move on to the end. We'll look first at the words *finish* and *final*, which both come from the Latin *finis*, meaning end. To finish, of course, means to bring to an end, and something that is final occurs at the end or the conclusion—it is the last. A finale (fuh-NAHL-ee) is the close or termination of something. It might be the last section of an instrumental musical composition, or the last, often climactic, event in a sequence. A fireworks display, for instance, usually ends with a stunning, extravagant burst of pyrotechnics called the *grand finale*.

term

A synonym for *finish* is *terminate*. It comes from the Latin word *terminum*, meaning limit, boundary or end. This origin is directly reflected in the definition of the word, which is to bring or put to an end. This lesson is approaching termination. A related word is *terminus*. A terminus is an ending place—a goal, end or final point. It is most often used more specifically, however, to refer to a terminal—either end of a railroad, bus, or air line.

ulti

Lastly, we could say that this is the ultimate lesson on roots in this book. Descended from the Latin *ultimus*, meaning last or final, *ultimate* means coming at the end, final, the last possible thing. It also has the meaning of fundamental or basic—*We have yet to discover the ultimate source of life.* Still another, related, meaning is greatest—*In giving his life for freedom, he made the ultimate sacrifice.*

When someone issues an ultimatum (UL-tuh-MATE-um), he makes a final proposal or statement of condition, which must be accepted if a relationship or negotiations are to continue. An ultimatum is the person's last word on a matter. A parent, for instance, might issue the ultimatum that either a child cleans up her room by five o'clock on Friday afternoon or she will be grounded for the weekend. Ultimatums often bring results. They certainly bring about the termination of arguments or debates in one way or another.

This brings us to the ultimate sentence in this lesson. May you enjoy your future explorations into the world of words.

4:1 Write each word or root listed on the left beside its meaning on the right.

proto- 1. _____ last

agonist 2. _____ active supporter

protagonist 3. _____ finish

terminate 4. _____ first

ultimate 5. _____ actor or contestant

4:2 Mark each statement as either true or false.

_____ 1. *Ultimate* can mean final or it can mean the greatest, as in "the ultimate sacrifice."

_____ 2. In drama, the protagonist is always a man.

_____ 3. Something that is the first of its kind may be described as being prototypical.

_____ 4. According to the meaning of the word *terminal,* each stop on a train line is called a terminal.

_____ 5. An ultimatum is a casual, open-ended request.

4:3 Put an *x* in front of the answer choice you think is correct.

1. If *ultima* means the last syllable in a word, the last syllable of ultima is
   - ☐ a. ul.
   - ☐ b. ti.
   - ☐ c. ma.

2. The primitive beings who were the first humans are sometimes called
   - ☐ a. protohumans.
   - ☐ b. protagonists.
   - ☐ c. protozoans.

3. The Times Square shuttle, a subway line in New York City, originates at Times Square and ends at Grand Central Station, which means that Grand Central is the shuttle's
   - ☐ a. ultimatum.
   - ☐ b. terminus.
   - ☐ c. protagonist.

4. If you know that *ultimate* means last and that *pen* means almost or next to, what do you think *penultimate* means?
   - ☐ a. before the first
   - ☐ b. next to the last
   - ☐ c. never-ended

5. Outer space has been called the last, or ultimate,
   - ☐ a. frontier.
   - ☐ b. playground.
   - ☐ c. battlefield.

5: Extending Your Word Power

5:1 Multiple Meanings

The five vocabulary words listed below have meanings other than the ones they held in the reading passages. Those alternate meanings are given in the exercise that follows. On the line in front of each definition, write the vocabulary word that holds that meaning. Refer to the glossary for the meanings of any words you are unsure of.

amplify   brevity   discriminating   imperative   draft

1. _____ : giving a particular person or group distinct and usually unfair treatment

2. _____ : selection of persons without their consent for a specific purpose

3. _____ : expressing a command

4. _____ : shortness (of time)

5. _____ : make greater, larger, louder, etc.

6. _____ : a current of air in a confined space

7. _____ : to increase the strength of (electric power, voltage or current)

8. _____ : to write out a rough copy of

9. _____ : an order or command

5:2 Roots Review

The incomplete sentences below contain words that you learned in the two roots lessons in this unit. Complete each sentence so that it makes sense and shows the meaning of the boldfaced vocabulary word.

1. The **ultimatum** that Ms. Hood gave her secretary was _____ _____ _____ .

2. When Jenny's **duplicity** was discovered, _____ _____ .

3. As a **protagonist** of women's rights, Anne _____ _____ .

4. For many people, personal satisfaction is the **ultimate** _____ _____ .

5. At the **terminus**, Stewart _____
   _____.

6. Everyone agreed that the **finale** _____
   _____.

7. The **multiplicity** of creative ideas _____
   _____
   _____.

8. Felicia found the **polyglot** message intriguing because _____
   _____.

9. Greg's constant use of **polysyllabic** words _____
   _____
   _____.

10. As a **prototype**, the device was _____
    _____
    _____.

5:3 Choosing Just the Right Word

Many of the words you have worked with in this unit have a number of synonyms. In some cases the synonyms convey different shades of meaning.

Following are synonym studies for three of your vocabulary words. Use either the vocabulary words or their synonyms to complete the sentences in the exercise that follows. In some cases you may need to use a past tense. Refer to the synonym studies as you decide which word carries the best meaning for the specific context of each sentence.

distinguish   differentiate   discriminate

Distinguish, differentiate and *discriminate* mean to recognize or show the differences among or between things. *Distinguish* means to recognize the features that set a thing apart from others. *I was able to distinguish the violins from the violas when I listened to the recording.* Differentiate means to point out the exact differences between one thing and others of the same class. *The teacher differentiated between Euripides' tragedies and those of Sophocles.* Discriminate stresses the ability to select what is true or appropriate. *The pediatrician urged us to discriminate when buying toys, so as to avoid breakable or unsafe products.*

hesitant   reluctant   loath

Reluctant, hesitant and *loath* mean lacking the desire or will to do something. *Reluctant* implies unwillingness. *If Ms. Lewis is reluctant to take the job, offer her a higher salary.* *Hesitant* suggests that one is holding back because of uncertainty or fear. *I was hesitant to walk down the icy stairs.* *Loath* implies strong unwillingness because the thing to be done is very disagreeable or hateful. *Hector was loath to give up his freedom in order to take a summer job.*

validity   cogency

Validity and *cogency* mean soundness with respect to truth, rightness or reasoning. *Validity* is the quality of being based on fact and supported by strong reasoning. *I question the relevance but not the validity of your claim.* *Cogency* implies that an argument or contention is so valid as to be convincing. *The cogency of the defense's closing argument inspired the jury to hand down a verdict of "not guilty."*

1. People who are color-blind may find it difficult to _____ red from green.

2. The market research firm was called upon to defend the _____ of its statistics.

3. Most parents are _____ to believe that their children would ever do anything illegal.

4. It was difficult to _____ among the many well-qualified applicants for the job.

5. We assured Milly that the rollercoaster was safe, but she was still _____ to ride on it.

6. The _____ of her sales pitch was such that Jeanne received more orders than the company could fill.

7. For his students, the chef _____ between lobsters and crayfish.

8. I was _____ to get up and answer the phone after I'd settled myself in front of the fire.

9. The _____ of your reasoning will be evaluated in the debate.

10. You'll have to _____ among the answer choices on this multiple-choice exam.

5:4 Recognizing Word Forms
The words listed below are other forms of vocabulary words you have worked with in this unit. Fill in the blank in each sentence with the appropriate word from the list. Use what you have learned in this unit to help you figure out what the words mean.

drafted imperious relegated adorned odiousness invalid
disclosure nonconformist amplification briefs discrimination reluctance

1. That is an important point that merits _____.

2. The university was found guilty of _____ against women on the faculty, and was ordered to pay over a million dollars in back salaries.

3. I can't understand Bud's _____ to see the play tonight; he usually loves to go to the theater.

4. When the fire alarm sounded in the middle of the night, Toby ran out of the dorm wearing only his _____.

5. One of the brothers enlisted in the army, and the other was _____.

6. Because of her _____ manner, her coworkers referred to Bernice as "her royal highness."

7. Saying that she had nothing to hide, the congresswoman agreed to make full _____ of her investments.

8. Despite the _____ of the task, Peggy cleans the cat's litterbox frequently.

9. The tiara was _____ with emeralds and rubies.

10. An _____ can be cared for at home by a private-duty nurse.

11. A lot of kids like to follow the crowd, but Frank is a _____.

12. When the Merkels bought a new livingroom set, their old furniture was _____ to the attic.

5:5 Putting Your Vocabulary to Use

In this exercise you will create rhyming phrases using vocabulary words from this unit and the preceding one. The phrases will complete humorous definitions of the words.

Examples: A seafood dinner is marine cuisine.
A fish doctor might be a sturgeon surgeon.

1. A person who conceals information won't _____ what he knows.

2. To keep track of how many miles you drive in Europe, use a _____ odometer.

3. A famous jester is a _____ clown.

4. Anyone who insists on being different won't _____ to the norm.

5. A painting of a cow has a beef _____ .

6. A carefree one-celled organism is an easygoin' _____ .

7. A brief suggestion would be _____ advice.

8. A horribly ugly baggy sweater is commodious and _____ .

9. A linguist's sailboat is a _____'s yacht.

10. Strong determination to change is _____ ambition.

11. A false impression that two things are joined is a _____ illusion.

12. A silly preliminary sketch is a daft _____ .

13. A summary of a conversation between a reporter and a famous personality is an interview _____ .

Portmanteau Words

Throughout history, as new objects and ideas have come into being, new words have been needed to name them. Once a substantial supply of words had been fabricated, it made sense to start using some of that inventory to build new words. One way this was done, of course, was by adding prefixes and suffixes, or both, to root words, thus making it possible to create from the single word *happy*, for instance, the words *unhappy*, *happiness* and *unhappiness*.

Combining parts of two or more words is another long-standing method of creating new ones. *Smog*, for instance, grew up naturally from the combination of *smoke* and *fog*, which is what smog is. Such terms have traditionally been called "blends," "blend words," "telescopings," or "portmanteau words," a portmanteau being a large traveling bag. That last name was invented by Lewis Carroll, and appears in *Through the Looking Glass:* "You see it's like a portmanteau . . . there are two meanings packed up into one word." In that book, Carroll coined such portmanteau words as *slithy* (from *lithe* and *slimy*) and *mimsy* (from *flimsy* and *miserable*)—both rather whimsical creations.

But some portmanteau words are practical ones that we use every day. They have become so ingrained in the language that we don't think of them as being blends. It's easy to forget, for example, that "motels" are *mo*tor *ho*tels, which came into being when motor travel became popular in the 1950s. People also regularly partake of "brunch" on a leisurely weekend morning—a meal that falls sometime between the regular hours for *br*eakfast and *l*unch. Botanists who experiment with fruit have brought us the tangelo, a hybrid between a tangerine and a pomelo, and those who experiment with animals have given us the beefalo (sometimes called cattalo), a cross between the American buffalo and domestic cattle.

Nowhere have portmanteau words so proliferated as in advertising and bureaucratic circles. The ad folks have given us *Frigidaire, cranapple* and *Band-Aid*. Technology has created *Digitronics* and *selectric* (among scores of others), and government has produced *technocrats,* people who are in charge of a *technocracy,* which is a government run by technicians. The abomination *stagflation,* coined during the American recession of the early 1970s, is a blend of *stagnant* and *inflation,* and means continuing inflation combined with stagnant consumer demand and relatively high unemployment. You needn't worry about remembering that one, for it's a word that never thrived beyond government and media reports on the state of the national economy of that recessionary period.

It is a sure thing that portmanteau words will continue to be created, for blending is a useful, descriptive way to name things that combine two ideas. Some of those words will become assimilated into the language, just as *motel* and *smog* have. Others, like *stagflation,* will have a short, limited life but will continue to bring color and vitality to the English language.

Student Words

Word	Definition

Word | **Definition**

Word	Definition

Word	Definition

Word **Definition**

Answer Key

UNIT ONE

1:1
1. scorned
2. sparse
3. ability
4. gloomy
5. following

1:2
1. prowess
2. meager
3. disdained
4. disdained
5. melancholy
6. melancholy
7. subsequent
8. meager
9. disdained
10. prowess
11. meager
12. subsequent
13. prowess
14. melancholy
15. subsequent
16. disdained

1:3
1. rubble
2. rituals
3. moratorium
4. pilgrimage
5. revered

1:4
1. rubble
2. pilgrimage
3. rituals
4. revered
5. moratorium

2:1
1. ocul-
2. monochromatic
3. monogamy
4. chroma
5. monotone

2:2
1. false
2. false
3. true
4. true
5. true

2:3
1. one
2. movement from a distance
3. one
4. one
5. marriage to two people at the same time

3:1
1. d
2. b
3. b
4. c
5. d

3:2
1. simultaneously
2. bestowed
3. contenders
4. augment
5. vied

3:3
1. pinnacle
2. factor
3. comprised
4. prestige
5. traverse

3:4
1. pinnacle
2. comprised
3. traverse
4. factor
5. prestige

4:1
1. uni-
2. unify
3. prime
4. uniformity
5. bicameral

4:2
1. false
2. false
3. false
4. true
5. true

4:3
1. b
2. b
3. b
4. c
5. c

5:1
| 1. a | 2. b | 3. b | 4. b | 5. a |
| 6. b | 7. c | 8. a | 9. a | 10. b |

5:2
Answers will vary.

5:3
1. revere	2. revere	3. reverenced	4. delay	5. delay
6. postponement	7. moratorium	8. postponement	9. voyage	10. pilgrimage
11. journey	12. voyage	13. journey		

5:4
1. disdain	2. prestigious	3. meagerness	4. factors	5. reverent
6. augmented	7. simultaneous	8. ritualistic	9. traversed	10. contender
11. comprises	12. subsequently	13. vying		

5:5
1. subsequent
2. unicycle
3. pilgrimage
4. pinnacle
5. monarch
6. rubble
7. disdained
8. prima donna
9. revered
10. unite
11. melancholy
12. monotonous
13. monoplane
14. augment
15. unique

UNIT TWO

1:1
| 1. d | 2. b | 3. c | 4. b | 5. d |

1:2
| 1. apprehension | 2. abyss | 3. subterranean | 4. impel | 5. allure |

1:3
| 1. flourish | 2. examining | 3. openings | 4. doubts | 5. thrill |

1:4
1. fissures
2. misgivings
3. thrive
4. exhilaration
5. scrutinizing
6. exhilaration
7. misgivings
8. scrutinizing
9. exhilaration
10. thrive
11. fissures
12. thrive

2:1
1. dual
2. biannual
3. -ennial
4. duplicity
5. binocular

2:2
1. false
2. true
3. false
4. false
5. true

2:3
1. b
2. a
3. b
4. c
5. b

3:1
1. large amount, abundance
2. wise, careful
3. provide
4. irritation, scraping
5. roomy

3:2
1. afford
2. capacious
3. profusion
4. abrasion
5. prudent

3:3
1. provocative
2. ensure
3. paraphernalia
4. banter
5. labyrinth

3:4
1. banter
2. labyrinth
3. provocative
4. ensure
5. paraphernalia

4:1
1. manus
2. diplomacy
3. pteron
4. -sauros
5. dichotomy

4:2
1. true
2. true
3. true
4. false
5. true

4:3
1. the hands
2. thunder lizard
3. two
4. the eyes
5. walking or running

5:1
1. apprehension 2. apprehension 3. thrive 4. afford 5. banter
6. allure 7. afford

5:2
Answers will vary.

5:3
1. apprehension 2. wise 3. ensure 4. prudent 5. fear
6. insure 7. prudent 8. alarm 9. fear 10. wise

5:4
1. capacity, ensuring
2. apprehensive, exhilarating
3. afforded, abrasive
4. bantering (or abrasive), provoked
5. impulse, profusely
6. scrutinized, ensure

5:5
1. dipterous 2. prowess 3. bestowed 4. vied 5. monograph
6. thrive 7. scrutinizing 8. exhilaration 9. biannual 10. biennial
11. prudent 12. disdain 13. biped 14. provocative 15. telegram
16. subterranean 17. duet 18. augment 19. banter 20. duplicate

UNIT THREE

1:1
1. supporters 2. adjust 3. restore 4. slight 5. credit

1:2
1. orient 2. replenish 3. subtle 4. advocates 5. attribute

1:3
1. hinder 2. speed 3. error 4. escape 5. guessed

1:4
1. surmised 2. impede 3. elude 4. misconception 5. velocity

2:1
1. -dent 2. trimonthly 3. tribunal 4. tributary 5. triangulation

2:2
1. false 2. true 3. true 4. false 5. true

2:3
1. c 2. b 3. a 4. b 5. a

3:1
1. adequate 2. optimal 3. imperiled 4. paramount 5. restored

3:2
1. renovate   demolish
2. enough   insufficient
3. most important   trivial
4. endangered   unjeopardized
5. best   worst

3:3
1. thought of
2. significantly
3. near
4. a vast amount
5. established

3:4
1. myriad 2. imminent 3. perceived 4. initiated 5. substantially

4:1
1. quadrennium 2. twi- 3. twilight 4. -gon 5. poly-

4:2
1. true 2. false 3. true 4. false 5. false

4:3
1. many gods
2. a flat figure having ten angles
3. four
4. three
5. four

5:1
1. attribute 2. elude 3. adequate 4. restore 5. Orient
6. initiated 7. perceived 8. restore 9. initiated 10. advocates
11. orient

5:2
Answers will vary.

ANSWER KEY 203

5:3

1. restore
2. renovate
3. renew
4. paramount
5. impede
6. escape
7. eminent
8. dominant
9. elude
10. imminent
11. impending
12. prevent
13. perceived

5:4

1. restorative
2. inadequate
3. imperceptible
4. initiative
5. attributes
6. advocating
7. Oriental
8. restoration
9. eludes
10. substantial
11. adequately
12. oriented
13. replenished
14. attributed
15. eluding

5:5

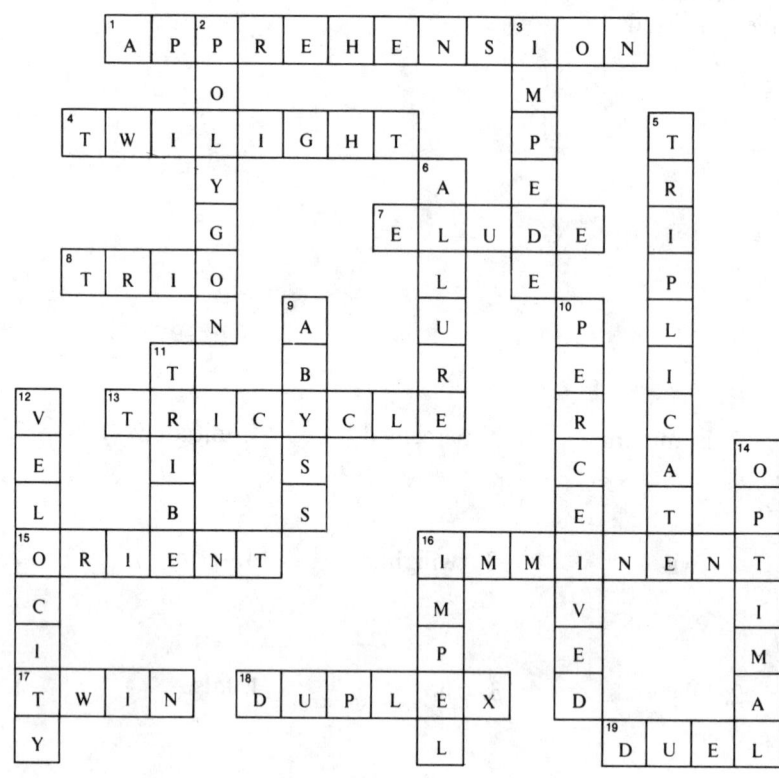

UNIT FOUR

1:1

1. c
2. b
3. a
4. d
5. a

1:2

1. spurious
2. concur
3. artifacts
4. dispute
5. intrigued

1:3

1. believable
2. prevented
3. difficult
4. suggest
5. wonder

1:4
1. formidable 2. speculate 3. credible 4. imply 5. thwarted

2:1
1. hydro 2. androgynous 3. andro- 4. tetralogy 5. gyn-

2:2
1. false 2. false 3. false 4. true 5. true

2:3
1. a 2. c 3. b 4. b 5. a

3:1
1. skilled 2. installed 3. imprisoned 4. acquired 5. important

3:2
1. incarcerated 2. integral 3. instituted 4. proficient 5. amassed
6. integral 7. amassed

3:3
1. chronicled 2. allies 3. vestiges 4. subjugation 5. tributes

3:4
1. chronicled 2. allies 3. subjugation 4. tributes 5. vestiges

4:1
1. de- 2. defoliate 3. foliage 4. quintessence 5. ethereal

4:2
1. true 2. true 3. false 4. true 5. false

4:3
1. a 2. b 3. c 4. b 5. c

5:1
1. a 2. b 3. a 4. b 5. a
6. b 7. b 8. a

5:2
Answers will vary.

5:3
1. credible 2. accumulated 3. implied 4. inferred 5. vestiges
6. traces 7. dispute 8. debate 9. amassed 10. credulous

5:4
1. vestigial 2. alliance 3. incarceration 4. integer 5. disputatious
6. credibility 7. implying 8. speculator 9. indisputable 10. intriguing
11. concurred 12. speculation 13. implication 14. incredible 15. implicit

5:5

1. contribute	2. misconception	3. speculate	4. formidable	5. vestiges
6. quartet	7. credible	8. surmised	9. quadrennium	10. androgynous
11. subtle	12. dehydrate	13. adequate	14. spurious	15. artifacts
16. restored	17. substantially			

UNIT FIVE

1:1
1. concept	2. technology	3. discipline	4. scope	5. liaison

1:2
1. liaison	2. technology	3. scope	4. concepts	5. disciplines

1:3
1. development	2. prohibitive	3. extreme	4. strict	5. important

1:4
1. drastic	2. stringent	3. stringent	4. stringent	5. crucial
6. exorbitant	7. drastic	8. crucial	9. evolution	10. crucial
11. exorbitant	12. evolution	13. exorbitant		

2:1
1. -morphic	2. anthrop-	3. anthropomorphize		
4. sapient	5. homo-			

2:2
1. false	2. true	3. true	4. true	5. true

2:3
1. a	2. b	3. c	4. b	5. c

3:1
1. serenely	2. aft	3. apparatus	4. dissipated	5. console

3:2
1. console	2. aft	3. dissipated	4. serenely	5. apparatus

3:3
1. b	2. c	3. a	4. d	5. c

3:4
1. elapsed	2. bay	3. remotely	4. configuration	5. components

4:1
1. pathos	2. anti-	3. synthesis	4. syn-	5. thesis

4:2
1. false	2. false	3. false	4. false	5. true

4:3
1. its opposite idea
2. the arranging of words together in a sentence
3. sharing with, sound
4. You are expected to feel pity or compassion.
5. an antirevolutionary

5:1
1. liaison
2. bay
3. discipline
4. dissipated
5. console
6. bay
7. discipline
8. bay
9. remotely

5:2
Answers will vary.

5:3
1. scattered
2. range
3. ingredient
4. components
5. dissipated
6. scattered
7. ingredients
8. range
9. exorbitant
10. component
11. dissipated
12. excessive
13. scope

5:4
1. remote
2. stringently
3. evolved
4. technological
5. exorbitance
6. dissipating
7. drastically
8. conception
9. remotest
10. inconsolable
11. disciplinarian
12. consolation

5:5
1. chronicled
2. athletics
3. defoliate
4. drastic
5. anthropoid
6. folios
7. evolution
8. ethereal
9. tributes
10. concepts
11. allies
12. scope
13. amassed
14. console
15. quintessence
16. homonyms
17. incarcerated

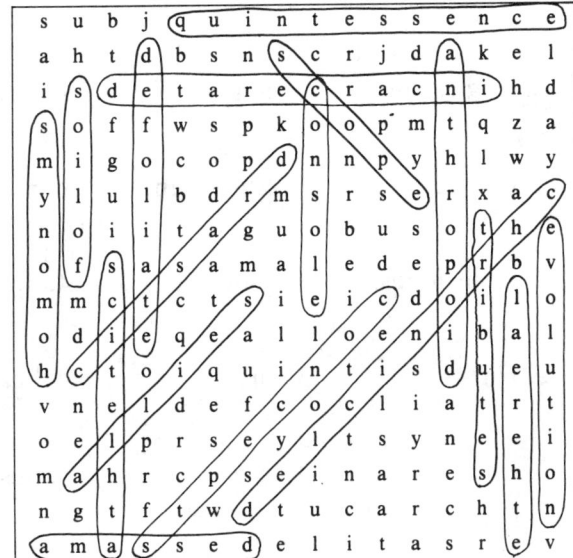

UNIT SIX

1:1
1. b
2. c
3. d
4. d
5. c

1:2

1. host	2. asunder	3. asunder	4. adversary	5. host
6. adversary	7. adversary	8. civility	9. civility	10. adversary
11. civility	12. tempered	13. asunder	14. tempered	15. tempered

1:3

| 1. search | 2. checks | 3. liable | 4. confer | 5. undertaking |

1:4

| 1. subject | 2. quest | 3. negotiate | 4. endeavor | 5. stays |

2:1

| 1. biology | 2. geo- | 3. zo- | 4. micro- | 5. -ology |

2:2

| 1. false | 2. true | 3. true | 4. true | 5. true |

2:3

| 1. b | 2. c | 3. b | 4. b | 5. c |

3:1
1. unjust treatment
2. essence
3. burned
4. shackles
5. living powerlessly

3:2

| 1. manacles | 2. languishing | 3. content | 4. oppression | 5. seared |

3:3

| 1. appalling | 2. discords | 3. self-evident | 4. momentous | 5. withering |

3:4

| 1. discords | 2. momentous | 3. self-evident | 4. appalling | 5. withering |

4:1

| 1. antipathy | 2. hepta- | 3. virile | 4. apathy | 5. septemvir |

4:2

| 1. false | 2. true | 3. true | 4. false | 5. false |

4:3

| 1. c | 2. c | 3. c | 4. b | 5. c |

5:1

1. negotiate	2. content	3. content	4. stays	5. subject
6. tempered	7. languishing	8. negotiate	9. endeavor	10. host
11. subject	12. subject	13. tempered	14. stays	15. host
16. subject	17. discords	18. withering		

5:2
Answers will vary.

5:3
| 1. civility | 2. effort | 3. opponent | 4. adversary | 5. courtesy |
| 6. adversary | 7. opponent | 8. endeavor | 9. effort | 10. courtesy |

5:4
1. subjected	2. adverse	3. negotiating	4. civil	5. stay
6. languidly	7. manacled	8. oppressive	9. discord	10. appallingly
11. withered	12. civilities			

5:5
| 1. apparatus | 2. virile | 3. endeavor | 4. configuration | 5. quest |
| 6. host | 7. bay | 8. seared | 9. appalling | 10. serene |

UNIT SEVEN

1:1
| 1. devalued | 2. cooperation | 3. covertly | 4. refrain | 5. unspoken |

1:2
1. abstain	2. tacit	3. tacit	4. furtively	5. tacit
6. furtively	7. tacit	8. abstain	9. depreciate	10. abstain
11. furtively	12. abstain	13. compliance	14. depreciate	

1:3
| 1. entreated | 2. mutual | 3. alleviating | 4. void | 5. stowed |

1:4
| 1. void | 2. mutual | 3. alleviating | 4. stowed | 5. entreated |

2:1
| 1. genesis | 2. generate | 3. genus | 4. oct- | 5. genre |

2:2
| 1. true | 2. true | 3. false | 4. false | 5. false |

2:3
| 1. degeneration | 2. beginning | 3. generic | 4. sixty-four | 5. a genealogist |

3:1
| 1. tentatively | 2. arbitrary | 3. enunciating | 4. plaintive | 5. breadth |

3:2
| 1. enunciating | 2. breadth | 3. plaintive | 4. arbitrary | 5. tentatively |

3:3
1. change 2. decisions 3. mass 4. rest 5. contemplation

3:4
1. repose 2. resolves 3. metamorphosis 4. bulk 5. reflection

4:1
1. cosmic 2. -naut 3. cosmo 4. nona- 5. astro

4:2
1. true 2. true 3. false 4. true 5. true

4:3
1. Not many people live to be ninety years old.
2. No. There wouldn't be many clouds on a starry night.
3. cosmic dust
4. because a person inside can look up and see the stars
5. the sea

5:1
1. b 2. c 3. a 4. c 5. d
6. b 7. a 8. a 9. b 10. a 11. b

5:2
Answers will vary.

5:3
1. decision 2. rest 3. allay 4. resolve 5. alleviate
6. decision 7. repose 8. resolve 9. alleviate 10. repose

5:4
1. alleviate, abstaining
2. furtive, tacitly
3. abstained, resolve
4. comply, voided
5. enunciation, reflects
6. arbitration, mutually
7. plaintively, entreaty
8. stowing, bulky

5:5
1. empathy
2. alleviating
3. void
4. mutual
5. octagon
6. appalling
7. seared
8. discords
9. entreated
10. genus
11. stowed
12. pathos
13. generate
14. tacit
15. withering
16. generation
17. manacles
18. genealogy
19. content
20. abstain
21. antipathy
22. genes

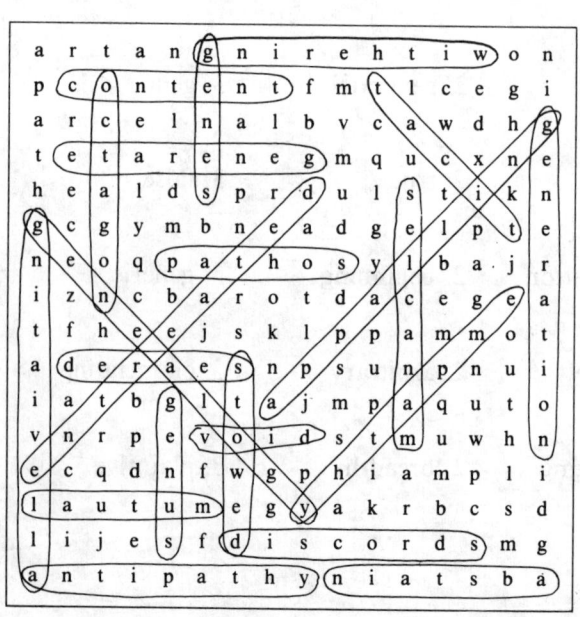

210 ANSWER KEY

UNIT EIGHT

1:1
1. young
2. seriousness
3. economic success
4. break
5. slump

1:2
1. success   poverty
2. inexperienced   seasoned
3. cut   connect
4. drop   rise
5. sincerity   pretense

1:3
1. diversified
2. secluded
3. nurture
4. isolation
5. innovative

1:4
1. isolation
2. nurture
3. secluded
4. diversified
5. innovative

2:1
1. monologue
2. deca-
3. demo-
4. dia-
5. -logue

2:2
1. false
2. false
3. true
4. true
5. true

2:3
1. b
2. b
3. b
4. b
5. b

3:1
1. found out
2. unrefined
3. fervent
4. sensible
5. continuation

3:2
1. intense
2. sober
3. perpetuation
4. unearthed
5. unearthed
6. sober
7. intense
8. crude
9. perpetuation
10. unearthed
11. perpetuation
12. crude
13. sober
14. intense
15. unearthed
16. sober
17. crude
18. unearthed
19. perpetuation

3:3
1. conviction
2. destined
3. reared
4. harried
5. semblance

3:4
1. harried
2. conviction
3. semblance
4. reared
5. destined

4:1
1. bicentennial
2. retro-
3. gradual
4. -grade
5. cent-

4:2
1. false
2. false
3. false
4. true
5. true

4:3

1. c   2. a   3. c   4. a   5. c

5:1

1. reared   2. earnest   3. unearthed   4. crude   5. decline
6. sober   7. conviction   8. fledgling   9. decline   10. decline

5:2

Answers will vary.

5:3

1. staid   2. sentiment   3. sober   4. decline   5. deterioration
6. serious   7. earnest   8. conviction   9. belief

5:4

1. prosper   2. declined   3. severed   4. innovators   5. intensified
6. sobriety   7. seclusion   8. earnestly   9. innovations   10. destiny
11. crudeness   12. convict   13. resemblance   14. diversity   15. perpetuate

5:5

UNIT NINE

1:1
1. confirm   2. ridiculed   3. typical   4. extreme   5. famous

1:2
1. renowned   2. radical   3. derided   4. attest   5. attest
6. renowned   7. radical   8. derided   9. renowned   10. derided
11. representative   12. attest   13. representative   14. attest   15. radical
16. derided   17. representative

1:3
1. a   2. b   3. b   4. a   5. c

1:4
1. asserted   2. depict   3. dissident   4. theme   5. milieu

2:1
1. kilocycle   2. milli-   3. myria-   4. myriad   5. kilo-

2:2
1. false   2. false   3. false   4. false   5. true

2:3
1. the year 2000
2. 1,000
3. myriad
4. one-thousandth of a degree
5. the millipede

3:1
1. stimulated   2. warranted   3. accepted   4. combination   5. diminished

3:2
1. justified   2. conventional   3. spurred   4. fusion   5. marred

3:3
1. surrogates   2. presume   3. editorialized   4. spontaneous   5. identified

3:4
1. editorialized   2. surrogates   3. spontaneous   4. identified   5. presume

4:1
1. semiliterate   2. demigod   3. semicircle   4. hemi-   5. hemisphere

4:2
1. false   2. false   3. true   4. false   5. false

4:3
1. b   2. c   3. b   4. b   5. a

5:1
1. b   2. d   3. e   4. f   5. h
6. c   7. b   8. f   9. b   10. g
11. a   12. i

5:2
Answers will vary.

5:3
1. justify   2. noted   3. assert   4. famous   5. declare
6. renowned   7. conventional   8. ridicule   9. deride   10. formal
11. warrant

5:4
1. dissidents *or* radicals
2. represent
3. radicals *or* dissidents
4. assert
5. spur
6. attested
7. fuse
8. unidentified
9. derision
10. presumptuous
11. depiction

5:5
1. reared
2. semblance
3. spurred
4. surrogates
5. marred
6. myriad
7. kilocycle
8. perpetuation
9. conviction
10. sober
11. spontaneous
12. retrograde
13. justified
14. editorialized
15. mil
16. gradual
17. unearthed
18. destined

UNIT TEN

1:1
1. a   2. c   3. d   4. c   5. b

1:2
1. overview
2. brevity
3. anecdotes
4. expository
5. reluctant

1:3
1. segmented   2. change   3. selective   4. expand   5. consign

1:4
1. discriminating   2. transition   3. amplify   4. relegate   5. subdivided

2:1
1. polyglot   2. multi-   3. polygamy   4. multiplicity   5. multifaceted

2:2
1. true   2. false   3. true   4. true   5. false

2:3
1. rhythms
2. multilayered
3. It has many colors.
4. a great number
5. He or she has many spouses.

3:1
1. detestable
2. major
3. brief
4. necessary
5. plain

3:2
1. concise
2. imperative
3. odious
4. foremost
5. unadorned

3:3
1. draft
2. validity
3. conform
4. substantiate
5. disclose

3:4
1. validity
2. draft
3. disclose
4. substantiate
5. conform

4:1
1. ultimate
2. protagonist
3. terminate
4. proto-
5. agonist

4:2
1. true
2. false
3. true
4. true
5. false

4:3
1. c
2. a
3. b
4. b
5. a

5:1
1. discriminating
2. draft
3. imperative
4. brevity
5. amplify
6. draft
7. amplify
8. draft
9. imperative

5:2
Answers will vary.

5:3
1. distinguish
2. validity
3. loath
4. discriminate
5. hesitant
6. cogency
7. differentiated
8. reluctant
9. validity
10. discriminate

5:4
1. amplification
2. discrimination
3. reluctance
4. briefs
5. drafted
6. imperious
7. disclosure
8. odiousness
9. adorned
10. invalid
11. nonconformist
12. relegated

5:5
1. disclose
2. kilometer
3. renowned
4. conform
5. motif
6. protozoan
7. concise
8. odious
9. polyglot
10. transition
11. fusion
12. draft
13. overview

Glossary

abrasion *noun.* A place scraped or worn by friction.

abrasive *adjective.* Causing something to be worn or scraped by friction.

abstain *verb.* (1) To deny oneself indulgence in an action or practice. (2) To refrain from voting. **abstaining**

abyss (ə-bĭs′) *noun.* A very great depth; a chasm.

accumulate *verb.* To collect, little by little, over a period of time. **accumulated**

adequate *adjective.* (1) Enough; sufficient. (2) Competent; suitable.

adequately *adverb.* Sufficiently; satisfactorily.

adorned *adjective.* Decorated.

adversary *noun.* A person who is openly fighting or actively opposing another in a spirit of hostility.

adverse *adjective.* Harmful or unfavorable.

advocate (ăd′və-kĭt) *noun.* A defender or supporter. *verb.* (ăd′və-kāt′) To support, speak or write in favor of. **advocating**

afford *verb.* (1) To provide. (2) To have the money for. (3) To manage to give, spare or have. **afforded**

aft *noun.* The rear section of a boat or ship. *adjective.* Rear.

agonist Root meaning actor or contestant.

alarm *noun.* Fright brought on by the awareness of danger.

allay (ə-lā′) *verb.* To lay to rest; to quiet or to soothe that which is excited.

alleviate *verb.* To lighten; to make more bearable.

alleviating *adjective.* Making more bearable.

alliance *noun.* A union formed by mutual agreement to protect mutual interests.

allure *noun.* The power of attraction; charm. *verb.* To attract someone by appealing to the senses.

ally (ăl′ī′) *noun.* A person, group or nation united with another. *verb.* (ə-lī′) To unite with or form a connection between. **allies**

amass *verb.* To gather a large amount of something within a relatively short time. **amassed**

amplification *noun.* Further explanation that expands a statement, narrative, etc.

amplify *verb.* (1) To expand a statement through further explanation. (2) To make greater, larger, louder, etc. (3) To increase the strength of, as in electric power, voltage or current.

andro- Root meaning man.

androgynous (ăn-drŏj′ə-nəs) *adjective.* Having the characteristics of both male and female.

anecdote *noun.* A short account of an interesting, humorous, or biographical incident.

anemia *noun.* A condition resulting from too little hemoglobin or too few red blood cells, or from a loss of blood. Its characteristics are weakness, pallor, palpitation of the heart and a tendency to fatigue.

annual *adjective.* Yearly.

anthrop-, anthropo- Root meaning human being.

For a guide to the pronunciation symbols used in this glossary, refer to *The American Heritage Dictionary,* or to *Dictionary Drills,* by Jamestown Publishers.

anthropoid *noun.* Any of the large, tailless or short-tailed apes such as chimpanzees, gorillas and orangutans. *adjective.* (1) Resembling a person, especially in shape. (2) Resembling an ape, especially in action.

anthropologist *noun.* An expert in the science of human beings, especially as it involves the study of their origins, races, environmental and social relations, and cultures.

anthropology *noun.* The science of human beings, especially as it involves the study of their origins, races, environmental and social relations, and cultures.

anthropomorphic (ăn′thrə-pō-môr′fĭk′) *adjective.* Described or thought of as having human form or human qualities.

anthropomorphize (ăn′thrə-pō-môr′fīz′) *verb.* To attribute human form or qualities to animals or objects.

anti- Root meaning against or opposite.

antipathy *noun.* A strong dislike or aversion; a feeling of intense dislike.

antiseptic *noun.* A substance that prevents the growth and spread of microorganisms that cause infection.

antisocial *adjective.* (1) Not sociable; not open to friendliness and companionship. (2) Opposed to or hostile to the principles of society.

antitrust *adjective.* Opposed to trusts or monopolies.

antonym *noun.* A word that has the opposite meaning of another word.

apathetic *adjective.* Indifferent; having or showing little or no interest, concern or feeling.

apathy *noun.* Indifference; lack of interest, concern or feeling.

appalling *adjective.* Horrible or dreadful.

appallingly *adverb.* In a horrible or dreadful manner.

apparatus *noun.* Equipment.

apprehension *noun.* (1) A fear of something evil happening in the future. (2) Legal seizure; arrest. (3) Understanding on a superficial level.

apprehensive *adjective.* Fearful.

arbitrary *adjective.* Not based on sense, reason or fixed law; based rather on random individual preference or whim.

arbitration *noun.* Settlement of a dispute by a person whose decision the conflicting parties agree to accept.

-arch Root meaning rule.

artifact *noun.* Man-made object.

-ary Root meaning pertaining to.

assert *verb.* To state vigorously, often without proof or in spite of proof to the contrary.
   asserted

asterisk *noun.* A small star symbol (∗) used in writing and printing.

asteroid *noun.* One of thousands of small planets that revolve around the sun, mainly between the orbits of Mars and Jupiter.

astro Root meaning star.

astrology *noun.* The study of the various aspects and positions of the stars and planets to try to determine their supposed influences on human affairs.

astronaut *noun.* A person who travels into outer space.

astronomer *noun.* An expert in astronomy, or the science of the celestial bodies.

astronomical *adjective.* (1) Related to astronomy. (2) Enormously large or great.

astronomy *noun.* The science of the celestial bodies.

asunder *adverb.* Into separate parts.

athlete *noun.* A person trained and skilled in sports or games requiring physical skill, coordination and strength.

athletics *noun.* Exercises of physical strength, coordination and skill.

-athlon Root meaning contest.

attest *verb.* To confirm; to bear witness. **attested**

attribute (ăt′-rə-byo͞ot′) *noun.* A characteristic or trait. *verb.* (ə-trĭb′yo͞ot) (1) To regard as belonging to. (2) To give credit for. (3) Regard as an effect of. **attributed, attributing**

augment *verb.* To make or become greater in size, number, amount or degree; increase. **augmented**

banter *noun.* Playful teasing. *verb.* To tease playfully. **bantering**

bay *noun.* (1) A division or compartment of a structure. (2) A part of the sea extending into the land. (3) The position of a pursuer who is being held off. *verb.* To howl.

bestow *verb.* To present as a gift. **bestowed**

between *adverb.* (1) In the space or time separating. (2) In the middle.

bi- Latin prefix meaning two.

biannual *adjective.* Occurring twice a year.

bicameral *adjective.* Having or consisting of two legislative chambers, or houses.

bicentennial *noun.* A two-hundredth anniversary.

bicuspid *noun.* A double-pointed premolar tooth that tears and grinds food.

biennial *adjective.* Occurring every two years.

bifocal *adjective.* Having two focuses, or focal lengths, as in bifocals.

bifocals *noun.* Eyeglasses that have bifocal lenses.

bimanual *adjective.* A physical task that is done with or that requires two hands.

bimonthly *adjective.* (1) Occurring twice a month. (2) Occurring every two months.

binary *adjective.* Made up of two parts.

binocular *adjective.* (1) For both eyes at once. (2) Using both eyes at once.

binoculars *noun.* A double telescope that is joined for use by both eyes at once.

bio- Root meaning life.

biography *noun.* An account of a person's life.

biology *noun.* The scientific study of plant and animal life.

biosphere *noun.* That part of the earth's crust, water and atmosphere in which life can exist.

biped *noun.* A two-footed creature.

biweekly *adjective.* (1) Occurring twice a week. (2) Occurring every two weeks.

breadth *noun.* Width.

brevity *noun.* (1) Shortness of duration. (2) Shortness in speech or writing.

briefs *noun.* Underpants.

bulk *noun.* Enormous mass.

GLOSSARY

bulky *adjective.* Large; taking up much space.

capacious *adjective.* Large and roomy.

capacity *noun.* The ability to receive and hold.

cent- Root meaning one hundred.

cent *noun.* A coin worth one-hundredth of a dollar.

centenarian *noun.* A person who is one hundred years old or older.

centennial *noun.* A one-hundredth anniversary.

centi- Root meaning either one hundred or one-hundredth.

centigrade *adjective.* Based on or according to a scale for measuring temperature on which 0 degrees marks the freezing point of water and 100 degrees marks the boiling point.

centigram *noun.* A unit of mass equal to one-hundredth of a gram.

centiliter *noun.* A unit of volume equal to one-hundredth of a liter.

centimeter *noun.* A unit of length equal to one-hundredth of a meter.

centipede *noun.* A multi-legged crawling creature having a long, flattened, many-sectioned body, with each section bearing one pair of legs.

century *noun.* A period of one hundred years.

chroma Root meaning color.

chronicle *verb.* To record or write down.
   chronicled

civility *noun.* Politeness; courtesy.

cogency *noun.* The quality of being forcefully convincing.

compliance *noun.* Cooperation.

comply *verb.* To cooperate; to obey.

component *noun.* A part that joins with other parts to form a unit.

comprise *verb.* (1) To include within a particular scope. (2) To be made up of.

concept *noun.* Something conceived in the mind; an idea.

conception *noun.* A general idea; an impression.

concise *adjective.* Brief and to the point.

concur *verb.* (1) To be of the same opinion; to agree. (2) To occur at the same time.
   concurred

configuration *noun.* The arrangement of parts or elements; the shape.

conform *verb.* To be in agreement with or to comply with generally accepted standards.

consolation *noun.* (1) A person or thing that gives comfort. (2) Comfort.

console (kŏn′sōl) *noun.* A panel with dials and switches to control electronic or mechanical equipment. *verb.* (kən-sōl′) To provide comfort.

contend *verb.* (1) To compete. (2) To state as a fact. **contended**

contender *noun.* A contestant.

content (kŏn′tĕnt) *noun.* (1) What is contained in anything. (2) Facts and ideas as opposed to physical form. (3) Subject matter of a field of study. *adjective.* (kən-tĕnt′) (1) Satisfied. (2) Willing.

conventional *adjective.* (1) Following generally accepted patterns. (2) Unoriginal, trite.

convict *verb.* To prove a person to be guilty of a crime.

conviction *noun.* (1) A belief that is unshakable and undoubting. (2) The act of finding or proving that a person committed a crime.

cosmic *adjective.* Related to or characteristic of the cosmos, or the whole universe.

cosmo Root meaning order or universe.

cosmology *noun.* A branch of astronomy that deals with the origin and structure of the universe.

cosmonaut *noun.* A Soviet astronaut, or space traveler.

cosmopolitan *adjective.* (1) Having a worldwide rather than a limited perspective. (2) Worldly; sophisticated. (3) Composed of persons or elements from many parts of the world. (4) Belonging to or found in most parts of the world.

cosmos *noun.* An orderly, harmonious, systematic universe.

courtesy *noun.* Politeness in consideration of the feelings and wishes of others.

credibility *noun.* The quality of being believable.

credible *adjective.* Offering reasonable grounds for being believed; believable.

credulous *adjective.* Too ready to believe something.

crucial *adjective.* Critical, decisive; very important.

crude *adjective.* (1) Incompletely developed; unpolished. (2) Rude; lacking taste.

cycle Root meaning wheel.

de- Prefix meaning the reverse of or to remove.

debate *noun.* A discussion of reasons for and against a question or topic. *verb.* To discuss a question or topic by considering opposing arguments.

deca- Greek root meaning ten.

decade *noun.* A period of ten years.

decagram *noun.* A unit of mass equal to ten grams.

decaliter *noun.* A unit of volume equal to ten liters.

decalogue *noun.* A basic set of rules that carries binding authority.

Decalogue *noun.* The Ten Commandments.

decameter *noun.* A unit of length equal to ten meters.

decapod *noun.* A mollusk, or shellfish, with ten legs.

decathlon *noun.* An athletic contest comprising ten track-and-field events.

decem- Latin root meaning ten.

deci- Prefix meaning one-tenth.

decigram *noun.* A unit of mass equal to one-tenth of a gram.

deciliter *noun.* A unit of volume equal to one-tenth of a liter.

decimate *verb.* (1) To destroy or kill a large part of. (2) To take or destroy one-tenth of.

decimeter *noun.* A unit of length equal to one-tenth of a meter.

decision *noun.* A conclusion that is reached following the consideration of a matter.

declare *verb.* To state firmly and openly.

decline *noun.* A gradual decrease. *verb.* To decrease gradually. **declined**

defoliate *verb.* To remove the leaves from, especially prematurely.

degrade *verb.* To bring into dishonor or contempt; to debase.

dehydrate *verb.* To remove the water from.

delay *noun.* The state of being put off until a later time; being caused to be late.

demi- French prefix meaning half.

demigod *noun.* (1) A mythological being with more power than a mortal but less than a god. (2) A person so outstanding as to approach the divine.

demitasse *noun.* (1) A smaller-than-average cup used to serve strong black coffee. (2) A small cup of black coffee.

demo- Root meaning people.

dent- Root meaning tooth.

depict *verb.* To show, describe or portray.

depiction *noun.* A description or portrayal.

depreciate *verb.* (1) To lessen the price or value of. (2) To become less valuable or expensive. **depreciated**

deride *verb.* To make fun of in contempt. **derided**

derision *noun.* Contemptuous ridicule.

destined *adjective.* Designated, assigned or dedicated in advance.

destiny *noun.* Fate.

deterioration *noun.* A making or growing worse.

di- Greek prefix for two.

dia- Root meaning between or across.

diagonal *adjective.* Crossing at an angle; slanting.

dialogue *noun.* A conversation or discussion between two or more people.

dichotomy (dī-kot′ə-mē) *noun.* A division into two parts, especially a division into opposing groups.

differentiate *verb.* To point out the exact differences between one thing and others of the same class.

dioxide *noun.* A compound in which each molecule has two atoms of oxygen.

diploma *noun.* A document bearing record of graduation from a school, university or college.

diplomacy *noun.* The art and practice of conducting negotiation between nations.

diplomat *noun.* A person skilled in conducting relations between nations.

diplopia *noun.* A vision disorder in which two images of a single object are seen; double vision.

dipole *noun.* (1) A pair of equal and opposite electric charges or magnetic poles of opposite sign, usually separated by a small distance. (2) A type of radio or television antenna having two horizontal conducting rods that are parallel and separated slightly.

dipterous *adjective.* Having two wings.

diptych *noun.* A work of art consisting of a picture or series of pictures painted or carved on two hinged tablets.

disciplinarian *noun.* A person who enforces rules.

discipline *noun.* A field of study. *verb.* (1) To train. (2) To punish.

disclose *verb.* To reveal or expose.

disclosure *noun.* The act of revealing or exposing.

discord *noun.* Lack of agreement or harmony between persons or factions.

discriminate *verb.* (1) To select what is true, appropriate or best. (2) To unfairly favor or mistreat a person or group.

discriminating *adjective.* Discerning, selective; able to choose what is true or appropriate.

discrimination *noun.* The unfair favoring or mistreatment of a person or group.

disdain *verb.* To scorn, treat with contempt. **disdained**

disputatious *adjective.* Inclined to argue or disagree.

dispute *noun.* An argument or debate. *verb.* (1) To argue about; to call into question. (2) To disagree with.

dissident *noun.* One who disagrees or dissents. *adjective.* Disagreeing or dissenting.

dissipate *verb.* To spread apart to the point of disappearing. **dissipated, dissipating**

distinguish *verb.* To recognize the features that set a thing apart from others.

diversified *adjective.* Varied.

diversity *noun.* Variety.

dominant *adjective.* Most powerful or influential.

downgrade *verb.* To lower in position, quality, value or reputation.

draft *noun.* (1) A version; a rough sketch. (2) A current of air in a closed-in space. (3) The selection of persons without their consent. *verb.* To write a preliminary version. **drafted**

drastic *adjective.* Extreme, severe.

drastically *adverb.* Extremely, severely.

du- Latin prefix meaning two.

dual *adjective.* (1) Two. (2) Consisting of two parts or elements, or having two parts that are alike; double.

duel *noun.* A formal fight between two people.

duet *noun.* A piece of music composed for two voices or instruments.

duo *noun.* Two singers or musicians who perform together.

duplex *noun.* A two-family house. *adjective.* Having two main elements or parts.

duplicate (d/y/o͞o′plĭ-kĭt) *noun.* One of two things that are exactly alike; an exact copy. *verb.* (d/y/o͞o′plĭ-kāt′) Make an exact copy of; repeat exactly.

duplicity *noun.* Doubleness of thought, speech or action; a form of dishonesty whereby a person deceives by saying things or acting in ways that are not in keeping with his or her true intentions, or by acting one way in private and another way in public.

earnest *noun.* A serious, eager attitude. *adjective.* Strong and firm in purpose; eager.

earnestly *adverb.* Eagerly and purposefully.

effort *noun.* Use of mental or physical power to do something.

elapse *verb.* To pass or slip by (as in time). **elapsed**

elude *verb.* (1) Avoid. (2) Baffle. **eluding**

eminent *adjective.* Distinguished, prestigious.

empathy *noun.* The action of fully understanding, being sensitive to, and experiencing the thoughts, feelings and experiences of another without their having to be fully explained.

endeavor *noun.* A long, difficult and sincere effort.

ennea- Greek root meaning nine.

enneagon (ĕn′ē-ə-gŏn′) *noun.* A closed plane figure having nine sides and nine angles; nonagon.

enneahedron (ĕn′ē-ə-hē′drən) *noun.* A polyhedron having nine faces, or sides.

-ennial A form of the root annual, meaning yearly.

ensure *noun.* To guarantee.

entreat *verb.* Ask; make a plea to. **entreated**

entreaty *noun.* Request; plea.

enunciate *verb.* To speak clearly. **enunciating**

enunciation *noun.* Clear and articulate speech.

epi- Root meaning after, on or upon.

epidemic *noun.* (1) The rapid spread of a disease upon the people. (2) The spread of anything that affects many individuals within an area. *adjective.* Affecting many people at the same time; widespread.

epidemiology *noun.* A branch of medicine dealing with the causes, distribution and control of the spread of diseases in a community.

epiglottis *noun.* A small valvelike piece of cartilage at the top of the glottis (an opening at the top of the larynx, behind the tongue), which closes off the opening when we swallow.

epilogue *noun.* (1) A speech at the conclusion of a play. (2) A concluding section of a literary work.

escape *verb.* To get away.

ethereal *adjective.* (1) Of or relating to the regions beyond the earth. (2) Heavenly; spiritual. (3) Light, airy, delicate.

evolution *noun.* Development; process of change.

evolve *verb.* To develop through gradual change. **evolved**

excessive *adjective.* Going beyond what is appropriate in amount or extent.

exhilarate *verb.* To put into high spirits.

exhilarating *adjective.* Enlivening, exciting.

exhilaration *noun.* High spirits.

exorbitance *noun.* Excessiveness.

exorbitant *adjective.* Unreasonably excessive.

expository *adjective.* Explanatory.

factor *noun.* (1) Something that tends to produce a result. (2) A number which, when multiplied with another, produces a product.

famous *adjective.* Widely and usually favorably known.

fear *noun.* Any feeling of being afraid.

finale (fĭ-năl′ē) *noun.* The close or termination of something, as in the last section of a musical composition, or the last, often climactic, event in a sequence.

fissure *noun.* A long, narrow opening; a crack.

fledgling *noun.* A young bird. *adjective.* Young, inexperienced.

fleet *noun.* A number of automobiles, ships, airplanes or the like that are under unified control. *adjective.* Quick, swift.

fleetness *noun.* Quickness, swiftness.

foliage *noun.* The leaves of a plant.

foliate *verb.* (1) To decorate with leaves. (2) To put forth leaves.

folio *noun.* (1) A page number. (2) An oversized book.

folium Root meaning leaf.

foremost *adjective.* Of greatest importance; dominant.

formal *adjective.* In strict accordance with prescribed methods and procedures.

formidable *adjective.* Difficult, intimidating.

furtive *adjective.* Covert; stealthy.

furtively *adverb.* Stealthily; covertly.

fuse *noun.* A slow-burning wick used to set off an explosive device.

fusion *noun.* A union formed by or as if formed by melting.

-gamos Root meaning marriage.

gen- Root meaning birth, race or kind.

gene *noun.* A part of a chromosome that influences the inheritance and development of some characteristic.

genealogy *noun.* (1) The study of family ancestries or histories. (2) An account of the descent of a person or family from an ancestor; family tree.

generate *verb.* To bring into existence; to produce.

generation *noun.* (1) The action or process of coming or bringing into being. (2) A group of people constituting a single step in the line of descent from an ancestor.

generic *adjective.* (1) Characteristic of a genus, kind or class. (2) Having to do with a group of similar things; general; not specific or special.

genesis *noun.* The origin or coming into being of something.

Genesis *noun.* The first book of the Old Testament, which gives an account of the creation of the world.

genetic *adjective.* (1) Having to do with origin and natural growth. (2) Of or having to do with genes or genetics.

genetics *noun.* The branch of biology that deals with the principles of heredity.

genre (zhän′rə) *noun.* A kind or sort, especially a kind or category of art, music or literature that is characterized by a particular style or form.

genus, gener Root meaning birth.

genus *noun.* Any group of similar things, especially a kind or class of related plants or animals.

geo- Root meaning earth.

geologist *noun.* An expert in geology.

geology *noun.* The study of the history of the earth and its life, especially as recorded in rocks.

glottis *noun.* The opening at the top of the larynx, behind the tongue.

-gon Root meaning angle.

gradation *noun.* A series that forms connected stages, steps or degrees, each leading directly to the next.

-grade Root meaning step.

gradient *noun*. A part sloping upward or downward; inclination.

gradual *adjective*. Taking place by steps or degrees; little by little.

graduate *verb*. (1) To pass from one stage or level to a higher one. (2) To finish a course of study at a school or college and receive a document testifying to the accomplishment.

graduation *noun*. The act of graduating, or receiving a diploma or degree from a school or college.

-gram Root meaning writing or drawing.

-graph Root meaning something written or an instrument for making or transmitting records.

gyn- Root meaning woman.

harried *adjective*. Beset by worries.

hedra Root meaning face.

hemi- Greek prefix meaning half.

hemisphere *noun*. Half of a round solid body, or sphere.

hepta- Greek root for seven.

heptagon *noun*. A closed plane figure having seven sides and seven angles.

heptahedron *noun*. A polyhedron having seven faces, or sides.

Heptateuch (hĕp′tə-to͞ok) *noun*. The name of the first seven books of the Old Testament.

hesitant *adjective*. Holding back from doing something because of uncertainty or fear.

hex- Greek prefix meaning six.

hexachloride *noun*. A chloride containing six atoms of chloride in each molecule.

hexadecimal *adjective*. Relating to, or being a number system with a base of 16.

hexaemeron (hĕk′sə-ĕm′ə-rŏn′) *noun*. The six days of the creation.

hexagon *noun*. A closed plane figure having six angles and six sides.

hexagram *noun*. A six-pointed star made by drawing an equilateral triangle out from each side of a regular hexagon.

hexahedron *noun*. A polyhedron having six faces, or sides.

hexameter *noun*. A line of verse having six metric feet.

hexapod *noun*. An insect.

homo- Greek root meaning same. Latin root meaning man.

homogeneous *adjective*. (1) Having the same nature. (2) Having a uniform structure.

homogenize *verb*. To blend into a uniform mixture.

homograph *noun*. One of two or more words that are spelled alike but are different in meaning or pronunciation. The noun *content* (kŏn′tĕnt) and the adjective *content* (kən-tĕnt′) are homographs.

homonym *noun*. One of two or more words that are spelled and pronounced alike but have different meanings; homophone.

homophone *noun*. One of two or more words that are spelled and pronounced alike but have different meanings.

Homo sapiens *noun*. Human beings.

host *noun*. (1) A large number. (2) A living plant or animal in or on which a parasite lives. (3) A person who receives another person as a guest.

hydra, hydro Root meaning water.

hydrant *noun*. A large, upright cylinder with a valve for drawing water directly from a water main.

hydrate *noun.* A compound formed by the union of water with some other substance. *verb.* To cause to take up or combine with water or the elements of water.

hydraulic *adjective.* Operated by the pressure of water or other liquids in motion.

hydrophone *noun.* An instrument for listening to sounds transmitted through water.

hydroplane *noun.* (1) A seaplane; an airplane that can both land and take off on water. (2) A kind of boat that has planes, or winglike surfaces, on the bottom, which lift the hull partly or completely out of the water for greater speed.

hydrotherapy *noun.* The use of water in the treatment of diseases.

-illion Latin suffix meaning thousand.

imminent *adjective.* About to occur.

impede *verb.* To hinder.

impel *verb.* To drive or force.

impending *adjective.* Likely to happen any time in the near future.

imperative *noun.* An order or command. *adjective.* (1) Necessary, required. (2) Expressing a command.

imperceptible *adjective.* Unable to be detected.

imperil *verb.* To put in danger; jeopardize. **imperiled**

imperious *adjective.* Haughty and overbearing.

implication *noun.* An indirect suggestion; a hint.

implicit *adjective.* Meant, but not openly stated.

imply *verb.* (1) Signify, mean, suggest. (2) Express indirectly. **implied, implying**

impulse *noun.* A sudden inclination to act.

inadequate *adjective.* Insufficient.

incarcerate *verb.* To imprison. **incarcerated**

incarceration *noun.* Imprisonment.

inconsolable *adjective.* Broken-hearted.

incredible *adjective.* Amazing, unbelievable.

indisputable *adjective.* Too evident to be disputed; certain; unquestionable.

infer *verb.* To conclude; find out by reasoning. **inferred**

ingredient *noun.* One of the parts of a mixture or combination.

initiate *verb.* (1) To start or establish. (2) To admit with formal ceremonies to a group. (3) To introduce into knowledge of an art or subject. **initiated**

initiative *noun.* An active part in taking the first steps in an undertaking.

innovation *noun.* A new idea, method, or invention.

innovative *adjective.* Characterized by or using new ideas or methods.

innovator *noun.* One who introduces new ideas or methods.

institute *verb.* To establish. **instituted**

insure *verb.* To arrange for money to be paid in case of loss, accident or death.

integer *noun.* Any positive or negative whole number or zero.

integral *adjective.* Essential.

intense *adjective.* Feeling deeply by nature or temperament.

intensify *verb.* To increase in degree. **intensified**

intrigue *verb*. To fascinate, to arouse the curiosity. **intrigued**

intriguing *adjective*. Fascinating.

invalid (ĭn′və-lĭd) *noun*. A person who is weak because of injury or sickness.

isolation *noun*. The state of being alone or set apart.

journey *noun*. A long or tiring trip.

justify *verb*. (1) To give reasons that excuse an action, remark, etc. (2) To make (lines of type) the proper length. **justified**

kilo- Greek prefix meaning thousand.

kilocycle *noun*. A unit of measure equal to one thousand cycles per second. Used to measure the frequency of radio and television waves.

kilogram *noun*. A unit of mass equal to a thousand grams.

kiloliter *noun*. A unit of volume equal to a thousand liters.

kilometer *noun*. A unit of distance equal to a thousand meters.

kilowatt *noun*. A unit of electric power equal to a thousand watts.

labyrinth *noun*. A confusing or complicated arrangement.

languid *adjective*. Sluggish or listless.

languidly *adverb*. In a sluggish or listless manner.

languish *adverb*. (1) To suffer harsh treatment. (2) To be or to become weak or weary; droop. **languishing**

liaison (lē-ā′zŏn′) *noun*. (1) A connection or communication to improve cooperation. (2) An illicit love affair.

loath *adjective*. Strongly unwilling to do something that is considered very disagreeable or hateful.

-logue Root meaning word or speech.

lure *verb*. To tempt; to lead into something bad.

manacle *verb*. (1) To handcuff. (2) To restrain. **manacled**

manacles *noun*. (1) Handcuffs or fetters. (2) Anything that restrains.

manicure *noun*. The care of the hands and fingernails, especially the trimming and polishing of the fingernails.

manus Root meaning hand.

mar *verb*. To spoil or detract from. **marred**

matri- Root meaning mother.

matriarchy *noun*. A family or group that is ruled or dominated by a woman.

meager *adjective*. Poor or scanty; sparse.

meagerness *noun*. Deficiency; scantiness.

melancholy *adjective*. Gloomy; sad.

metamorphosis *noun*. Transformation.

meter Root meaning measure.

micro- Root meaning small.

microbe *noun*. Germ; microorganism.

microbiologist *noun*. An expert in microbiology.

microbiology *noun.* A branch of biology that deals with microorganisms, which are microscopic animal or vegetable organisms, or microbes.

microscope *noun.* An optical instrument consisting of a lens or a combination of lenses for magnifying things that are invisible or unclear to the naked eye.

mil *noun.* A unit of measurement equal to one-thousandth of an inch.

milieu (mē-lyœ′) *noun.* Setting, environment.

mill *noun.* A monetary unit equal to one-thousandth of a dollar, or one-tenth of a cent.

millenium *noun.* A period of a thousand years.

milli- Latin prefix meaning thousand.

milligram *noun.* A unit of mass equal to one-thousandth of a gram.

milliliter *noun.* A unit of volume equal to one-thousandth of a liter.

millimeter *noun.* A unit of length equal to one-thousandth of a meter.

million *noun.* A thousand thousands.

millipede *noun.* A multi-legged crawling creature having a cylindrical many-segmented body, with two pairs of legs attached to each segment.

misconception *noun.* A mistaken idea or notion.

misgiving *noun.* A feeling of doubt, suspicion or anxiety.

momentous *adjective.* Of great consequence.

monarch *noun.* One who rules alone.

monarchy *noun.* A state having a single ruler.

mono- Root meaning one.

monochloride *noun.* A substance whose molecules each contain a single chloride atom.

monochromatic *adjective.* Having or showing only one color.

monocle *noun.* Eyeglass for one eye.

monocular *adjective.* Affecting or involving only one eye.

monogamy *noun.* The state of being married to only one person at a time.

monograph *noun.* A written document on one subject; a book or an article, usually a scholarly one.

monologue *noun.* (1) A long speech by one person, especially one that monopolizes conversation. (2) A part of a play in which a single actor speaks alone. (3) Entertainment by a single speaker.

monoplane *noun.* An airplane with only one pair of wings.

monorail *noun.* Railway in which cars run on a single track.

monotone *noun.* Sound or repetition of sounds that is unvaried; manner of speaking or singing without change of pitch.

monotonous *adjective.* (1) Continuing in the same tone or pitch. (2) Wearying or boring because of its sameness.

moratorium *noun.* Officially granted delay or interruption.

-morphic Root meaning form, or having a form.

motif (mō-tēf′) *noun.* A theme.

multi- Latin prefix meaning many.

multifaceted *adjective.* Having many aspects, or facets; complex.

multifarious *adjective.* Having many different parts or forms; many and varied; diverse.

multiple *adjective.* Many.

multiplex *adjective.* (1) Multiple. (2) Of a system for sending two or more messages or signals over the same wire, circuit or air wave at the same time.

multiplicity *noun.* (1) A diversity. (2) A great many; great number.

mutual *adjective.* Shared in common.

mutually *adverb.* Commonly, reciprocally.

myria- Root meaning ten thousand.

myriad (mîr′ē-əd) *adjective.* Countless; innumerable.

myriagram *noun.* A unit of mass equal to ten thousand grams.

myrialiter *noun.* A unit of volume equal to ten thousand liters.

myriameter *noun.* A unit of length equal to ten thousand meters.

-naut Root meaning sailor.

nautical *adjective.* Pertaining to sailors, navigation or ships.

negotiate *verb.* (1) To discuss or confer. (2) To arrange for. (3) To get by or around something. **negotiating**

-nomy Root meaning system of laws or arrangement.

nona- Latin root meaning nine.

nonagenarian *noun.* A person in his or her nineties.

nonagon *noun.* A closed plane figure having nine sides and nine angles; enneagon.

nonconformist *noun.* A person who refuses to conform to a given church or social group.

noted *adjective.* Well-known for a particular talent or accomplishment.

nove- Latin root meaning nine.

novemdecillion (no′vəm-dĭ-sĭl′yən) *noun.* A number that is written as 1,000 followed by nineteen groups of three zeros.

novena *noun.* A Roman Catholic devotion that lasts for nine days.

nurture *verb.* To foster; to encourage the development of.

oct- Root meaning eight.

octagon *noun.* A closed plane figure having eight sides and eight angles.

octahedron *noun.* A solid figure having eight faces, or sides.

octave *noun.* A span of eight notes in a musical scale.

octet *noun.* (1) A group of eight, especially eight singers or musicians who perform together. (2) A musical composition for eight voices or instruments.

octogenarian *noun.* A person in his or her eighties.

octopus *noun.* A sea mollusk that has eight arms, or tentacles, with suckers on them.

odious *adjective.* Distasteful.

odiousness *noun.* Hatefulness.

-oid Root meaning appearance or form.

-ology Root meaning science or study of.

-onym Root meaning name or word.

-opia Root meaning eyes or vision.

opponent *noun.* A person on the other side of an argument, game, contest, etc.

oppression *noun.* Cruel or unjust treatment.

oppressive *adjective.* Hard to bear, burdensome.

optimal *adjective.* Most desirable or satisfactory.

orient *verb.* (1) Adjust to a particular direction. (2) Adjust to a new situation.
    oriented

Orient *noun.* The region in Asia that is south and southeast of the Himalayas. **Oriental**

overview *noun.* A summary.

parallelogram *noun.* A quadrilateral whose opposite sides are parallel and of equal length.

paramount *adjective.* Of highest importance.

paraphernalia *noun.* Equipment; gear.

pathetic *adjective.* Having the ability to move a person to either compassion or scornful pity.

pathological *adjective.* Related to disease; often changed or caused by disease.

pathology *noun.* The study of the nature of diseases.

pathos, path, pathy Root meaning suffering, experience or emotion.

pathos (pā′thŏs′) *noun.* A quality or an element in speech or in a work of art, literature or music that evokes pity or compassion.

patri- Root meaning father.

patriarchy *noun.* A family or group that is ruled or dominated by a man.

ped- Root meaning foot.

pedal *noun.* A lever pushed by the foot to move any kind of machinery.

pedestrian *noun.* One who travels on foot.

pedicure *noun.* The care and treatment of feet, toes and nails.

penta- Greek root meaning five.

pentagon *noun.* A closed plane figure having five sides and five angles.

pentagonal (pĕn-tăg′ə-nəl) *adjective.* Having five angles and five sides; five-sided.

pentagonoid *adjective.* Somewhat pentagonal.

pentagram *noun.* A five-pointed star made with alternate points connected by straight lines.

pentathlon *noun.* An athletic contest consisting of five different events.

perceive *verb.* (1) To take in with the mind; observe; understand. (2) To be aware of through the senses. **perceived**

perpetuate *verb.* To make something last indefinitely; to keep from being forgotten.

perpetuation *noun.* (1) Immortalization. (2) The act of making something last or continue indefinitely.

pilgrimage *noun.* (1) A journey to a sacred place. (2) A long journey.

pinnacle *noun.* (1) A small turret or steeple attached to a building. (2) The peak of a form or structure. (3) The highest point of development or achievement.

plaintive *adjective.* Melancholy; mournful.

plaintively *adverb.* Mournfully, sorrowfully.

-plex Root meaning fold.

-plic Root meaning fold.

-plo From -ply and -plex, meaning fold.

pod- Root meaning foot.

poly- Greek prefix meaning many.

polygamy *noun.* Marriage to several people at the same time.

polyglot *noun.* A person who knows several languages. *adjective.* Containing material in several languages.

polygon *noun.* A closed plane figure having three or more straight sides and angles.

polygraph *noun.* A lie detector; an instrument for recording changes in a number of involuntary body activities at one time.

polyhedron *noun.* A solid figure having four or more faces, or sides.

polysyllabic *adjective.* Of more than three syllables (referring to a word).

postponement *noun.* A putting off until a definite future time.

prestige *noun.* Reputation, influence or distinction founded on what is known about one's abilities, achievements, etc.

prestigious *adjective.* Having prestige.

presume *verb.* (1) To dare or venture. (2) To go beyond what is right or proper. (3) To take for granted.

presumptuous *adjective.* Acting without right; too bold.

prevent *verb.* Stop from happening.

prima donna *noun.* (1) The principal woman singer in an opera. (2) A temperamental person.

prime, prima Root meaning first.

prime *adjective.* (1) First in rank or importance; chief; principal. (2) First in time or order. (3) First quality; first-rate; excellent.

primer (prĭm'ər) *noun.* (1) A first book in reading. (2) (prīm'ər) Material used in priming, or preparing, a surface for a finish coat of paint.

primogenitor *noun.* Ancestor; forefather.

primogeniture *noun.* (1) Fact of being the firstborn of the children of the same parents. (2) Right of inheritance or succession by the firstborn, especially the inheritance of a family estate by the eldest son.

proficient *adjective.* Advanced in any art, science, or subject; skilled, expert.

profuse *adjective.* Abundant.

profusely *adverb.* Abundantly.

profusion *noun.* Great abundance.

prologue *noun.* (1) A speech addressed to the audience by one of the actors at the beginning of a play. (2) A preface or introduction to a piece of literature. (3) Any introductory act or event.

prosper *verb.* To flourish economically.

prosperity *noun.* Economic well-being.

provocative *adjective.* Tending to call forth action, thought, laughter, anger, etc.

provoke *verb.* (1) Call forth; cause. (2) To make angry.

prowess (prou'ĭs) *noun.* Outstanding skill.

prudent *adjective.* Having or showing good judgment.

pteron (tĕr'ŏn) Root meaning wing.

pterosaur (tĕr'ə-sôr') *noun.* Pterodactyl: an extinct flying reptile.

quad-, quatr-, quadri- Root meaning four.

quadrangle *noun.* (1) A closed plane figure having four sides and four angles. (2) A four-sided area of land surrounded by buildings.

quadrant *noun.* (1) A quarter of a circle; an arc of 90 degrees. (2) A quarter of any plane figure that is divided by intersecting lines that meet to form a 90-degree angle. (3) An instrument with a scale of 90 degrees, used in astronomy, surveying and navigation for measuring altitudes.

quadrennial *adjective.* (1) Occurring every four years. (2) Continuing for four years.

quadrennium *noun.* A period of four years.

quadrilateral *noun.* A quadrangle; a closed plane figure having four sides and four angles.

quadruped *noun.* A four-footed creature.

quadruple *verb.* To make or become four times as great or as many. *adjective.* (1) Fourfold. (2) Four times as great.

quadruplet *noun.* One of four children born at the same time to the same mother.

quadruplicate *adjective.* Fourfold.

quart Root meaning four.

quart *noun.* One-fourth of a gallon.

quarter *noun.* (1) One of four equal parts into which a thing may be, or is, divided. (2) One-fourth of a dollar, or twenty-five cents.

quartet *noun.* A group of four, especially a group of four singers or musicians performing together.

quest *noun.* A search or hunt.

quinque- A form of the root *quint,* meaning five.

quinquefoliolate (kwĭn′kwə-fō′lē-ə-lāt′) *adjective.* Having clusters of five leaflets.

quinquennial (kwĭn-kwĕn′ē-əl) *adjective.* (1) Lasting for five years. (2) Taking place every five years.

quinquennium (kwĭn-kwĕn′ē-əm) *noun.* A period of five years.

quint Root meaning five.

quintessence *noun.* (1) The essence of a thing in its purest form. (2) The most typical or representative example of something.

quintessential *adjective.* Being the most typical or representative example.

quintet *noun.* (1) A group of five, especially a group of five singers or musicians performing together. (2) A piece of music for five voices or instruments.

quintuple *adjective.* Being five times as great or as many.

quintuplets *noun.* Five babies born at the same time to the same mother.

quintuplicate (kwĭn-tōō′plĭ-kĭt) *noun.* Five copies all alike. (kwĭn-tōō′plĭ-kāt′) *verb.* To make five copies or examples of a thing. *adjective.* Fivefold, or consisting of five corresponding or identical parts or examples.

radical *noun.* (1) One who favors extreme change or reform. (2) In math, the sign √⁻, which is placed before an expression to show that the square root is to be extracted. *adjective.* (1) Favoring extreme change or reform. (2) Extreme. (3) Fundamental.

range *noun.* The extent; the scope.

rear *verb.* (1) To raise. (2) To rise up. **reared**

reflect *verb.* To show the result or effect of.

reflection *noun.* Contemplation; meditation.

relegate *verb.* Assign to a low position or status. **relegated**

reluctance *noun.* A lack of willingness.

reluctant *adjective.* Unwilling.

remote *adjective.* (1) Distant. (2) Slight (as in possibility). **remotest**

remotely *adverb.* Distantly.

renew *verb.* (1) To give or get for a new or additional period of time. (2) To make new again; restore.

renovate *verb.* To put in good condition by cleaning, repairing, redecorating, etc.

renowned *adjective.* Having great and enduring fame and honor.

replenish *verb.* To fill again; to renew. **replenished**

repose *noun.* The state of complete freedom from mental or physical activity.

representative *noun.* An agent. *adjective.* Typical.

resemblance *noun.* Similarity in appearance.

resolve *noun.* (1) A firm decision to do or refrain from doing something.
(2) Resoluteness. *verb.* (1) To settle or find an answer to. (2) To reach a firm decision.

rest *noun.* A ceasing of activity to provide recuperation from mental or physical fatigue.

restoration *noun.* A bringing back to a former condition.

restorative *adjective.* Tending to renew health or strength.

restore *verb.* (1) Return something to its original condition. (2) To give back or put back. (3) To establish again. **restored**

retro- Root meaning backward.

retrograde *adjective.* (1) Moving backward. (2) Becoming worse; deteriorating. (3) When referring to a satellite, moving in a direction opposite to the body that is being orbited.

revere *verb.* To feel deep respect mixed with love. **revered**

reverence *verb.* To feel deep respect and love mixed with awe and wonder.

reverent *adjective.* Feeling or showing deep respect mixed with love. **reverence**

ridicule *verb.* To make fun of in an attempt to make someone or something seem little or unimportant.

ritual *noun.* A form or system of rites or ceremonies.

ritualistic *adjective.* Having to do with a form or system of rites or ceremonies.

rubble *noun.* Broken fragments, of stone, brick, etc.

sapient (sā′pē-ənt) *adjective.* Wise.

sauropod (sôr′ə-pŏd′) *noun.* A suborder of dinosaurs that ate plants and had a long neck and tail, small head, and five-toed limbs. Sauropods were the largest land animals known.

sauros Root meaning lizard.

scatter *verb.* To separate so that an original group is disbanded. **scattered**

scope *noun.* The area over which an activity extends.

scrutinize *verb.* To examine closely. **scrutinizing**

sear *verb.* To burn or char the surface of. **seared**

secluded *adjective.* Set apart; private.

seclusion *noun.* Privacy and solitude.

self-evident *adjective.* Apparent; needing no proof.

semblance *noun.* Appearance or form.

semi- Latin prefix meaning half, almost, partly or somewhat.

semiannual *adjective.* Occurring every six months, or twice a year.

semiautomatic *adjective.* Not fully automatic; operated partly automatically and partly by hand.

semicentennial *noun.* A fiftieth anniversary.

semicircle *noun.* A half circle.

semiconscious *adjective.* The state of being only partly conscious, or mentally aware.

semiliterate *adjective.* Able to read and write on only a limited level.

semipermanent *adjective.* Intended to last for a long time, but not permanently.

semisweet *adjective.* Slightly sweetened.

sentiment *noun.* An attitude or view prompted by feelings.

sepsis Root meaning decay.

sept- Latin root meaning seven.

septemvir *noun.* A member of a ruling group of seven men. Specifically, one of seven men who ruled in ancient Rome.

septemvirate *noun.* A group of seven men called septemvirs who governed ancient Rome.

septic *adjective.* (1) Decaying. (2) Relating to a toxic condition resulting from the spread of bacteria caused by an infection.

septicemia (sĕp′tĭ-sē′mē-ə) *noun.* An illness in which the bloodstream is infected by disease-causing bacteria.

septuagenarian (sĕp′tyo͞o-ə-jə-nâr′e-ən) *noun.* A person in his or her seventies.

serene *adjective.* Tranquil.

serenely *adverb.* Tranquilly.

serious *adjective.* Thoughtful or subdued in appearance or manner.

sever *verb.* To break, cut or separate.

severed *adjective.* Cut off, cut apart.

sex-, sexi- Root meaning six.

sextant *noun.* An instrument used to measure angular distances, used especially in navigation to observe the altitudes of celestial bodies in order to determine latitude and longitude. The measuring portion of the instrument is one-sixth of a circle.

sextet *noun.* (1) A group of six, especially a group of six singers or musicians performing together. (2) A musical composition for six instruments or voices.

sextuple *adjective.* Being six times as great or as many.

sextuplet *noun.* One of six babies born at one time to the same mother.

sextuplicate (sĕks-to͞o′plĭ-kĭt) *noun.* Being one of six things that are exactly alike. *verb.* (sĕks-to͞o′plĭ-kāt′) To repeat or copy six times.

simultaneously *adverb.* Happening at the same time.

sober *adjective.* (1) Restrained, realistic and reasonable. (2) Not drunk.

sobriety *noun.* The state of not being drunk.

speculate *verb.* (1) To wonder or meditate. (2) To buy or sell at great risk, hoping to realize a large profit.

speculation *noun.* Guessing; conjecture.

speculator *noun.* One who buys or sells at great risk intending to profit from future price changes.

speedometer *noun.* An instrument for measuring speed.

sphere *noun.* A round solid body; globe.

spontaneous *adjective.* (1) Natural, uncontrived. (2) Arising from a momentary impulse.

spur *verb.* To stimulate, goad, motivate.
   spurred

spurious *adjective.* (1) False. (2) Deceitful.

staid *adjective.* Showing prim self-restraint; serious.

stay *noun.* Something that supports or holds something else up. *verb.* (1) To restrain or check. (2) To remain in a place. (3) To continue to be. **stays**

stow *verb.* To pack, store or load. **stowed, stowing**

stringent *adjective.* Strict, harsh.

stringently *adverb.* Strictly, harshly.

subdivide *verb.* To divide again; to separate into smaller parts. **subdivided**

subject *noun.* (1) A course of study. (2) Something discussed, thought about and referred to. (3) A person under the control of another. (4) A figure or scene depicted by an artist. *adjective.* Liable. **subjected**

subjugation *noun.* A bringing under complete control.

subsequent *adjective.* (1) Close after. (2) Later, following.

subsequently *adverb.* Closely.

substantial *adjective.* Large; important; ample.

substantially *adverb.* Largely.

substantiate *verb.* To support with facts.

subterranean *adjective.* Underground.

subtle (sŭt′l) *adjective.* Elusive; not obvious.

surmise *verb.* To imagine or infer, especially with only a little evidence to go on. **surmised**

surrogate (sŭr′ə-gĭt) *noun.* Substitute. *verb.* (sŭr′ə-gāt) To put in the place of another.

sym- Root meaning with or together with.

symbiosis *noun.* The living together in close association of two or more different kinds of organisms.

sympathy *noun.* (1) A sharing of another's sorrow or trouble. (2) An agreement in feelings or thoughts between people.

syn- Root meaning with or together with.

synchronize *verb.* (1) To occur at the same time. (2) To make events or actions coincide, or to make things exist at the same time.

synchronous *adjective.* (1) Occurring at the same time; simultaneous. (2) Moving or taking place exactly together and at the same rate.

synonym *noun.* A word that has the same or almost the same meaning as another.

synonymous *adjective.* Having the same or nearly the same meaning.

synthetic *adjective.* Made artificially through the joining of chemical elements or compounds; not natural.

synthesis *noun.* (1) The combination of parts or elements to form a whole. (2) The formation of a substance through the joining of chemical elements or compounds.

tacit (tăs′ĭt) *adjective.* (1) Unspoken. (2) Implied.

tacitly (tăs′ĭt-lē) *adverb.* Wordlessly; silently.

technological *adjective.* Of or pertaining to the science of industrial or mechanical arts.

technology *noun.* The science of the industrial and mechanical arts.

tele- Root meaning distant, at a distance, or over a distance.

telegram *noun.* A message sent by telegraph.

telegraph *noun.* An apparatus for communication at a distance by coded signals. *verb.* To send or communicate a message by telegraph.

telemeter *noun.* An instrument for measuring the distance of an object from the observer.

temper *verb.* (1) To toughen. (2) To moderate or soften. (3) To moisten, mix and prepare in the proper consistency. **tempered**

tentative *adjective.* (1) Not definite; not completely worked out. (2) Uncertain; hesitant.

tentatively *adverb.* (1) Hesitantly. (2) Not definitely.

terminal *noun.* (1) Either end of a railroad line, airline or bus line at which are located a station and offices for the handling of freight and passengers. (2) The station at the end of a railroad line, airline or bus line. *adjective.* At the end; forming the end part.

terminate *verb.* To finish; end.

termination *noun.* An ending; a conclusion.

terminus *noun.* (1) An ending point; a goal; an end. (2) Either end of a transportation line; also the town, city or station at such a place.

tetra Root meaning four.

tetragon *noun.* A closed plane figure having four sides and four angles.

tetrahedral *adjective.* Having the form of a tetrahedron (a polyhedron having four faces, or sides).

tetrahedron *noun.* A polyhedron having four faces, or sides.

tetrahydrate *noun.* A chemical compound having four molecules of water.

tetralogy *noun.* A series of four related works, such as novels or plays.

tetrameter *noun.* A line of verse consisting of four feet.

tetrandrous *adjective.* Having four stamens, or male parts.

tetrapetalous *adjective.* Having four petals.

tetrarch *noun.* A ruler of one-fourth of a state.

tetrarchy *noun.* Rule by four people.

thesis *noun.* A proposition or statement to be proved or supported.

thetic Root meaning to put or lay down, or to place.

thrive *verb.* (1) To grow vigorously. (2) To be successful; prosper.

thwart *verb.* To interfere with, defeat or frustrate. **thwarted**

-tonous Root meaning tone.

trace *noun.* Any noticeable indication left by something that has happened or been present.

transition *noun.* A progression, shift or change.

traverse *verb.* To go across. **traversed**

tri- Root meaning three.

triangle *noun.* A plane figure having three sides and three angles.

triangulation *noun.* (1) Survey or measurement done by means of trigonometry. (2) The series or network of triangles laid out for such measurements.

tribe *noun.* A group of people united by common customs and traditions and following the same leaders.

tribunal *noun.* (1) Court of justice; place of judgment. (2) A deciding authority.

tributary *noun.* A stream or small river that feeds into a larger river.

tribute *noun.* (1) A tax or forced payment. (2) An acknowledgment of thanks or respect, often in the form of a gift or service.

trident *noun.* A fork having three teeth, or prongs.

triennial *adjective.* (1) Consisting of or lasting for three years. (2) Occurring every three years.

trigonometry *noun.* The branch of mathematics that deals with the relations between the sides and angles of triangles and the calculations based on these.

trillion *noun.* A number written as 1,000 followed by three sets of three zeros; a million millions.

trimonthly *adjective.* Occurring every three months.

trio *noun.* Three singers or musicians who perform together.

triple *verb.* To make three times as great or as many. *adjective.* Being three times as great or as many.

triplet *noun.* One of three children born at the same time to the same mother.

triplex *noun.* A three-unit dwelling.

triplicate *noun.* Three copies all alike. *adjective.* Consisting of three corresponding or identical parts or examples.

twe- Root meaning two.

twenty *noun.* Two times ten.

twi- Root meaning two.

twice *adverb.* Two times.

twilight *noun.* The light from the sky between sunset and full night, or between full night and sunrise, when the sun is just below the horizon.

twin *noun.* One of two babies born at the same time to the same mother.

twine *noun.* A strong cord made up of two or more strands.

ultimate *adjective.* (1) Coming at the end; last. (2) Fundamental; basic.

ultimatum *noun.* A final proposal or statement of condition, which must be accepted if a relationship or negotiations are to continue; a person's last word on a matter.

unadorned *adjective.* Plain, simple.

unearth *verb.* (1) To discover. (2) To dig up. **unearthed**

uni- Root meaning one or single.

unicameral *adjective.* Having or consisting of a single legislative chamber, or house.

unicycle *noun.* A single-wheeled vehicle that is usually propelled by pedaling.

unidentified *adjective.* Unnamed; anonymous.

uniform *noun.* The distinctive clothes worn by the members of a group, and by which they may be recognized as belonging to that group. *adjective.* (1) Always the same; not changing. (2) All the same.

uniformity *noun.* The quality or state of being the same.

uniformness *noun.* The quality or state of being the same.

unify To unite or bring together as one.

union *noun.* (1) An act of uniting, or bringing together, two or more things into one. (2) A group of people, states, etc., united for some special purpose. (3) A group of workers joined together to protect and promote their interests.

unique *adjective.* (1) One of a kind. (2) Having no equal.

unisex *adjective.* (1) Not distinguishable as male or female. (2) Suitable or designed for both males and females.

unit *noun.* (1) A single thing or person. (2) Any group of things or persons considered as one.

unite *verb.* Join together; make one; combine.

upgrade *verb.* To move up in rank or level of importance; to advance.

validity *noun.* Soundness based on accurate reporting of facts and strong reasoning.

velocity *noun.* Speed.

vestige *noun.* An actual remnant of something that existed in the past.

vestigial *adjective.* No longer fully developed or useful.

vie *verb.* To compete. **vied, vying**

vir Root meaning man.

virile (vĭr′əl) *adjective.* (1) Manly; masculine. (2) Vigorous; forceful.

virility *noun.* (1) Masculinity. (2) Manly vigor and energy.

void *noun.* An empty space. *verb.* To invalidate. *adjective.* Not valid. **voided**

voyage *noun.* A long trip, especially by water.

warrant *verb.* To provide a reason for something, based on precedent, merit or necessity.

wither *verb.* (1) To cause to lose hope. (2) To intimidate. (3) To droop. **withering**

zo-, zoo- Root meaning animal, animal kingdom or kind.

zoo *noun.* A zoological garden, or place where living animals are kept and put on display for the public.

zoology *noun.* The branch of biology that deals with animals and animal life.